The Art of Resilience
Phoenixes Rising

T.S. Continue's

No matter what life looks like dream big and never give up on your dreams

The author of this book does not dispense medical advice or prescribe the use of any technique as a form of treatment for physical, emotional, or medical problems without the advice of a physician, either directly or indirectly. The intent of the author is only to offer information of a general nature to help you in your quest for emotional and spiritual well-being. This book is not meant as a replacement for medical care. Please consult your pastor, priest, physician, or health-care provider for treatment. This book is based on my experiences and my opinion and in no way is meant to degrade anyone's religion, beliefs, or spiritual practices. In the event you use any of the information in this book for yourself, which is your constitutional right, the author and publisher assume no responsibility.

Adult: Non-Fiction / Dr. Joy T. Vaughan
ISBN 978-1-889306-04-9
Edited by: Dr. Judith Swartz-Galician, Contributing Editors - Alice Wujciak, Jason Rainford, Dawnay St. John

Cover Design by: Tia Liburd, Empire Design Inc.,
Fort Lauderdale, FL

Published by: Baroness Productions Inc. and Digislate Inc.

This book is graphically designed with typography to accommodate people with learning and visual disabilities.

Table of Contents

Foreword

Some years ago, I interviewed a Kung Fu master in Vietnam who described resilience as a small flame. He said, "You can nurture your flame by learning new skills. You can rely on it in times of darkness. Most importantly, you can use your flame to illuminate the path for others."

Mainstream media would have us believe that the world is a dark and dangerous place when, in reality, people are far more similar than we are different. We are born, we grow, we age. We pick things up and leave things behind. While incalculable variables shape our experience of life, it is how we respond to challenges that counts. Some of us crumple under pressure, succumbing to our default nervous system responses of fight, flight, or freeze. Others activate calm amidst the storm, align with purpose, engage emotions, and find their way.

Resilience is the ability to not only endure adversity but to emerge stronger.

I had the pleasure of connecting with Dr. Vaughan and hearing about her incredible global adventure. To embark on such a journey alone, with an open heart and mind, is a story of resilience. But she didn't stop there. Dr. Vaughan met and interviewed inspirational women from all walks of life. From a bus driver in New Zealand to the President of Barbados, she captured the essence of what enabled these women to survive and thrive—often against all odds.

The Art of Resiliency shines the flame of resilience brightly, providing inspiration, insight, and practical wisdom for life.

Bradley Hook, Co-founder, and Partner at the Resilience Institute Global, New Zealand. Author of *Resilience Mastery: 11 Keys to Upgrade Human Performance* and *Surfing Life Waves.*

Dedication

The Art of Resilience: Phoenixes Rising is dedicated to my heavenly Father, the foundation of my resilience. This book is also dedicated to my parents and resilient teachers, Hilton and Thelma Vaughan of Barbados. Mom, Dad, this is a continuation of your legacy. It is upon your shoulders that I proudly stand after so many years of struggle, hardship, and loss. Thank you for being the solid rock of my resilient journey. I also dedicate this book to my co-parent Dr. Eric Brown who taught me how to put a book together so many years ago, and how to finish the mission.

To our late son, Eric Hilton Vaughan Brown in heaven, who left us too soon at the age of thirty-five, thank you for the honor and privilege of being your mom while you were here on earth. To my daughter-in-law Erica Vaughan Brown, my grandchildren, Summer, and Riley Vaughan Brown, and my family in Barbados and abroad, this book is also dedicated to you because it is our turn now to continue to put God first as we keep the resilient torch burning brightly, and move forward to fulfill our God-given purpose. One love, one heart always.

Joy

Acknowledgements

With profound gratitude and humility, I acknowledge all the ladies who generously contributed to this anthology, *The Art of Resilience: Phoenixes Rising Project*. From Fiji to the United States of America, I acknowledge you for the patience and courage that it took to share your stories, poems, and voice with the world. Every person who reads your story or poem will be touched in their soul by what you have shared about your life or declared in your poem about your true self. I particularly acknowledge Te Aroha Martin, Lucille Chance, and Charlotte Blumstein for sharing their story. These ladies have transitioned. Although they are no longer with us, their spirit, and legacy live on.

They say that it takes a village to raise a child. As part of the Resilience village, I also acknowledge the following persons without whom this project would not have happened: President Dame Sandra Prunella Mason for her commitment to excellence and our country, Barbados, Ginny Jolly for sponsoring our first book launch, The Resilience Institute Global, New Zealand, Tia Liburd for her graphic design prowess and powerful book cover, publisher Dave Vasudevan, my editors Dr. Judith Galician, Alice Wujciak, Jason Rainford, and reader Dawnay St. John. I especially acknowledge Steve Pivin, my Digital Partner, who handles my social media.

My personal village consists of Tamera Lowe and her coaches at Kingdom Builders Academy, the many Pastors who cover me in prayer, Dana Cahn from F.A.C.E.S, my Time to Thrive Mastermind Group of seven spearheaded by Naveed Bhatti and Rich Kelly, and my faithful accountability partners Gail Birks, Colleen Dupont, and Woodie Lesesne. For your selfless contribution to my life, I thank you. I love and appreciate you all so much, you don't even know. As we soar, let us move forward in spirit and truth to uplift and inspire downtrodden souls and impact the world.

My resilient journey

Dr. Joy Vaughan

"Beautiful gems can emerge from dirt. Struggle can teach you self-discipline and resilience."
Dipa Satanani

My resilient journey started in my home, Barbados, as the only child of Hilton and Thelma Vaughan. We are a family of legacy builders. My dad was one of our country's statesmen who helped to write the constitution for Barbados and then, in his later years of life, represented our country at the United Nations. My dad published his first book of poems in 1943. My mom established her legacy in social welfare for Barbados. I pay tribute to her resilience in Chapter 6 of this book. I am a product of their legacy. I watched and learned how to keep going in the face of adversity. I learned what it meant to know your purpose and to finish your mission. Both my parents fulfilled their God-given purpose and finished their mission before they transitioned. Now it is my turn.

I also come from a family of teachers. It was no surprise to my mother when she found me lining up my dolls and playing the role of teacher to lifelike figures who just stared back at me. To all teachers, you have my deepest respect as I am sure that you may have experienced the same with your human students. Teaching can be challenging as some days you are left wondering "What on earth?"

Growing up as an only child, my parents made sure that I had many friends. However, as the only child of my parents, my special and sacred friends were God and the angels with whom I had many conversations. Hence, I have always maintained my connection to the spirit world.

At one point I had a near-death experience and can tell you that heaven is real and wonderful. I got to hang out with Jesus, and He is pure unconditional love. Although I wanted to stay, they sent me back to finish my work and mission.

Throughout my life, I have had my share of hardships beginning with the loss of my mother at age thirteen, my dad later in life, other family members, and finally the recent death of my son, who also finished his mission and left his legacy in the Christian Spoken Word genre. Through it all, I have pulled on my faith, my understanding of the spirit world, and my relationship with God to see me through. Hence, I have developed the ability to have peace in my storms. Everything in life is temporary. You just must be patient.

Along the way, I was fortunate to gain a scholarship to Columbia University to study occupational therapy, special education, and subsequently, neuropsychology under Dr. Catherine Best—a noted pioneer in Developmental Neuropsychology at Yale and Columbia Universities. Together, we were able to prove that what is poured into a child in the first three years of their lives—regardless of their economic status, sets the foundation of neuronal patterns in the brain that determines the trajectory for the rest of their lives. Our research was the foundation of my masters' thesis.

As life would have it, there would be many more twists and turns, tragedies and triumphs. One of my biggest tragedies was being paralyzed after a wisdom tooth extraction which left me with a rapid onset of rheumatoid arthritis and fibromyalgia. Through God's grace and acupuncture, I was able to walk again. Although my hands and feet are deformed, it has not stopped me from being resilient and following my mother's advice:

"Joy, plan your life in decades and reinvent yourself every five years."

Another very valuable piece of advice that she imparted to me before she transitioned was,

"I named you Joy because I was so happy to have you, so don't let anyone steal your Joy."

Armed with these two mantras, I joined these (mantras) with my faith and allowed myself to be led by the spirit. While praying during my darkest hour, spirit led me to pick up the phone and call Landmark Education. Who answered the call was a lady named Dotty Olsen-Dehon who simply said,

"We've been waiting for you."

Landmark Education's programs were instrumental in my resilient journey. As part of Landmark's leadership body, I was granted the profound privilege to lead their seminars in Florida under my mentors, Mollie Partridge and Ina Lee.

The technology of Landmark Education laid the foundation for my work with the Academy of College Excellence (ACE) under the leadership of Diego Navarro. This organization, formerly backed by the Carnegie and Bill and Melinda Gates Foundations, provides transformational technology that impacts the executive functions in the frontal lobe of college freshmen. The result is that they become more focused, raise their grades, become leaders of themselves and others, and go on to do great work in their communities. Along with a handful of trained practitioners, I was honored to lead their college Foundational and Social Justice Curricula, and to train fellow faculty members in this transformational technology.

As life goes, the Academy of College Excellence (ACE) program ended at the college. However, in the spirit of resilience, I have learned that when one door closes, a better one opens. The door that opened was none other than the door to Nova University's Doctoral Program. What was not possible earlier in my life became possible in my late fifties.

I secured permission from Diego Navarro to conduct the study on the Academy of College Excellence students at a Southern College in Florida, and from Dr. Russel Barkley—a pioneer in Executive Functions, to use his empirically-based tool BDEFS Scale of Executive Functions. Building on my earlier research at Columbia University with Dr. Best, I set out to prove that shifts do happen in the brain with the right input, particularly in college freshmen.

Hence, college students or youth, despite what anyone thinks, can with the right input be motivated to improve their brain's executive functions, lead themselves and others, but more importantly, finish what they start. This is the phenomenon of neuroplasticity.

It took me seven years to complete my dissertation, but I finished. I thank my Dissertation Chair, Dr. Sheri Bennett, and Co-chair, Dr. Judith Schwartz Galician for hanging in there with me for 7 years. Now that is resilience!

Well, you guessed it—after I completed my dissertation, I expected to be hired at a college or university where I might make an impact in the field of Higher Education. However, when door after door slammed in my face, I understood "not my will but yours Lord." Spirit had other plans for me that were better aligned with my purpose and mission.

I am not one to network extensively but, I found myself at a particular networking event where I met a lady named Dana Cahn. She had the vision to start her own company that would help children and families in South Florida. Needing to earn an income, I joined her and veteran counselor, Connie Harrell first at the Mental Health Association of Broward, then as a Co-parenting consultant at her company, F.A.C.E.S (Family and Co-parenting Enrichment Services) in Fort Lauderdale. I continue to provide co-parenting classes to court-ordered and voluntary couples, who are experiencing the trauma of separation, divorce, or life. I focus on improving their emotional intelligence and executive functions so that their children can get the best of them as parents and people.

I recently launched Dr. Joy Coaching where we provide brain-based and emotional intelligence coaching, and counseling services to female executives, entrepreneurs, and veterans. I also work with organizations and their personnel to help them reinvent themselves and plan for their resilience. This training is done online either individually or in small groups. At Dr. Joy Coaching, we give you the brain-based Reinvention, Resilience, and Sustainability tools. These three areas are not automatic but if people are willing, they can be taught how to reinvent themselves, be resilient, and then, how to sustain their newfound success over time.

Specifically, we do the deep work needed for you to shift your mindset. We also hold our clients accountable for improving their performances and for achieving the results that they want to produce.

Oh, I almost forgot to mention the zenith of my resilience to date. After graduating with my doctorate, I needed to perk myself up a bit. Correction, let us say that I needed to bolster my spirits a lot. The doctoral journey is not for the faint of heart. After seven years of mental and psychological grinding, I was wiped, skewered, stick-a-fork-in-me, done! Well, you get the picture.

My cousin, Jan Hackett who is a world traveler herself inspired me to take my journey around the world. So, with God and His angels on my side, I packed my three suitcases and laptop, fortified my arthritic body with vitamins and all things good, and on

March 30, 2019, I jetted off on my once-in-a-lifetime around my almost solo world trip.

My first stop was Fiji, followed by New Zealand, Australia. I even tracked down and managed to have lunch with my former professor, Dr. Catherine Best in Australia. We hadn't seen each other in 30 years. Egypt was next with my friends Gail and Lorena who joined me for an exciting trip up the Nile and Pyramid exploration. Then off I went to Dubai, England, and several countries in Europe beginning with Paris where I, along with my three suitcases, hopped off and on trains which took us to my next destination. At each juncture, God and His angels showed up and showed up big. From helping me with the luggage to directing me safely to where I needed to go, there was never a time when I felt afraid or alone. When I asked and was patient, help arrived.

Another treat was to have dinner with my family in London and my childhood friend, Andre in Germany. We hadn't seen each other in 50 years. A delicious side to friendship is that if you have not seen a person for a long time when you do connect it is like you saw them yesterday. That's the funny aspect of time and relationships. Two months, twenty countries, and several climate changes later I arrived back in the United States refreshed, rejuvenated, and ready to rock and roll.

People often asked me where did you find all these people for my book?

There is a saying which goes,

> *"Ask, and it shall be given you; seek, and ye shall find; knock, and it shall be opened unto you: For every one that asketh receiveth; and he that seeketh findeth; and to him that knocketh it shall be opened."*— **Matthew 7:7-8**

Following the spirit's direction, I did what was instructed in the above quote. This was how this book *The Art of Resilience: Phoenixes*

Rising was born. I asked, and people were only too willing to tell their stories. From Fiji to the United States, what you will learn is that humans are resilient no matter where they are in the world. Our brains are wired to adapt to anything life throws us. The key is to believe.

Thank you for allowing me to tell this aspect of my resilient story. As we move on in *The Art of Resilience: Phoenixes Rising*, I can't wait to begin our journey around the world and to introduce you to the wonderful and amazing ladies in this anthology. I invite you to find your resilient path as you read each story and poem. If you would like to learn more about how to be resilient, the work I do, or how I can serve you, please contact me at: linkedin.com/in/dr-joy -vaughan-ab18179 https://www.facebook.com/' info@drjoycoaching .com https://drjoycoaching.com 786-209-3918

My Epic Camel Ride in Egypt

Our Phoenixes

Like my camel ride in Egypt, every story in this anthology is an account of each Phoenixes' resilience. The I AM Poem format is courtesy of The Academy of College Excellence. Each poem in this anthology is a declaration of our Phoenixes' unique, cultural essence as resilient women. Consider that once you know who you are, and Whose you are, no one can take that away from you. In addition to understanding your purpose, who you are at your core drives the fulfillment of your legacy. That is what makes you unique and awesome.

In this anthology, we will travel around the world. We may not see every country, but enough places that you can discover your resilience through the eyes of these fabulous Phoenixes. Don't look for a logical path as we may bounce from Egypt to Guyana, then back to the US, followed by a visit to Ecuador. Life is not linear, or even at times logical. However, being able to roll with the unpredictable and ever-changing direction of life is what makes you resilient. As you read our Phoenixes' stories and poems, we invite you to discover and reflect on the message of resilience echoed in each of their submissions.

The Art of Resilience: Phoenixes Rising is designed to be interactive. Throughout this book, we are curious to know what you are getting (i.e.what is your takeaway?) from the stories and poems. We do this because your answers could help others. Thank you in advance for sharing your takeaways in our Phoenixes Rising Facebook Group. Throughout the anthology, we have provided you with our #PhoenixesRising, and QR Code that when scanned with your phone, will take you to our Phoenixes Rising Facebook Group. If you are having difficulty with the QR Code, you can also access our Facebook group with this link https://bit.ly/phoenixesrising.

Joining the group allows you to interact with the Phoenixes and the anthology's content. Please post your comments on our Phoenixes' stories and poems, and network at your leisure.

So, what is your takeaway so far?

#PhoenixesRising

https://bit.ly/phoenixesrising

Question: What kind of Phoenix do you want to be?

ON RESILIENCE

"I no longer feared the darkness once I knew the phoenix in me would rise from the ashes."
—William C. Hannan

Preface

"Resilience is knowing that you are the only one that has the power and the responsibility to pick yourself up."—**Mary Holloway**

What does it take? I mean take to come back from those guaranteed curve balls that life throws you, time and time again? Have you ever wondered how some people can get knocked down or deal with adversity and seemingly, not miss a beat? Now we know that no two people are exactly alike. But what is that thing, yeah, that one thing that would have a person not quit, not give up, but emerge stronger, often, dare I say better, time and time again?

It's called *resilience*. Said another way, resilience is the ability to quickly spring back from the difficulties caused by life. In other words, it is the ability to take a licking and keep on ticking, because truth be told, what doesn't kill you makes you stronger—that is, if you let it. Notice I said, "IF YOU LET IT!" Consider that the ability to emerge victoriously is a conscious choice that one makes based on their wants, desires, and core beliefs.

In this chapter, we will talk about three things: First, resilience: What it is, and what it is not. Second, the 3 Tenets of Resilience, and third, we will offer some tips on how you can increase your capacity to be resilient—Sound good?

According to Jessica Schaffer, a Nervous System Educator who focuses on stress management, resilience is not an automatic phenomenon. It does not involve mustering up the courage to power through unfavorable situations or crises. And it is not a fixed or unchangeable characteristic.

Rather resilience is a powerful practice grounded and fueled by your belief system that gets expressed via words and actions that demonstrate "I will get through this," and more importantly—"I must get through this, followed by the corresponding actions that will quickly lead me out of my adversity!" Said another way, it is what you tell yourself, based on the degree to which you believe, that you will be victorious.

Resilience then is equivalent to going to a mental gym where you develop your positive mindset and trust your internal and external resources to bring you through whatever adversity you are dealing with. Internal resources are your will, positive emotions, and self-talk, based on your belief that you will be victorious. External forces are your support system of your family (if applicable) and positive friends that you choose to have in your inner circle. The marriage of external and internal forces creates a synergy, if you will, that catalyzes your success.

Resilience is a daily practice that involves building up your ability to cope with life itself. Consider that every day, we are faced with something that we must deal with. Yet, how we deal with our challenges is equal to the amount of emotional resolve that we have built up over our lifetime. For truth be told, nothing lasts forever, and everything in life is temporary—even your crisis. Remember that time is a great healer.

Resilience is what we call a nature vs nurture internal training gleaned from your childhood. Although resilience can be taught, it must be practiced daily. For example, in my life, I learned how to be resilient from my mother. Said another way, resilience is the ability to create a new paradigm and quickly pivot.

My Mother, Thelma Vaughan, was a chronic asthmatic whose heart stopped several times but who was revived by her mother every time. I will share more about my mom in Chapter 6. Later in life, my dad supported those efforts during their marriage. My mother died at age forty-three, having been the first Barbadian and Woman of Color to be the Director of the Social Welfare Department in Barbados.

Later in life, I developed syncope, which is a condition where your heart slows down, and then, finally stops for a few minutes, only to start again. I remember my second or third incident of syncope— what I call 'THE BIG ONE'. I was going through seemingly never-ending crises in my life and to get through it, I was busy taking care of everyone but myself. Hence, I was suffering from severe physical, and more so, emotional burnout. How many of you can relate?

I remember walking to lunch with my then boss and on the way, I felt a tug but no, it was more like a strong pull into another dimension. Before I knew it, I had left my body and was in this magnificent, beautiful garden with the most exquisite and brilliantly colored flowers, foliage, and the greenest grass that stretched for miles and miles. Close by, there was a waterfall that sang the most beautiful song that I had ever heard. But what was incredibly profound was the unspeakable peace I felt, like I had never felt before. They call it the peace that "passeth all understanding." I knew then that I wanted to stay in that place forever. People call this a near-death experience.

Then, before I knew it, I was lying on my back and three huge angels (their heads alone were about six feet tall) were peering down at me.

"It's not your time yet." They said softly, "You have to go back." I bemoaned,

"NOOOOOO, I don't want to go back."

They said,

"Yes, you have work to do."

Now, I am a spiritual person, but at that moment I understood the meaning of "On earth as it is in heaven." I woke up on a gurney in the emergency room to the concerned and worried looks on everyone's faces. However, I knew at that moment my life had changed forever. That experience helped me to reinvent my life as an author, speaker, professor, transformational specialist, solo traveler of the world. My near-death experience also helped me to master the art of resilience because it gave me a deeper understanding of resilience's three tenets, with reinvention being the cornerstone of resilience mastery.

So, what are the three tenets of resilience? Previously, I shared that resilience was the capacity to pull from your internal and external resources to bring you through whatever crises or adversity you face or are facing. These resources are built over time. Consider that your internal resources are predicated on these three things: Your purpose or WHY that is, why you are here on this planet? Furthermore, what is your true purpose for being here? For me, my WHY is as follows:

Dr. Joy Vaughan's WHY

"The Purpose of my life is to die completely by leaving a legacy of Joy, Peace, and Freedom to all those that I have the honor and privilege to touch within my lifetime,"

The vehicle through which my WHY gets expressed is that of being a teacher, Reinvention and Resilience coach, and counselor. Every day, I share the knowledge with which I have been gifted, with others so that they can discover and fulfill their God-given purpose. I am at the point of my life where my commitment is to be happy, at peace, and to live a stress-free life. Do you want to know a secret? Focus on your purpose and your WHY, keep walking in faith, and I promise you true happiness will naturally follow! If you want to know more about how to discover your purpose, your WHY, or how to live a stress-free life, then go to https://www.drjoycoaching.com/ to learn more.

Now you probably heard about purpose and WHY before, but you have not understood that they are intricately tied to your ability to be resilient. Consider that your purpose could be something as tender as your children or as complex as to better humanity globally (e.g., the Hunger Project, saving an animal species from extinction, or World Peace). Here's the good news; your purpose just must be bigger than you because it is what brings you out of your adversity, time and time again.

In my travels around the world, I had an opportunity to interview women from various countries on what made them resilient. Most of them said their purpose for living and what kept them resilient was their children or a cause that brought them happiness. So, what is your purpose for being on Mother Earth, and does that purpose bring you happiness?

Now, let's talk about how your WHY is tied to your purpose for living. Simply put, your WHY is your legacy. What do you want people to say about you when you find yourself in the beautiful garden as I did? What was your contribution to anyone other than yourself? The pandemic has taught us that your next breath is not guaranteed, and a personal reset is necessary to thrive.

So, we've spoken about your purpose and your WHY. Now let us speak about your happiness. What makes you happy? Do you have a happy place? For me, my happiness comes from seeing people with whom I have had the honor to coach, teach or work with, succeed. My happiness comes from connecting with my faith because that is what gives me peace. Also playing with my grandkids. Nothing beats a warm hug and tummy tickles! My happiness comes from traveling where and when I so choose because as I have gotten older, I have chosen to simplify my life. How about you? Where can you create happiness and joy every day in your life?

In closing, I shared what resiliency is and what it is not. I also shared about the Three (3) Tenets of Resiliency—your Purpose, your WHY, and your Happiness. I gave you some insight as to how my own resilience was shaped by my mother and family.

So as promised, here are some tips to support your resilience journey.

1. If you don't already have one, find the purpose that is bigger than you that you want to fulfill. It should be something that you would do even if you are not getting paid for it. Don't get it twisted. There is nothing wrong with getting paid and paid well for what you do. In other words, there is no shame in the game. Amen? Amen!

2. Find a WHY that creates a legacy that will last and be remembered, long after you are gone.

3. Every day, manage your internal state of mind and external resources to support your happiness. This includes giving yourself a time limit in which you will bounce back, by being in action, to deal with your crises.

4. Finally, let no one mess with your peace. My mother always told me "Don't let anyone steal your Joy," This was one of the best pieces of advice that she ever gave me. Finally, be gentle and compassionate with yourself, understanding that everything in life is temporary and in divine order.

Stay blessed always! Dr. Joy
https://www.drjoycoaching.com/ 786-209-3318 (QR FB Code)
As you read this preface on Resilience, what is your takeaway?

#PhoenixesRising

https://bit.ly/phoenixesrising

Question: What kind of Phoenix do you want to be?

Well readers, are you ready to take your resilient journey around the world? Here we go! As we hear from our fabulous ladies. I invite you to be inspired and to learn from their stories and poems. All aboard! Our first stop is my beautiful island of Barbados where we will meet President Dame Sandra Prunella Mason.

BE RESILIENT

Chapter 1

"Like tiny seeds with potent power to push through tough ground and become mighty trees, we hold innate reserves of unimaginable strength. We are resilient."—**Catherine DeVry, The Gift of Nature**

Leading yourself and others can be a daunting task. In the spirit of resilience, you must be willing to be disappointed, but not stay disappointed. You also need to have a purpose and an understanding of what you were put on this planet to achieve. Everyone's path is different. However, once you get crystal clear on your path, the fire in your belly will be lit and you will become unstoppable. It is my honor and privilege to introduce our first, fearless, and unstoppable, Phoenix—our President of the Republic of my country Barbados, Dame Sandra Prunella Mason. I invite you as you read her story to allow her words and life of resilience to light a fire within you.

Dame Sandra Prunella Mason
Former Governor General and First President of
The Republic of Barbados

Dame Mason as Governor
General With Her
Majesty Queen Elizabeth II

President Sandra Mason and
Prime Minister Mia Amor
Mottley

The Making of a President
From my Beloved Parents, Doreen and Lionel Mason

"You can be anything that you want to be."

What does it take, I mean really take, to come from humble beginnings and rise to be the first President of the Republic of my country, Barbados? It takes knowing your purpose, developing and sustaining a passion for that purpose, and resilience. Who would have thought that this little girl from the Parish of St. Philip would fulfill her dream to be a pioneer in fields where women were previously rare gems? My name is Dame Sandra Prunella Mason, and this is my resilience story.

I was born to two amazing parents. There were nine of us—four boys, five girls. Our parents always told us that we could do anything. As a typical middle-class family of that time, my father was a joiner and artisan who created much of the antique furniture found in the Great Houses of Barbados, today. My mother was a homemaker. Like many couples in the 1950s, most married women did not necessarily work outside of the home. Instead, their job was to be the stabilizing force of the household, while their husbands were the family's financial pillars.

My dad was my first advisor. The day I got my results to go on to high school I was 9 years old. He pulled me aside and gave me the best advice that a father could give a daughter. His words did not mean much at the time, but they resonated in my later years and have remained with me to this day. His guidance was reflective of Plato's observation that human behavior flows from three things: desire, emotion, and knowledge. My father urged me to seek knowledge because it was the best protection in the world, and once gained, it was something that no one could take from or take advantage of me.

Knowledge, if used correctly, would stand me in good stead for the rest of my life. My dad wanted me to become a leader and not a follower, because in his mind, the person who had no opinion of their own but depended on the opinion and taste of others, was destined to be a slave.

The relationship I had, with not only my dad but my family, has played a significant role in the person I am today. I was fortunate to have benefitted from their steadfast support at every stage of my life. It is this which provided an effective bulwark against some of life's more cruel vagaries, proving the idiom once stated by American lawyer and politician Brad Henry,

"Families are the compass that guides us. They are the inspiration to reach great heights and our comfort when we occasionally falter."

In addition to my family, I have had many compasses in my life that have guided me to where I am today. Every trial and test that I have been through, has helped me to survive the male-dominated fields of law and politics. Each experience, coupled with my parents' mantra of

"You can do whatever you want to be,"

has made me stronger, and yes, may I dare say, resilient.

My journey to becoming a fierce, courageous, unstoppable lawyer started with my primary education in Barbados at St. Catherine's School in the Parish of St. Philip. I credit my teachers for providing me with a solid foundation, steeped in rigor and the practice of critical thinking. I was fortunate enough to continue my secondary education at Queens College. There I was further shaped and guided by my formidable principals, one of them being Dame Elsie Payne and her team of brilliant faculty. I was also influenced to become a lawyer through the many lawyers portrayed in Shakespeare's plays—*The Merchant of Venice* in particular. Shakespeare's work is fraught with legal arguments and resolve. The in-depth analysis of *Merchant of Venice* as well as Shakespeare's other plays was standard practice at school. I also loved French and became quite adept in the speaking and writing of this beautiful language.

From an early age, I knew that I did not want to be a homemaker. I wanted more. That desire was profoundly sparked by two significant people in my life. The first person was Ms. Nellie, our school conductress on our Number 10 Transport Bus. Every morning she greeted me before we started our daily trek back and forth from St. Philip to Queens College in pursuit of this knowledge of which my father spoke. Ms. Nellie always looked out for me. I was fascinated by the fact that she was a working woman who earned a living. She was solicitous, earnest, dedicated to her duty, and was always happy and smiling. She was my veritable angel. I wanted to be exactly like her when I grew up. So convinced was I that this was the life for me, I went home one evening and declared to my mother, and anyone else that would listen, that I was going to become a conductress. My mother never batted an eyelid or admonished me for my choice. She simply said.

> **"Well, if that's what you've decided to become, promise me that you'll become the best conductress in the world."**

On later reflection, I recognized that she was reinforcing what my father had advocated previously: that while my future depended on many things, it would be mostly because of me and my decisions. As the truism goes:

> **"We are free to choose, but we are not free from the consequences of those choices."**
> **—Anthony Ashley Cooper**

As Conductress Nellie was my first influencer to become a job-holder, believe it or not, my second influencer was Portia Blake—a popular character from a radio program called *Portia Faces Life*. In those good old days (which for me were the 1960s), before television and the ubiquitous internet, one relied on the radio for both information and entertainment. It was through the prominently perched Rediffusion box, that we learned the latest pop songs, were introduced to classical music, learned the names of the English Premier League football teams, heard the cricket scores and listened to plays by Shakespeare.

Portia Faces Life was a procedural drama that chronicled the exploits of an erudite and engaging female lawyer who was fierce, courageous, unstoppable, and victorious in her intent to fight crime and corruption. A feisty attorney, widow, and single parent, Portia was constantly under assault with her issues, as she overcame an onslaught of hardships, while single-handedly raising her son. I became fascinated by the cleverness of the law and a woman portrayed through Portia's capacity, to use law and her femininity to battle and solve the many forces of crime, injustice, and civic corruption in her city. Somehow, with the shrewdness of her namesake in Shakespeare's *Merchant of Venice*, Portia always managed to outwit her opponents in the courtroom. The older I got, the more I saw myself being able to take on that role, not as a voice-over actress on Rediffusion, but as a lawyer. Growing up, there were only a handful of female lawyers who were making their mark in this male-dominated field. I wanted to join them and to help shake up the field a little.

Having settled on becoming a lawyer, I pestered my father who at that time was living in the United Kingdom, to let me join him so that I could pursue my law studies there. He adamantly refused, citing the discrimination which was rampant in the United Kingdom at that time. As a caring dad, he wanted to shield me from that type of negativity. I was upset and instead of pursuing studies in Latin, as was recommended for the study of Law, I switched to French as my aspirations focused on entering the diplomatic corps. The French language was one of the gateways to being a part of the diplomatic service. The other gateway I was not privy to knowing or entering for other reasons. I had to manage my dashed hopes and come to grips with the fact that working in the foreign services seemed to be reserved for "specially selected" persons. Once I realized that the decision-makers found me neither special enough for nor in the realm of selection consideration with respect to, the diplomatic service, I turned my attention to teaching. One of the biggest factors in resilience is the ability to pivot quickly before resignation, cynicism or depression settle in your spirit. Those emotions will make you give up on your dreams, and I, Sandra Prunella Mason, was not about to give up.

Hence, despite Portia's influence as a lawyer, and my rejection from the diplomatic corps, I began my career as a teacher. Growing up, our then Prime Minister, later National Hero, The Right Excellent Errol Walton Barrow, drilled into our brains the value of being educated. He knew that knowledge was, and is power, and insisted that all Barbadians be educated and educated well. He was one of the many male lawyers who rose to become one of our formidable Prime Ministers and to lead our country into Independence in 1966. He understood that education was the way out of poverty. For his people, poverty was not an option. It should be noted that nearly all our Barbadian Prime Ministers, prior to and post- Mr. Barrow, have been brilliant barristers and lawyers. Another little piece of history that you might also find interesting is that post-slavery, Barbados was the only island where the slaves were educated by the Quakers, despite the objection of the slave owners.

With this knowledge of history coupled with the positive experience of school, I was excited to start my first job as a teacher at the Princess Margaret Secondary School. I quickly found out that teaching was not for me, as the curriculum did not reflect us as a people, our culture, or our history. My need to rebel against what was being taught also did not sit well with my principal, who was hell-bent on following the rules. We amicably parted ways. There is a saying that you are always being prepared for your next assignment.

"Hmmm," I thought. *"Now what?"*

Since my teaching career was thwarted, a career in banking would work. In 1969, I entered the banking industry as a clerk and spent about a year in banking, learning the ins and outs of finance. Banking turned out to be a fun but challenging job. Within a year of working at Barclays, the opportunity presented itself in 1970, when the University of the West Indies established its law faculty in Barbados. Before this date, anyone wanting to study law had to travel to England and qualify there before returning to Barbados to be admitted to the Bar in Barbados. I was one of the first students admitted to the university's undergraduate program where I graduated with honors in 1973. From there, I went on to law school in Trinidad and Tobago and graduated with a certificate in Legal Education in 1975. I also became the first female to be admitted to the Bar in Barbados under this new system.

After qualifying as a lawyer, I returned to Barclays, because truth be told, I was so afraid to appear in court. Nevertheless, I was appointed as a Trust Administrator in Barbados and Jamaica. I returned to Barbados from Jamaica in 1976 where I worked in the mortgage finance department.

In February 1977, I made up my mind that I was going to face my fears, and consequently, I put up my shingle and stepped out in faith as a practicing attorney. I quickly learned that while studying law and attending law school had set the foundation, the actual practice of the law was a completely different animal. Furthermore, as a sole practitioner, the entrepreneurship learning curve was steep, and I was forced to adjust quickly. I also began teaching Family Law at the University of West Indies. I practiced as a solopreneur for about a year when God must have seen fit to end my misery.

In 1978, I heard via the radio that the government was looking to hire a lawyer with 5 years of experience to work as a magistrate. I considered it opportune given my interest in family law that my first assignment was in juvenile and family court.

Being a magistrate in family court helped me recognize that although we are all made in God's image, we are all different people, with different strengths, different attitudes, and aptitudes. I considered that although some of the persons appearing before me might be charged with serious offenses, it was my duty as magistrate to consider each one according to that person's peculiar circumstances before determining that person's fate. I learned very early on to make allowances for everyone, for at some point we will all make mistakes, but we should never let those mistakes overwhelm us to the point where we cannot recover from them.

I spent 17 years as a magistrate, including 4 years as Chief Magistrate, moving through all the island's magisterial districts. My stories of the magistrate's courts are legendary; some humorous, some distressing but thought-provoking, leaving me to frequently reflect there but for the Grace of God go I.

As if life was not complicated enough, I fell in love. Yes, folks, it does happen. Did I mention that I also discovered that I was pregnant which was a total game-changer for my life? As a struggling magistrate, I accepted a teaching position at the University of West Indies in Barbados which meant that I worked two jobs and raised my son. Thank God for loving parents, family, and my son's dad (co-parent) who supported me unconditionally. Over time, working two jobs took its toll and so I decided to quit my teaching job at the University of the West Indies. Courageously moving forward as a single parent, I chose to focus on the area of family law. Much like Portia, quitting my teaching job gave me the flexibility to be a mom, and to grow my practice. My child made me realize the importance of family and the healing of particularly fractured families.

My purpose and passion shifted from just being a lawyer to leaving a legacy for my son, and future children of color.

You have no idea the level of scrutiny, backlash, and ostracism in a small society that had little tolerance for unwed mothers. There were days when I felt that it was me against the world. This feeling became my reality as I continued to battle societal norms, male egos, and whatever else was hurled at me. With God and family at my back, I became the first female single-parent lawyer in Barbados. A child changes everything. What my son did for me was to help me understand the plight of single mothers in general. At the end of the day, you still must hold your head high and muster through the stares, pretentious smiles, and scathing gossip.

As I previously stated, having my own child fueled my passion for children in general. I also became the first Barbadian woman and one of 10 experts to serve on the United Nations Committee on the Rights of the Child from 1992–1998. The high profile of the Committee's Convention in Geneva and the fervor of the members ensured that the various governments took seriously their obligation to improve the lives of the children in their care. The volume of work necessitated expanding the membership to 18 experts. By the time I had left the Committee, all the countries in the world except for Somalia and the United States had ratified the Convention—a remarkable feat in the history of United Nations conventions. No other convention has ever achieved that. I was therefore honored to serve as the Committee's chairman for the last two years of my tenure.

While in Geneva attending a Committee meeting in 1992, I received a telephone call from Barbados enquiring whether I would consider sitting on the West Indian Commission as a replacement to Dame Nita Barrow who had been appointed as Barbados' first female Governor-General. Headed by Sir Shridath Ramphal, I was one of two women on a committee of 13 to look at the issue of regional integration. This was followed by being the first woman to serve on the Barbadian Court of Appeals. My work with the United Nations Committee had not gone unnoticed.

In 1994, I served as the first Barbadian Ambassador to Venezuela and four of its surrounding countries. I quickly learned that being a diplomat required a very different level of resilience than that learned as a magistrate. As a diplomat, you have first to seek permission from headquarters before making a statement and any decision made, had to coincide with the policy of the Government. The lesson I learned therefore is that adaptability is critical. I did all this while continuing to raise my son. Like Portia, I was on a mission.

After my Venezuelan Ambassadorship, I returned home and accepted a position as Chief Magistrate. Over the next 10 years, I focused on my work, career, and my son. My climb up the judicial ladder resulted in my being appointed Chief Magistrate followed by Registrar of the Supreme Court. This was a shift from being a litigator to now one of an administrator of our highest court. I was now responsible for a staff of over 200 persons in the different legal areas including the operation of the Magistrates' Courts from which I had recently departed as well as the Supreme Court to which I was aspiring. My resilience depended on my ability to adapt and to delegate. Sometimes we as women have difficulty with these skill sets; yet, they are critical to our buoyancy and burnout prevention. I also firmly believe that God does not give you more than you can bear. You just must trust Him.

In 2005, I was appointed as a High Court Judge on the Supreme Court of the Eastern Caribbean. This appointment took me to the French-Creole Island of St. Lucia where my knowledge of French served me well during my 3 years of service. Those years brought another realization: the love which Caribbean people genuinely have for each other. I was very warmly received and, in the process, learned about the closeness between our countries—Barbados and St. Lucia, which exceeds geography.

In 2008, after completing my 17 months as Ambassador to Venezuela, I returned to Barbados and was appointed as our country's first female Justice of Appeal; I felt that I had reached my zenith. I must admit that I have always craved to reach the zenith of my profession and have been constant in that quest. Despite this, and more probably because of this, I did not consider the position to be a sinecure. I felt that as the only woman among men I had to prove myself. That feeling turned out to be oh so wrong, and not at all necessary. The Honorable Chief Justice did not mollycoddle me. He accepted that I had come to the job duly qualified and so I had to hit the ground running. With this acceptance and the support of the other justices, I did my part. As the older justices retired and were replaced, collegiality and camaraderie heightened. Teamwork continued to be the order of the day and the judgments we delivered have stood the test of time.

In 2014, while fulfilling my duties as a Justice of Appeal, another offer came my way. I was elected for a 4-year renewable term to the Commonwealth Secretariat Arbitral Tribunal which is charged with the responsibility of adjudicating any action brought by a member of the Secretariat's staff against the organization.

I was settling in nicely in my multiple roles when I got "THE CALL."

"What call?" You might ask?

Before I share what kind of call this could be, please realize that although you see yourself climbing the ladder and reaching your Zenith, you never expect to get the call of a lifetime. However, for our readers, I want to share at this point that people are always watching and in Barbados, that is particularly true.

Looking back on my life, little did I know that subconsciously and all along, I was being prepared for my role as acting Governor General of Barbados. I remember getting a call from the Prime Minister's office asking if I would temporarily assume the position of Governor General. What was an unexpectedly pleasant surprise was my permanent appointment as the second female Governor General of Barbados!

My appointment as Governor General took me back to my childhood. I remember being around 8 or 9 years of age when I first took notice of, and became curious about a large white house known as Government House on my island of Barbados. Every morning, my journey in our Number 10 Transport bus took us past Government House en route to Queens College. To my young eyes, I was fascinated and curious about this white castle guarded by policemen in their crisp black and white uniforms. As a child, I had no idea who lived in that house, how they lived or their fundamental role in shaping our nation. Although I had no desire to live there, ironically, this is where I have found myself living as Governor General and the Queen of England's representative of our country.

Built in the colonial days, Government House was once the main house of a Quaker plantation. It had been purchased by the Monarchy in 1906 and became the official place of residence for the—then Governor and future Governor Generals. For those who are not aware, Barbados was under British Colonial rule until 1966 when our country achieved its independence from Great Britain. Previously, the office of Governor or Governor General was held by British males dating as far back as 1627. A female Governor, or Governor General, far less one of color, was not even remotely considered as a possibility. That did not stop me. I realized that I needed to make history not only for myself, but for any child, and (in particular) a female of color who wanted to break stereotypical barriers to achieve their dream.

Please indulge me a little as I share a little history about our beautiful Barbados and the importance of the Office of Governor General to our island and its people. As I share my story of resilience, my journey to Governor General will become more significant, as you will then begin to understand the degree to which I had to overcome racial, and gender barriers to become the second female Barbadian, to officially take the office of Governor General on January 8, 2018.

In terms of gender, I was called to follow the legacy of our first female Barbadian Governor General of color, Dame Ruth Nita Barrow. She reigned as Governor General from 1990 until her death in 1995. A formidable woman, and personality in her own right, I knew that I not only had big shoes to fill, but that I was perfectly capable of filling them. To fully understand the role and office of the Governor General, it is important to understand that the Governor General is regarded as the most important person as the Head of State in the Government of Barbados.

Under Chapter 1V of the Barbadian Constitution, the Governor General is recommended by the Prime Minister, and appointed by the Queen of England to be the Monarch's legal and administrative representative. Some of the duties include diplomatic hosting of world leaders, representing the Queen at the opening of Parliament, and disciplining civil servants when necessary. One of the rewards of being the second female Governor General, was being knighted by the Queen and given the title of Dame.

At this point you might be wondering when did I sleep, or how did I accomplish so much? As I shared before, my goal was to accomplish something great in life. To fulfill that, I had to learn everything about the role and duties of a Governor General. I had to learn not only what they did, but what they did to get… and stay there. Even more important, I had to learn the journey of this woman of color. Dame Nita had paved the way but now, I, Dame Sandra

Prunella Mason could not afford to let her good work go for naught. I would like to believe that she as well as my parents are smiling from heaven. On November 30, 2021, I was made the first President of the Republic of Barbados. I have been charged with overseeing the writing of the laws for our new Republic, as well as other duties by Prime Minister Mia Mottley; and I am honored to do so.

As women, we carry the world on our shoulders. However, it is our trials that make us resilient. As you read my story, you could say that I have accomplished a lot in my short lifetime. However, all my achievements pale in the face of my greatest gift—my son. I am so very proud of him. I am a single parent. My son has done well for himself and as an adult, he has thrived. As I look at my son, I am also reminded of my second love – children.

Yes, it is true that I have met dignitaries, settled disputes, represented the Queen of England at Parliament as Dame Sandra Mason; and now as the President of our country. However, my greatest joy is to give tours of Government House to our Barbadian school children. I let them know just like my parents told me, that they can be anything that they want to be. I tell them, particularly the girls, that they too can sit where I am sitting. As women, we no longer must hide in the shadows. We can fulfill our dreams and make a valuable contribution to our island, and the world at large. Barbados is only 166 square miles, but as a nation, we stand on the shoulders of the great, resilient, pioneering men and women who have ingrained in our DNA, that knowledge is the power that no one can take away from you.

I am content with the notion that the vast majority of what I did in my life, was essentially done my way, as Frank Sinatra famously crooned,

"Regrets, I've had a few, but then again, too few
to mention, I did what I had to do, and I saw
it through without exemption."
Frank Sinatra, My Way

So, to our readers, just remember that you just need to have the mindset to succeed and to always invoke the spirit of resilience. Aim high. Be determined. Pray often, be unstoppable, and stay humble. I am Dame Sandra Mason, proud mother of a very fine son, the second female Barbadian Governor General, the first female President of the Republic of Barbados, and I am resilient.

So, what's your takeaway from President Dame Sandra Prunella Mason's story?

#PhoenixesRising

https://bit.ly/phoenixesrising

Question: What kind of Phoenix do you want to be?

ON RESILIENCE

"Every morning we are born again. What we do today is what matters most"
Unknown

I hope that you enjoyed reading and were inspired by President Dame Sandra Mason's story. In her story, we saw what it took for Dame Sandra Mason to go from humble beginnings to become the President of Barbados. It takes courage to lead but resilience to maintain your position of leadership over time.

Sometimes you have no desire to be a leader. However, when your purpose and the villagers call you forth to step up and be bigger than you see yourself, what else is there to do but to answer the call of your ancestors. We say goodbye to my island home Barbados and travel to Fiji.

It is my pleasure to introduce you to our second Phoenix, Miriame Lestale. Her story is similar, but different from President Dame Sandra Mason's story. Ms. Miriame is one of two female leaders on the island of Vitalevu in Nawaka Village in Fiji.

Short back story. When I went around the world, I started my journey in Fiji and wondered if there were any female leaders. As I inquired at the hotel and restaurants, I was asked why a female and not a male leader. When I shared that I was writing a book about Resilience, the villagers arranged for me to meet Miriame Lestale, as they felt that she embodied the spirit of resilience. Fiji for the most part is a closed society, so being granted an audience with a female leader was a big deal.

I will never forget meeting her for the first time. We looked at each other and just started crying. It was as if we had known each other and had been waiting for this moment all our lives. You see, Miriame has outlasted … Well, read her story to discover what has made her the resilient leader of her two-hundred-member clan in Nawaka Village.

ON RESILIENCE

"Blessed is the one who perseveres under trial because, having stood the test, that person will receive the crown of life that the Lord has promised to those who love him."—**James 1:12**

Chapter 2

LEADERSHIP BY DEFAULT
Miriame Lestale
Leader of the Vunatopa Tribe – Nawaka Village Fiji

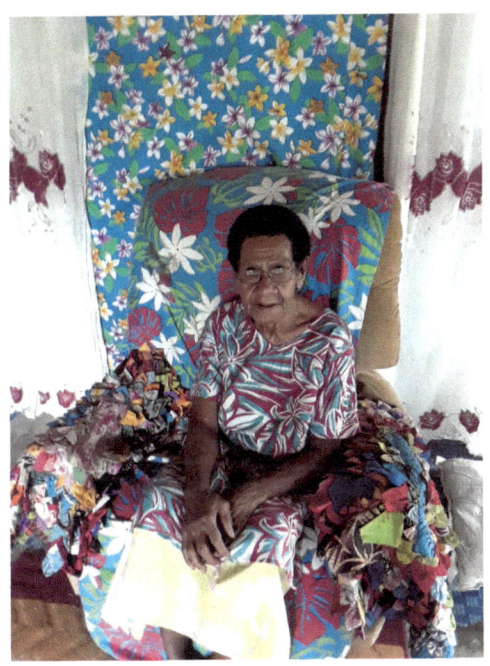

A quiet, gentle powerful soul, Miriame Lestale is one of two female leaders of her clan on the island of Viti Levu Fiji. The epitome of grace and strong leadership, Miriame Lestale serves as a consultant to the Chief of Nawaka Village.

Leadership By Default
Miriame Lestale
Leader of the Vunatopa Tribe – Nawaka Village, Fiji

"Pray not only for help in trials, but pray also for more resilience. Exodus 14:14 The LORD will fight for you, and you have only to be silent."

I became resilient the day my father died. Not just resilient but spiritually resilient. This kind of resilience stemmed from the depths of my soul, transcended my physical being, and wove itself into the fabric of my life. It was the only way that I could cope with the overwhelming grief and loss of someone whom I dearly loved and very much respected. As the leader of our growing Venutopa Tribe or Yesuva in our village of Nawaka, I watched my father lead us into a brighter future with power and grace. Tough yet compassionate, he was a tower of strength for all of us. His passing meant the end of one era and the beginning of another as we laid his mind, body, and soul to rest.

That day and subsequent days were a mixture of grief and celebration. Our humble home was filled with members of our Venutopa clan as well as those from the other eleven Yesuva. There was no shortage of food, music, and kind words were spoken. As the sweet pungent smell of roasted pig filled the air, each tribe brought their best Fijian dishes like Kokoda, Rourou, Palusami, and Lovo, along with their comfort, love, and support. As tears flowed down our cheeks, sorrow turned into joy as we remembered our leader, his contribution to our clan, and especially, to our family.

The passing of my father meant that my eldest brother was next in line to oversee our Yesuva. Leadership is determined by succession and passed from male to male within the Fijian culture. Like my dad, our eldest brother ruled our clan until he passed some years later. His passing opened the door for my second eldest brother to assume his leadership of our Yesuva. Several years later, my only remaining brother took his rightful place as head of our Venutopa clan.

My heart has become heavy over the years by the passing of the men in my family. Within the last fifteen years, I have buried my husband, three brothers, and one son. I have one son remaining who, God willing, will assume leadership of our Yesuva upon my passing. It is worth examining why in our patriarchal-governed village, our male leaders leave before we do.

However, that is a painful journey that I am not willing to take. Perhaps the complications and increasing pressures of life, coupled with the demands of leadership, took their toll. Governing our tribes can be a stressful process of marrying old and new traditions, without losing our identity as Fijians.

Given the patriarchal nature of Fiji, how then did this female leader emerge? I had no plans to lead our Yesuva. Why would I? In our patriarchal society, men are the leaders of our village and families. Female leadership of a Yesuva or village is rare, if non-existent. Yet, in my late fifties, and due to a series of unforeseen circumstances, I found myself being next in line and appointed as the rare and prestigious female leader of our two-hundred member Yesuva in Nawaka village.

To understand who I am, one needs to understand our Fijian culture and heritage.

Growing up in our humble abode, I was the only girl, with three male siblings. My role of leadership was relegated to household duties. Men may rule the village, but women rule the home. My mother and I assumed traditional female roles. Cooking, cleaning, supporting our men and each other were what we did happily. We understood that our survival depended on us praying together, working together, and maintaining our culture. In a tightly knitted community, tough times were made easy, problems got handled internally, and God was always our source.

It has been eighty-plus years since I was born on the beautiful Fijian island of Viti Levu. The largest island in the Republic of Fiji and home to over 600,000 inhabitants, we are proud indigenous descendants of Africa and India, who have existed since the 1600s. Viti Levu comprises a collection of villages and Nawaka village is one of them.

Resiliency runs in our veins as our search for opportunities and survival led our ancestors to leave their homeland many centuries ago to settle in the Polynesian islands in the South Pacific. Fijians are a tightly-knitted group who are committed to our community, our faith, and preserving our culture. I have watched as our island's untamed forestry and lush vegetation have succumbed to apartment buildings and varied resorts. Fiji's exponential growth over the years has spawned an exotic tourist getaway for the rich, famous, and not-so-famous. Yet, we as Fijians and particularly within our villages, continue our fight to maintain our private sanctity and traditions, even though the outside world is changing around us.

Throughout the centuries, we have had to be resilient as farmers, fishermen, business owners, faith keepers, and village leaders. Rich soil and current technology have allowed us to become organic farmers. We grow our food and raise livestock, but our dairy products come from the supermarket. There is an order and respect that guides our villages as each village has a chief and each chief has an assistant. One chief may oversee several villages with the help of the village's spokesperson and liaison.

In Nawaka, Chief or Tui (Tooey) Nawaka Ratu Asaeli (Asaylee) has the prestigious honor of overseeing five villages including the village of Nawaka. Viliame Sobumeuinavula (Bill) assists Chief Ratu Asaeli in overseeing Nawaka's 1,000 plus inhabitants who are divided into twelve Yesuva. The protocol requires that you meet with Bill before meeting Chief Ratu Asaeli or any of the Nawaka village leaders. One important tradition is the presentation of the Kava Root to the chief or leader with whom you are visiting. This presentation is followed by a short spiritual ceremony that welcomes the visitor. It is very important to know the order and structure of our culture, as many foreigners make the mistake of disrespecting who we are. I speak at length about our culture because, at eighty years of age, my primary duty is to be the cultural ambassador of our village. In other words, I am responsible for ensuring that we remain uniquely Fijian for as long as we can.

Fijians' physical, mental, spiritual, and emotional resiliency comes from our very strong sense of faith, community, and culture. We enjoy a simple and happy life. We rely on each other and limit outside influences on our community. In Nawaka, Fijians farm and grow their food which is shared by the tribe and/or village.

Typically, they are one or two key breadwinners in the family. Breadwinners can be both male and female. Within the village, women assume the traditional role of cooking, cleaning, taking care of the children, and supporting each other. Female leadership is relegated to the home but not as official community leaders. The church is where many of us exert our leadership abilities (e.g., bible study, small groups, outreach efforts to needy families). Having been converted to Christianity in the 1800s by the British, Fiji, although primarily Methodist and Protestant, is spiritually diverse as many religions coexist peacefully within one village. Fijians believe that God is God and that one should be free to worship and honor "source" in whatever way one chooses. In Nawaka, many religions are represented by churches and temples, either within the village or on the island itself.

The responsibility of guiding and taking care of every family within our village can be daunting. Our families are structured where one person in each family is the primary breadwinner, while the others take care of the family and village concerns. Our Chief and each tribal leader ensure that everyone in the village's needs are met.

Having been thrust into my leadership role after the passing of my brother, I learned very quickly how big a responsibility it was to lead our tribe. Where did we want to be ten, fifteen, or even twenty-five years from now? How could we preserve our culture and what is uniquely Fijian? Furthermore, how could I ensure that the younger generation who were steadily being influenced by technology and the glitz and glamour of life and not forget who we are as a people? These were just a few of the many questions that haunted me as a leader. We have many traditions that I along with the other Yesuva leaders are committed to preserving. The most important one is getting together and celebrating our families and community. Our culture is kept alive through storytelling, chants, and songs.

As the leader of our tribe, my responsibilities include ensuring that every member is, first and foremost, spiritually grounded. Our faith, my faith, keeps us spiritually resilient. I spend several hours a day before God in prayer for my tribe and village. There is much to pray for as the needs of our Yesuva are endless—health, financial stability, our crops, marriages, potential husbands, wives, and children to name a few. Most of the time, I spend praying for our chief Nawaka Ratu Asaeli.

Like the Royal Family, chiefs are chosen via bloodline succession. They must have a good moral and spiritual character, wisdom, excellent leadership abilities, and a strong vision for our village and/or the villages they govern. Potential chiefs are groomed and monitored closely throughout their lifetime. In the final analysis, only those with the aforementioned characteristics are considered for this lifetime role. As the elder statesperson of our village, part of my duties is to name the next chief after careful consideration and discussions with the village tribunal. I have named and appointed the last six chiefs. This is a tremendous honor as, much thought and prayer are involved in naming the next Tui (Tooey).

Although I could never be the next Tui because it is not in my bloodline, I am honored to be the leader of my 200-member-clan.

I like to think that I have done a good job so far as our Yesuva is growing. I stay humble and before God who gives me all the answers, I need to lead our tribe. I live a simple life because there is power and beauty in simplicity. I am also well respected, cared for, and supported by my tribe. Along with Nawaka Ratu Asaeli (Asaylee), Viliame Sobumeuinavula (Bill), and the village tribunal, we will continue to set the standards for our Nawakan Yesuva. As our village's ambassador, psychologist, spiritual guide, mentor, and Nana to many, I will continue to uphold our traditions and village life for as long as I can. I am Miriame Lestale, female leader of the Venutopia Tribe in Nawaka, Fiji and at eighty years of age, I am resilient!

So, what's your takeaway from Miriame Lestale's story?

#PhoenixesRising

https://bit.ly/phoenixesrising

Question: What kind of Phoenix do you want to be?

ON RESILIENCE

"Every adversity, every failure, every heartache carries with it the seed of an equal or greater benefit."—**Napoleon Hill**

Everyone finds the strength to be resilient from different places. For Miriame, it was her faith and relationship with God that have sustained her over the years. Also, she found her purpose as the official cultural ambassador of her village. It could not have been easy to step into a male-dominated role. However, she has done it with grace.

As we continue our resilience journey, we leave Fiji and travel to New Zealand. It is my honor to introduce you to our next Phoenix Te Aroha Martin—our Maori leader of her clan in New Zealand, who introduced me to the Maori culture. I invite you to discover what kept her resilient throughout the years.

ON RESILIENCE

"Whāia te iti kahurangi ki te tūohu koe me he maunga teitei"

"Seek the treasure you value most dearly: if you bow your head, let it be to a lofty mountain"

Chapter 3

FINDING STRENGTH THROUGH LOVE:
Te Aroha Martin, Clan Leader, New Zealand
ON RESILIENCE

Former Ambassador for Tamaki Maori Village in Rotorua, New Zealand, Te Aroha Martin was the epitome of love and grace. Devoted to her family and bringing joy to others through her songs and laughter, she will forever be in our hearts.

BE RESILIENT

What do you do when your life has been difficult? You find the courage to turn your tragedies into triumphs. I dedicate my story to my family and all at Tamaki Maori Cultural Village. Love truly does make the world go around. I hope that you enjoy my story of resilience as it comes from my heart to you

Finding Strength Through Love
Te Aroha Martin, Clan Leader, New Zealand

"Ko taku reo taku ohooho, ko taku reo taku mapihi mauria

My language is my awakening, my language is the window to my soul"

I descend from a culture known for its strength, and a people are known for their resilience: The Maori from Aoteroa] (aʊˌtelə'roʊə), — the Land of the Long White Cloud—known today as New Zealand.

The history of the Maori dates back to 1320 when groups of my ancestors migrated from Eastern Polynesia. They traversed the vast Pacific Ocean in handmade canoes, called Waka. The early Maori were adept navigators, perhaps the finest of their time. They monitored the tides, the winds, and the phases of the moon to make the perilous journeys, south. Their navigational skills, together with their masterful craftsmanship of carving out Waka, gave them the ability to conquer the elements.

As a result, tribal groups settled in Aotearoa. And with every Waka, a tribal group formed, finding land, and building palisaded villages to stake their claim. Aotearoa has rich soil and plenty of water sources. However, as tribes attempted to advantage themselves by claiming more territory, food sources, and women, tribal wars began.

The Maori are a proud warrior people, known for their creativity, grit, and survival skills. People across the globe had an opportunity to connect with our culture via the 2002 movie, Whale Rider. It tells of the schoolgirl who emerges as the leader of her tribe. The role of Rangatira, Chief, is traditionally held by a male.

My name is Te Aroha Martin and this is my story of resilience, and my emergence, as a woman, in a male-dominated world. Te Aroha means The Love. But people call me Aroha—Love. Being able to love others has been the cornerstone of my resilience. Love has seen me through the best and the worst times of my life.

I am a member of the Nga Tiawa tribe, and I grew up in a village called Wairaka—the only Maori village within the township of Whakatāne (pronounced *fah-kah-TAH-nə*). Whakatāne sits on the east coast of the North Island, in Aotearoa.

As a child, growing up in this area, I experienced a lot of hardship. I was one of sixteen children. And though we were not all from the same mother, our small home housed two adults, five girls, and eleven boys. My dad worked away, to earn a better living. It was a struggle to feed and care for the whanau (pronounced *'fa:naʉ*), the family. He would make his appearance when he could, but his absence was felt by my mother who was left to care for all the children.

My mother died when I was eleven and life became increasingly difficult for me. My older siblings had moved on, and the rest of us had been left to fend for ourselves. I became a mum, cook, cleaner, organizer, and supporter to my younger siblings when I was just eleven years old.

Over the next four years, day-to-day living became burdensome, unbearable, and frightening, with a combination of increased stress, exhaustion, and abuse—physical, sexual, and emotional. I will refrain from naming the perpetrators here.

Fiercely determined to survive and thrive, an unknown spirit rose inside of me. Enough was enough, and I knew something had to give—and it was not going to be me. "Kia Kaha," "Stay strong" is what I repeatedly told myself.

I ran away when I was fifteen and found shelter in the warmth and salvation of my older sister. Leaving my siblings behind was the hardest thing I've ever had to do. Looking back, I need to believe that someone took care of them. If you are one of my younger siblings, and you are reading this, I ask for your forgiveness for abandoning you.

I attended Whakatane High School and went on to work at several places. Eventually, I found my dream job in Rotorua, working as a tour bus driver for Tamaki Maori Cultural Village. Here, I met new people every day and shared with them our Maori culture.

Through my work, my love for my own personal family extends to families from across the globe. Of the many drivers employed by Tamaki, I am the only female. I drive a thirty-seater tour bus, and here I share my love of Maori culture with our international and local visitors to Tamaki Village.

I ensure that the guests on my Waka (my bus can be referred to as my canoe, or Waka), experience our Maori culture to the max. My bus tours are legendary. On our way to Tamaki Village we sing, play games, and make the whole experience fun, educational, and memorable. Along with my colleagues, I also sing and entertain our customers when we arrive at the village.

Over the years, very few of my passengers would have guessed that behind my smile and cheery disposition lay a hidden secret. As the matriarch of my family, I support four children, thirteen grandchildren, and four great-grandchildren.

One of my grandchildren—he is my heart—was born with developmental delays. I sensed something was wrong, but nothing could prepare me for the truth. My heart sank the day that he was diagnosed with Kabuki Syndrome, and we found out that he would never be normal.

That's when I told myself,

"You are Maori. We are warriors. Te Aroha, you are going to make it, and so will he. Kia Kaha (stay strong)."

For those who are not aware, Kabuki Syndrome is a rare type of genetic disorder that affects 1 in 32,000 people. This syndrome causes developmental and physical delays and there is no cure. Like other genetic diseases, children with Kabuki Syndrome face a myriad of challenges and health issues. As a family, we chose to do whatever was needed to have him thrive, despite his limitations.

My daughter agreed to let me raise him. He is my heart and joy and has exceeded our expectations. There are no words to describe what it is like to raise a child with special needs. There are days when your patience runs thin. You are exhausted, saddened, and will always ask yourself "Why this kid?"

Then the hugs, kisses, and smiles let you know that somehow, somewhere, everything will be alright. We were told that he might never walk. Well, he is resilient. Recently, he took his first steps, and each day he is improving.

In the meantime, I am having the time of my life, as I love what I do. When I am not driving the tour bus, I also work at our hospital in Rotorua, spreading love and happiness to our sick and infirm. My childhood was certainly not filled with the love that I would have liked. Yet I have learned that the secret to life is to give love even if you don't feel like it, or if you don't think others deserve it.

Somehow it returns ten-fold. I receive a lot of love from my husband, my children, grandchildren, and colleagues. The love I was denied in my childhood has returned in my adult years. I am grateful for the ability to drive my tour bus, make people happy, and take care of my family, especially my grandson. My name is Te Aroha Martin; wife, mother, grandmother, great grandmother, caretaker to the ill, driver, entertainer, and giver of Love … and I am resilient!

As of the writing of Te Aroha's story, unfortunately, she transitioned and is now driving her big, red Waka tour bus in the sky. Her spirit lives on in her children and grandchildren. Continued blessings to her family. It has been an honor and privilege to tell her story.

So, what's your takeaway from Te Aroha Martin's story?

#PhoenixesRising

https://bit.ly/phoenixesrising

Question: What kind of Phoenix do you want to be?

Te Aroha was a lovely lady who enjoyed introducing tourists and people to her Maori culture. Her passing reminds us to love the ones we are with. She left a great legacy for her family to follow. Thank you, Te Aroha, for your generous spirit and the joy that people felt just by being in your presence. To learn more about the Maori culture through Te Aroha's eyes, visit https://www.tamakimaorivillage .co.nz

I trust that you enjoyed reading about Te Aroha and getting a glimpse of her remarkable Maori culture. As we leave New Zealand, we are off to visit her friend and Phoenix, Poetess Erica Froggatt. Erica made my journey to these far-off lands amazing and memorable. As you read Erica's poem, see if you can glean a deeper appreciation of Maori culture through her eyes.

ON RESILIENCE

"Kia kaha, kia māia, kia manawanui"
"Be strong, be brave, be steadfast

I AM POEM

Erica Froggatt

Travel Ambassador, New Zealand/Australia

I AM WAHINE

I AM FROM

A Land
Abundant in natural beauty
Majestical, Spiritual, Haunting
I am made up of these things

I AM FROM

A Culture
Steeped in Mana
Steadfast, Enduring, Sacred
I am made up of these things

I AM FROM

A Community
Forged by the words, Kia Kaha
Sharing, Connected, Stoic
I am made up of these things

I AM FROM

A Family
Bound by Blood and Aroha
Robust, Spirited, Reflective
I am made up of these things

I AM

Wahine
Nature's Daughter

Compassionate, Gentle, Resilient
And this is my Whakapapa

*Wahine; Maori for Woman
*Majestical; in reference to the New Zealand movie
'Hunt for the Wilderpeople'
*Mana; a Maori word that is difficult to translate -
Imagine all positive feelings of 'Pride' and mix that with
Spiritual Strength
*Kia Kaha; Stay Strong
*Aroha; Maori word for Love
*Whakapapa; Maori word for Identity, Genealogy, Story

Erica Froggatt was born in Te Puke, New Zealand, and resides on the Sunshine Coast in Australia. Erica is a Travel Ambassador with a passion for family, health, nature, and culture. Her passion is editing books so that her customers' stories can provide the reader with the best possible experience.

So, what's your takeaway from Phoenix, Poetess Erica's poem?

#PhoenixesRising

https://bit.ly/phoenixesrising

Question: What kind of Phoenix do you want to be?

Together, Te Aroha's story and Erica's beautiful poem are a declaration of their truth and reflect their love for their Maori heritage, family, and culture. As we move from the region of New Zealand and Australia, our next stop is Egypt where we will meet Queen Pharaoh Hatshepsut – a fierce, 3000-year, take-no-prisoners, female Pharaoh. She is probably the most controversial, but influential Egyptian Queen Pharaoh in history.

As women, we are all queens in our own right. Queen Hatshepsut of Egypt is included in this anthology because she set the stage for women to assume leadership in an era where female governance was non-existent and taboo. For the love of her people and country, she made very bold and controversial moves upon assuming the role of Pharaoh in 1478 BC. As with any queen, the fight to achieve Queendom can be brutal. Consider that once your goal has been met, it takes resilience and fortitude to avoid being dethroned. I invite you to read the remarkable story of this controversial queen who was almost written out of the history books.

BE RESILIENT

Chapter 4

THE FORGOTTEN AND BOLDEST
QUEEN OF THE NILE
Queen Pharaoh Hatshepsut

ON RESILIENCE

*"She stood in the storm and when the wind did
not blow her way, she adjusted her sails."*
—Elizabeth Edwards

This story of Queen Pharaoh Hatshepsut has been modernized for *The Art of Resilience: Phoenixes Rising.* Many thanks to the Egyptologists who discovered her sarcophagus in 1872 and have continued to discover more and more about this amazing queen who lived over 3000 years ago. Special thanks also to Henry Golub, Egyptologist, who brought Queen Pharaoh Hatshepsut to life on our tour of Egypt.

Should you want to learn more about Queen Pharaoh Hatshepsut, here are some references that can provide you with more information on this amazing queen and Pharoah.

Hatshepsut - HISTORY

https://en.wikipedia.org/wiki/Hatshepsut

https://www.worldhistory.org/hatshepsut

https://www.tripsinegypt.com/queen-hatshepsut

https://www.biography.com/royalty/hatshepsut

https://www.metmuseum.org/art/collection/search/566763

Should you also want to learn more about Dr. Vaughan's work, please contact her at https://www.linkedin.com/feed/ info@drjoycoaching.com https://drjoycoaching.com 786-209-3918

The Forgotten and Boldest Queen of the Nile
Queen Pharaoh Hatshepsut
1479–1458 BC

"I have commanded that my titulary (title) abide like the mountains; when the sun shines its rays are bright upon the titulary of my majesty; my Horus is high upon the standard ... forever." **Hatshepsut**

More than anything else in the world, my title as Pharaoh meant everything to me. Everyone speaks about Cleopatra. There have even been books written and movies made about her. However, when it comes to myself, do you know that Thutmose III, that wicked and despicable person, had the nerve to try to erase me from the history books? Tell me, my people, how could you dare to erase the legacy of Queen Hatshepsut, the first female Pharaoh of the 18th Dynasty of the ancient Alkebulan civilization of Egypt. Yes, and yes folks, I was a bad sista. Hello again, in case you missed it, I am Queen Pharaoh Hatshepsut and this is my story of resilience.

I owe my place in the history books to a gifted team of archeologists. First, there was British archeologist Howard Carter who discovered my tomb in the Valley of the Kings in 1903. Of course, Thutmose III would bury me in some obscure place that was difficult to find, far less excavate. Howard Carter went as far as he could go. Then in 1989, Egyptologist Donald Ryan reopened my tomb but only found my wet nurse, some geese, and another unidentified body.

However, in 2007, it was our very own Dr. Zahi Hawass, Egypt's foremost archeologist, who discovered my body and tooth. It seemed that I was a mess when I died—overweight, with ovarian cancer and bad teeth. Apparently, since my death over 3000 years ago, humans had developed an advanced technology that could detect these things.

Dr. Hawass consulted noted dentist Dr. Galal El-Beheri from Cairo University, who confirmed that my tooth fit perfectly into the hole in my mouth from which it had fallen. I could only imagine their excitement. I forever will be grateful to these gentlemen and other archeologists throughout the years for helping me to find my voice in absentia, and for restoring my place in history.

I had no ambition to be a Pharaoh. Three thousand years ago, and traditionally, only men were Pharaohs, and that role was via succession from father to son. In my case that was not to be so. My mother Queen Ahmose was not able to give my dad the necessary male heir to the throne. She had my younger sister, Nefrubity, and me. My dad, on the other hand, had been married before, to Mutnofret, who gave him several sons. This meant that although my mom did not produce a male successor to the throne, one was guaranteed through the bloodline of my dad and Mutnofret. Unfortunately, my younger sister, Nefrubity died when she was young, which left me as the heir to the 18th dynasty, or so I thought.

In a male-dominated society, my stepbrothers were still placed before me because they were men. As they assumed leadership positions in the dynasty, I could only sit back and watch as they made a debacle of everything. However, being a girl, I was not to take my dad's place as Pharaoh. To continue the dynasty, and to preserve the already-built legacy, I found myself at age 12 being married off to my half-brother Thutmose II. There was no discussion. I was not even consulted. As the saying goes, "it was what it was."

My marriage to Thutmose II made me Queen. It was my dad's last gesture of goodwill before he transitioned in 1492 to the great beyond. That's how it was back then. For the gods and country, you did what was required of you.

Unfortunately, for our dynasty, Thutmose II and I had a daughter. We named her Neferure. Her name means "The Beauty of Ra", who is the God of the Sun. Well, when your wife cannot, or does not give you a son, what else is there for you to do but to get one from your concubine. It takes a special kind of resilience to sit back and watch another woman produce a male heir, and then be asked to raise that child as your own. One thing was clear. Concubines can never be queens. I was not sure if the reverse is true.

As a woman, I would find it very difficult to give my son up to someone else to raise. Again, that was the practice in those days. Shortly after that, I became Egypt's highest-ranking widow, and single mother as my husband Thutmose II died prematurely in 1479, leaving me to raise Neferure and Thutmose III. Of course, I had no shortage of help with the children. Any great leader is successful in part, because of her team. Since Thutmose III was a baby, although he was king, realistically, he was too young to govern our dynasty. Someone had to govern, and that person was me.

I became his regent. A regent is an appointed surrogate ruler who governs the state in place of a monarch that is too young, absent, or not able to rule their country. I became Thutmose III's regent and oversaw political affairs until Thutmose III reached the age of majority. When I took over as regent, our dynasty was in a sorry state. Thutmose II was not a good ruler. His decisions left our dynasty almost bankrupt. I, Queen Hatshepsut, decided to make it my mission to bring peace and prosperity to my people, restore trade relations, and oversee the construction of some of ancient Egypt's most stunning structures.

I was ambitious, driven, and determined. It would take being resilient to fulfill my mission. There have been many Pharaohs in the history of Egypt. Most of them have been male. The history books state that before me and Cleopatra, there was Sobekneferu. She ruled the 12th dynasty of Egypt from 1806 to 1802 BC. I was Pharaoh of the 12th Dynasty of Egypt and ruled from 1479–1458 BC. Cleopatra was the third female ruler of the Ptolemaic Kingdom of Egypt. She reigned from 51BC to 30 BC. BC means before Christ. After he came a lot changed. One key event occurred after Cleopatra's death. Egypt fell to Rome and as they say, the rest is history.

I was the Egyptian dynasty's longest-reigning indigenous female Pharaoh. I reigned for over 20 years as the second female in Egypt. It took everything for me to hold that position over time. I had to deal with the opposition of males who vehemently opposed female leadership. However, whatever mess they threw at me, I handled it with ease and grace like any queen would. Resilience is a muscle that, at least in my case, I had to exercise daily.

As I shared earlier, I was determined and unstoppable in my quest to bring prosperity and peace back to my people. Every day was a struggle to defend and hold onto my pharaonic power. No matter how many times I argued that my father had appointed me as his successor, no one listened to me. I even cited and reminded them of my royal ancestry; to no avail. As you know, a huge part of success is to bounce back from whatever life throws at you, and be determined to fulfill your purpose. I found myself taking extreme measures to fit in and to be one of the "good old boys." In an unheard and radical gesture for my time, I made myself look more like a man by growing a beard. If you notice you will see an oblong structure that extends from my bottom lip to beyond my chin. That is the beard that I grew.

I demanded that I be represented in statues and paintings as a male Pharaoh with a beard and huge muscles. In other photos, I appear in my typical feminine attire and I am pretty.

Life as Pharaoh was not all bad. I made sure to surround myself with powerful allies in my administration. My Chief Minister Senenmut became my right-hand person. One should never underestimate the power of a woman. In a series of carefully crafted maneuvers, I eventually obtained complete authority and became the de facto ruler of ancient Egypt and the fifth Pharaoh of Egypt's 18th Dynasty around 1473 BC. Before that, I was co-leader of our Alkebulan civilization. Not boasting, but boasting, I, Queen Pharaoh Hatshepsut am regarded as one of Egypt's most successful Pharaohs. I ruled over our dynasty for more than 20 years. Under my reign as Pharaoh, I oversaw the expansion of Egyptian trade, and the commissioning of large-scale architectural projects, including the Temple of Deir el-Bahri in western Thebes, where I would eventually be buried. I was known as "Lady of the Two Lands", possibly because of my work in Thebes and at home.

My greatest accomplishment was that I brought peace and prosperity, restored trade relations, and restored the infrastructure of a crumbling dynasty. I also oversaw the construction of some of ancient Egypt's most stunning structures. According to Egyptologist James Henry Breasted (1905), I, Queen Pharaoh Hatshepsut, am "the first famous lady in the history of whom we are aware." Here are a few of my accomplishments, other than fending off political enemies and protecting the crown for my stepson.

I commanded several large-scale construction and development projects, most of which may still be seen today, mainly in the Thebes area. I was a successful developer, with hundreds of projects under my belt. At Karnak's Great Temple Complex, I began by erecting two 100-foot-tall obelisks. At the time, they were the world's tallest obelisks. Around Thebes, I created and built our dynasty's Dynastic and Theological Center. I also built a network of spectacular processional routes and sanctuaries.

My most famous work perhaps is the vast Deir el-Bahri memorial temple, which is considered one of ancient Egypt's architectural marvels. The ancient Egyptian Mortuary Temple Complex of Deir el-Bahari is located on the Nile's west bank, immediately across from Luxor, Egypt. The Djeser-Djeseru, or Hatshepsut's Mortuary Temple, is located near the Temple of Mentuhotep II, beneath the cliffs of Deir el-Bahari. It is widely regarded as one of my most important accomplishments, as well as an architectural marvel of the ancient world. Scenes honoring my victories are carved onto my temple. Similar tributes as carvings can be seen on the various shrines I built to Anubis, the god of the dead, Hathor, the goddess of fertility, Amun, the king of gods, and Re, the sun god. Senenmut, the principal overseer of works at Deir el-Bahri, designed the temple. My construction projects were more extensive than those of my Middle Kingdom forebears.

Another notable achievement of my reign was the authorization of a trading voyage to Punt. What queen doesn't like to travel and travel well? My journeys brought incredible wealth to Egypt, including ivory, ebony, gold, leopard skins, and incense, from a faraway land known as Punt (possibly modern-day Eritrea).

The Land of Punt was an ancient kingdom and a trading city on the East African coast, located beyond the southernmost tip of the

Red Sea. Punt was known for producing and exporting gold, fragrant resins, blackwood, ebony, ivory, and wild animals, among other things. Hatshepsut was the one who authorized and directed Egypt's most famous voyage to the Land of Punt. In exchange for Egypt's linen, grain, papyrus, ebony, obsidian, myrrh trees, wild animals, and incense were sent back to Egypt. My Punt expedition was a diplomatic triumph, as no other Egyptian Pharaoh in history is regarded to have been as successful in Punt as I was. As a result of this successful voyage, historians believe Punt to be ancient Egypt's traditional trading partner.

History has me dying in 1458 BC. I think that I was in my mid-40s. I am buried with great company, as Tutankhamun is also buried in the Valley of the Kings. The Valley of the Kings is in the hills behind Deir el-Bahri. I shared earlier that every day I had to fight for my power. Even as I neared death, I found it imperative to legitimize my authority. As a final gesture of that quest, I reinterred my father's sarcophagus in my tomb so that we could both die together.

I could never have imagined that my stepson Thutmose III would turn out to be so spiteful and ungrateful. You never know about children. You can only pray that they turn out well. I am not sure what went wrong with that young man, but he took it upon himself when he took over the throne to erase my memory. My stepson was ambitious like I was, and a great warrior. He ruled for another 30 years after my death. However, in the later years of his reign, Thutmose III had almost all evidence of my authority destroyed. Can you imagine what It must have been like to have my portrayals of myself as Pharaoh on the temples and monuments I had created erased? Little by little, Thutmose III wanted to erase me as a formidable female ruler. Perhaps, he wanted to close the dynasty's male succession line.

My existence lay hidden until 1822 when Egyptian researchers were able to decode and interpret the hieroglyphics on the walls of Deir el-Bahri. While Cleopatra may be commonly regarded as the most famous woman in ancient Egypt, it was I, Queen Pharaoh Hatshepsut herself, who ruled Egypt for more than 20 years throughout the 15th century BC, and during this early period of the New Kingdom. My reign was far more significant as I brought an era of unparalleled artistic genius to Egypt, which was accepted by a thriving dynasty.

As I shared earlier, I am forever grateful to all the Egyptologists now and in the future who continue to keep my memory alive. My illustrious past in Egyptian history was all but lost until Egyptologists rediscovered and restored my rightful place in history. Since my sarcophagus (one of three I had made), was discovered by British archeologist Howard Carter in 1903, archeologists continue to excavate my most exquisite surviving edifice, and the temple I built in the Valley of the Kings at Deir el-Bahri, across the Nile from modern-day Luxor.

Thousands of stone fragments have been found surrounding the temple. They have been reassembled into magnificent Hatshepsut statues, some of which were enormous in scale. Today, discoveries are being uncovered, and academics' perceptions of me and my legacy have been altered as a result. A fresh team of archaeologists and Egyptologists continue to keep my spirit alive. My mummy is presently housed in Cairo's Egyptian Museum, and the New York City's Metropolitan Museum features a stunning life-sized statue of me seated that miraculously escaped my stepson's destruction. I hope that you have enjoyed reading my story as I have enjoyed bringing this modern version of my life to you. I am wife, mother, Queen, ruler, and first female Pharaoh of the 18th Dynasty of the ancient Alkebulan civilization of Egypt. My name is Queen Pharaoh Hatshepsut, and I am still resilient from my tomb.

WOW! What a story. Queen Pharaoh Hatshepsut certainly left her mark and blazed a trail for women leaders over 3000 years ago.

So, what's your takeaway from Queen Pharaoh Hatshepsut's story?

#PhoenixesRising

https://bit.ly/phoenixesrising

Question: What kind of Phoenix do you want to be?

As we continue our travels around the world, we will make a pitstop in Guyana, and the United States. Next, we will meet a feisty leader with a similar tenacious personality as Queen Pharaoh Hatshepsut. It took fortitude, courage, and resilience for a woman of color to build a real estate empire in the 1920s. Let us see how Lucille E. Chance Edwards achieved her success and legacy for her family and future generations

BE RESILIENT

Chapter 5

BUILDING A REAL ESTATE LEGACY:
Lucille E. Chance Edwards, Guyana

Lawyer, Real Estate pioneer, and powerhouse, Lucille E. Chance Edwards is the founder of Edwards Sisters Reality – the first Real Estate office in Harlem New York. Influencer, mover, and shaker of her time, she championed the rights of people of color to have a seat at the table of influencers.

ON RESILIENCE

"Hold yourself responsible for a higher standard than anybody else expects of you. Never excuse yourself. Never pity yourself. Be a hard master to yourself-and be lenient to everybody else."
—Henry Ward Beecher

Building a Real Estate Legacy
Lucille E. Chance Edwards, Guyana

"I have learned over the years that when one's mind is made up, this diminishes fear; knowing what must be done does away with fear."
—Rosa Parks, African American Civil Rights Activist

740 St Nicholas Avenue in Harlem, New York is where judges, ambassadors, politicians like Adam Clayton Powell Jr., Charlie Rangel (U.S. House of representatives), David Dinkins (former mayor of N.Y.), and many prominent persons of color wanted to be while launching their careers and engaging in the Civil Rights Movement in the 1960s.

Their mentor, supporter, and the champion was none other than a tiny, powerful, take-no-prisoners woman named Lucille E. Chance Edwards—our aunt and beloved family matriarch. Originally from Guyana, Aunt Lu was on an unstoppable mission to build, not only her real estate empire but to ensure that people of color took their rightful and deserving place in society, and even the highest offices of the land.

Born in the country of Guyana in 1898, to thirty-two-year-old parents, Aunt Lu was advanced for her time both in her thoughts and actions. As an emancipated slave, her father was educated in Barbados by church members in what was called the House of the Lessers. As the sugar industry declined in Barbados, her father answered the invitation to come to Guyana for a better life. Guyana was at that time and still is, rich in gold and minerals. He became a judge/legal assistant in Guyana, where he met and married Aunt Lu's mother. Together they had thirteen children.

What was remarkable about Aunt Lu's family was that she and all her siblings were successful. It is safe to say that the spirit of resilience was in their DNA and certainly in Aunt Lu's.

Aunt Lu was deemed to be one of the smartest of her siblings. Like her siblings and her parents, she was educated under the British system which put her two years ahead of the American School system. Her intellectual prowess did not go unnoticed. She was offered two scholarships to study in England and the United States. Married with a son, she accepted the United States offer, and began her journey to great success and power in a country that had little tolerance for people of color. She followed her sister, Millicent, and her husband, son, and other sister followed some years after. In 1921 she arrived in New York and entered Hunter College as an undergrad in 1929. From there she went on to attend New York University's Law School, graduated at the top of her class in 1932, and passed the bar on her first attempt. She was the first black female lawyer in the State of New York.

In the meantime, her sister Millicent, a proverbial entrepreneur, created an employment agency in lower Manhattan's 34th St for people of Caribbean descent. Many people from the various islands would find gainful employment as they came off the ships, working as maids and houseboys for the predominantly white and wealthy residents of Harlem.

In the 1920s, lower Manhattan was predominantly black because of the islanders who disembarked from the ships and settled there, whereas Harlem was predominantly Dutch, Caucasian, and void of black and brown cultures. This was just the beginning of a giant movement towards educational and financial independence for our people. Said another way, Aunt Millicent and Aunt Lu were the Harriet Tubman of the Caribbean. The sisters jump-started the careers of many famous people of color. In the 1930s Aunt Lu was left devastated by the loss of her sister, Millicent, and her father. However, she found the ability to carry on despite these setbacks.

Aunt Lu found love again with Al B. Chance, which helped her to cope with the loss of her sister and father. Together they had one son and two grandchildren. In her lifetime, she was fortunate enough to be a part of their lives. Her faith, fortitude, and her ability to see into the future played a huge part in her resilience journey.

As a lawyer, jobs for practicing lawyers were scarce or next to impossible. Aunt Lu decided to create her own law and real estate brokerage firm housed at 740 St. Nicholas Ave in the heart of Harlem. She was the first black to own property in what was then an all-white area. Over the years, blacks slowly migrated away from lower Manhattan and moved up to Harlem. On the flip side, whites were moving out of Harlem and closer to downtown Manhattan. In her community, Aunt Lu was known as a mover and shaker. Politically, she was very active and well-known among the "Harlemites." She even managed to have a few articles written about her in the local newspaper. She was named Outstanding Citizen of the Year several times and received commendations for her work in civil rights and the rights of people in general.

Due to redlining, a practice where the banks refused to give low-income families a mortgage, many low-income families could not purchase a home even if they had the down payment. Aunt Lu was on a mission to change that. She helped many persons of color to buy their first home in Harlem. She created the opportunity for landlords to hold or "buy back" the mortgages until the amount was paid off. This was a win/win for both parties.

She purchased the first family home—213 W 139th St. on the then known Strivers Row. Strivers Row was so named because of the people who were striving to be and do better in life. In addition to housing family members, 213 W 139th St. became the safe haven for those coming from the islands who needed a place to stay, and employment until they could achieve their own levels of independence. Over time, Aunt Lu's siblings migrated from Guyana to make a name for themselves in America. Her brothers, Phillip and King Edwards also attended New York University. Phil would go on to become a physician and Olympic champion in track and field, winning many bronze medals. He was known as "The Man of Bronze" because he had collected so many bronze medals from the many races he won. Phil even impressed Hitler during the Olympic games in Germany.

Aunt Lu had a lot of foresight. She had a knack for being able to predict trends and get ahead of them. I remember her telling us that when it came to real estate, buy in the areas where non-blacks are exiting, because sooner or later, they would want their property back. This foresight had her buy and sell several properties in Harlem and throughout New York.

This is how she and her family survived the aftermath of the Great Depression. This was a very difficult time for Aunt Lu and the family. Over the next thirty years, their ability to survive and thrive would be tested. Undaunted by prejudice and injustice, Aunt Lu continued to build her real estate empire. In 1944, she snagged the former German embassy in Hastings-on-the-Hudson in New York, and became the first black to move into this arena of opulence. Not wanting to be the only person of color in the neighborhood, she paved the way for other people of color such as Madam C. J. Walker, Drs. Kenneth and Mamie Clarke (Brown vs The Board of Education), and other doctors, lawyers, and prominent persons of color to buy property in the area. The area became known as "Nigger Hill" because that area was where all the up-and-coming blacks could buy real estate.

My cousin Judy loved to tell the story where our Caucasian neighbors would ring the doorbell. When she opened the door, they automatically assumed that she was the maid. They would ask to speak to the master or mistress of the house. She would politely ask them to wait a minute, return all dolled up, and confirm whom they wanted to speak to. Then in the sweetest voice would introduce herself as "I am she." Judy often shared that she loved to see the shock on their faces.

Very often, great success comes with a heavy price tag. Aunt Lu's resilience came from her purpose, passion, and profound commitment to have people of color not only survive, but thrive.

For her decision to be a real-estate pioneer, Aunt Lu endured cross burnings, ridicule, deceitful business practices from those she trusted, and other atrocities heaped on herself, family, and her neighboring colleagues and friends. Somehow, she understood that what she endured was a small price to pay for the gold at the end of her rainbow. It was only through God's grace that she and our family weren't killed.

This injustice did not phase Aunt Lu one bit, as she set her sights next on our family getaway in the Hamptons, New York. After all, you needed a place for the family to escape the pressures of the city, and life in general. She wisely befriended an Indian Chief at that time and bought several acres. Using the crew from her city real estate, they hand-built our family getaway in the Hamptons and the rest is history.

Other than real estate, Aunt Lu was one of the founding members, a trustee at Freedom National Bank, and a founding member of St. Martin's Church in Harlem. Joining other investors such as Jackie Robinson, Dunbar McLaurin, and Reverend Wyatt T Walker (Canaan Baptist Church), Freedom National Bank was an African-American-owned bank in Harlem (New York City) founded in 1964. It was one of the largest Black-owned banks in the U.S. that provided loans, investments, and other financial services to the people of color, who in those days, needed a safe place to conduct their banking and business. With its main office at 275 West 125th Street, Freedom National Bank lasted for twenty-six years, until it finally closed Its doors in 1990.

Aunt Lu was driven by her passion and purpose. In reflecting on what she would change, with her niece Ramona Grey-Harris, what she would change would be to not put the pressure on her family to succeed. Aunt Lu was absolutely intolerant of your failure or desire to not use your God-given talents and skills to better yourself and others. In her lifetime, she developed a system of success for our family and anyone else who wanted to pursue and master their purpose. Her philosophy was that anyone could attain anything or be someone, if they were willing to follow the blueprint. Perhaps what she could not understand was that success at a very high level or any level was not everyone's desire.

They were certain non-negotiables. The expectation was that everyone in our family must go to college. Aunt Lu had a system where the immediate family members were the "keepers of the flame." They were responsible for keeping and expanding the real-estate business and continuing to preserve what she fought so hard to build. Everyone else benefited from her turn-key system of success. She did that because she had a deep and personal mandate that post-slavery, people of color were not only going to thrive but become influencers and leave a legacy.

Aunt Lu lived to the beautiful age of 89. She left an indelible legacy and imprint on her family, community, and the world. 740 St. Nicholas Avenue still stands and is fully- operational today. It has been declared a historical landmark in Harlem. Aunt Lou's legacy lives on in her children, grandchildren, nieces, nephews, great-nieces, and great-nephews, not to mention all the thousands of people whose lives she has touched. Our mission as a family, should we decide to accept it, is to pass her spirit of purpose, passion, and success to the next generation and generations to come. Her name was Lucille Edwards Chance, lawyer, real estate creator, mover, and shaker, legacy maker, and she was resilient.

"Don't let anyone rob you of your imagination, your creativity, or your curiosity. It's your place in the world; it's your life. Go on and do all you can with it and make it the life you want to live."
—Mae C. Jemison,
First African American woman astronaut.

So, what's your takeaway from Lucille Chance Edward's story?

#PhoenixesRising

https://bit.ly/phoenixesrising

Question: What kind of Phoenix do you want to be?

Lucille E. Chance Edwards shared with her the story of resilience that had her be successful in the legal and real estate arenas. Her legacy lives on in her family as 740 St. Nicholas Avenue is and remains the first and oldest real estate business in Harlem.

To learn more about Lucille E. Chance Edwards, please contact Ramona Grey-Harris at 212-926-7200, Website: History - ESRA Realty, https://www.esrarealty.com.

I hope that you enjoyed Aunt Lu's story. She was quite something, and it was a privilege to learn from her as well. As we leave New York, we will return to Barbados where I want you to meet a very special Phoenix. I wonder what her resilience story is all about?

I would be remiss if I did not introduce you to my mom. Here she is with me as a baby. I hope that you enjoy reading about this incredible woman who also left a legacy for her family and country.

BE RESILIENT

Chapter 6

A TRIBUTE TO MY MOTHER,
Thelma Vaughan, Barbados

ON RESILIENCE
"It may sound strange, but many champions are made champions by setbacks."—**Bob Richards**

A Tribute To My Mother
Thelma Vaughan, Barbados

"When you were born, you cried and the world rejoiced; live your life so that when you die, the world cries and you rejoice." **Indian Proverb**

Born to an Amerindian father and Asian-Mulatto mother, Mummy was one of six children—four girls and two boys. Collectively, they were known as the Joseph Hacketts of Henry's Lane. Her father, Joseph Hackett was a stevedore from Guyana. Her mother Elizabeth Harvey was a homemaker and influencer in her community. Her parents stressed the value of education, hence their children not only needed to be educated, but to develop a gift in the arts. My mom played the piano, but preferred crafts such as embroidery, crochet, cross-stitch, and tatting (lace-making). Whether it was crafted, photography, music, drama, or art, the Joseph Hackett children were a well-educated and talented bunch.

As a child, my mother was a chronic asthmatic whose mother kept her alive through the application of mustard body wraps which opened her lungs and helped her to breathe. Granny was determined for her to live. Given the chronicity of her asthma, it is a miracle that she lived as long as she did. Granny's loving care and mustard wraps, helped my mom conquer school until graduation. Post-graduation, she began her teaching profession at St. Paul's Girls School in our country, Barbados. In one of our many mother/daughter chats, she shared that she wanted to be a nun when she grew up because she wanted to help people. However, at some point, she met my dad, and well, that nun dream became a fleeting thought.

My parents' paths crossed on several occasions as they were either going to England to study, or returning from studying in England. They agreed to wait for each other but kept their relationship alive through letters and messages from friends. Upon my dad's return from England, they married and started their careers. he rose in the legal profession to become a formidable judge, Attorney General, and a distinguished Minister of Government without portfolio.

Together they pledged that as a couple, they would work for the betterment of their country, and uplift and empower Barbadians to be educated and self-sufficient. For them, the focus was on ful-filling their purpose and leaving a legacy. My mother could have taken a back seat to my dad and assumed the role of housewife. However, that was not their agreement. My dad was a progressive man who celebrated professional women. My mom was no slouch as a homemaker, but he understood that she was much more than that. Hence, he fully supported her rise through the ranks to be-come the first Barbadian Director of Social Welfare in Barbados.

What I loved about my mom was that despite being a chronic asthmatic whose heart stopped, and was revived by my dad on several occasions, she carved a niche for herself , well beyond the shadow of my dad's politically illustrious career. Her social welfare journey satisfied her quest to help people.

After leaving St. Paul's Girls School, my mother entered the field of social work. In 1944, she went to Jamaica where she became involved in a social welfare course organized by Professor T. S. Simey, who at that time was Social Welfare Officer of the Colonial Development and Welfare Organization.

In 1946, she was awarded a scholarship to the London School of Economics (LSE). One year later she was appointed to the post of District Officer when the social welfare department was created. Upon her return to Barbados, she worked mainly in the island's par-ish of St. Andrew but gave her time freely to similar welfare commit-tees in other parishes throughout the island with special emphasis on daycare services for children. She obtained the Diploma in Social Science and returned to the island in 1948.

Mummy loved children. Growing up, there was no shortage of friends who would come to the house for sleepovers and my leg-endary birthday parties. When she was not hosting my birthday parties, high teas, or special luncheons for her friends, she would host her sister Daphne Hackett's plays in our garden. Of course, my cousins and I were automatic volunteers for my mom's and

Aunt Daph's escapades. We were also drafted for our uncle Carlton Hackett's photoshoots.

In her short lifetime, my mom devoted her life to helping those who were less fortunate, and fortunate to heal and get past their traumas. She created a cottage industry program—a work-to-wages initiative for women to financially support themselves. She also supported many families and friends in need, and created a safe passage along with my dad, for many to study abroad. What makes her special was that she was an awesome mom to my cousins, friends, and me. I still miss her from time to time, but her spirit and legacy live on in me, her grandchildren, and great-grandchildren. She is probably laughing in heaven at the fact that she is a great-grandma.

Her extended legacy lives on at The Thelma Vaughan Memorial Home for children with disabilities in Barbados. The Home recently celebrated its 50th anniversary. Several of those children raised in the Home are living independent lives. Some have become entrepreneurs. Please give the Home some love as they do amazing work with children whose families are unable to take care of their physically and developmentally-challenged offspring. At 43 years of age, my mother had fulfilled her purpose and left a legacy in the area of social welfare that stands to this day. On March 10, 1966, she handed the last client file to her successor and returned to her heavenly home around midnight. She was 43 years of age and complete.

"Heaven is my home. I just worked here on earth."—Unknown

Special thanks to the Thelma Vaughan Memorial Home for providing information on her career and for keeping her legacy alive. To learn more about the home visit Home - Thelma Vaughan Memorial home Inc. (tvmhdisability.com) or contact Dr. Joy Vaughan at:info@ drjoycoaching.com.

So, what's your takeaway from Thelma Vaughan's story?

#PhoenixesRising

Question: What kind of Phoenix do you want to be?

It was such a treat to share my mom with you. She transitioned when I was thirteen,but a marvelous part of her lives on, inside of me and she is the secondary source of my resilience.

As we continue our resilient journey, we leave Barbados and head back to the United States before heading to India. In the US, we meet Phoenix, Poetess Gail P. Birks. She has chosen to share the essence of her resilience through her I AM poem. As with Erica's poem which you read earlier, see if you can discover the root of her resilience.

I AM POEM—Gail Birks

I am from...
The sounds of church music from the choirs in which I sang and enjoyed, the concert flutist who played pages of black notes from memory yet found her passion sitting at the sewing machine enjoying the buzz of the creation coming together or the steam from the iron, and the concerts in the park where our families gathered just because. The smells of mom in the kitchen doing her thing with those "special" recipes. the sights of women of color always presenting themselves in such an elegant fashion of grace and love for the villages they nurtured.

I am from … meatloaf (with Lipton onion soup mix and an egg) and mashed potatoes, and corned beef and cabbage, grandma's scratch cooking where the recipe changes with her moods. My aunt who cooked breakfast, lunch, and dinner and always had the house smelling wonderfully appetizing. The homemade pound cakes that oozed of butter, lemon, and sugar and sometimes 7UP. yum. The spaghetti and sliced hot dogs and watered-down tomato Ketchup sauce that daddy made on Saturday when we gave mom the day off cooking. And the way he always had Chinese food waiting for me when I came home from college break because he knew that was my favorite. The complete meals that were always on the table even though mom worked hours as long as dad.

I am from … a family, intentional. My roots are from around the corner, as well as around the world. My talents range from music to art to the creation of something to wear for me and my sisters as we stepped out in style. From a nest where failure is not an option, and giving your all is expected even if the outcome is less than what you desired. The village mothers who embraced me when I thought I stood alone and said, "we got you, now go and do you!!!"

I am from … Barbara and Carl, Alma and Robert, Lucille and Walter, Sienie and Phillip, Cicero, "Big Mom" Suzie Jones and Grandpa Stephen, Fannie and Titus. The ancestors who whisper in my ear and say that "we lift you up so that no one can tear you down."

I am … the tour guide for my legacies, Courtney, Kenzo, Imani, and Kyron. And my gifted ones who just needed a village mother in their corner, when they felt alone or needed a push. I am the sista girl who loves her successful sistas that carry the torch for their ancestors and legacies but never forget that they, like me, are a *WOMAN FIRST*. You all know who you are, and I love you for that. My brothas from the village who walked beside me as we traveled through what life had placed on our pre-designed life paths. We give each other the feminine or masculine perspective to life lessons to fully understand what is being presented.

I am from … the ashes of Mother Earth who birthed me to make a difference while I am blessed to be here. I know that one day I will return, having finished my work. And when I am gone, those who remember my "walk" will say … "She did, because she is and for-ever will be … a woman of grace, virtue (and vices) but possessed love for all she encountered"

I am … Gail, Mommy, Maja, Wife, and Friend

Dedicated to my Village

Gail P. Birks, EMBA, LMDB, is President and Chief Solutionist for CMA Enterprise Incorporated. She serves business, industry, and government providing Results- Driven Organization & Cultural Transformation for executives and project teams. Ms. Birks is also a seasoned Independent Corporate Director. Her business passion is teaching my clients "how to fish" and building self-sufficiency through entrepreneurship. To contact Gail, visit Business Consulting & Advisory Solutions | CMA Enterprise Inc | Davie, FL. (cma-ent.com)

Like Erica's poem, Gail's poem reflected her culture and resilience essence. I hope that as you reflect on the I AM Poems and subsequent poems in this anthology, you will notice a common theme. Notice also the differences. Whether common or different, all roads lead to what has made these fabulous poetesses resilient.

So, what's Your Takeaway from Phoenix, Poetess Gail's poem?

#PhoenixesRising

https://bit.ly/phoenixesrising

As we say goodbye to Gail and continue our resilient journey, our next stop is India. I am so excited to introduce our next Phoenix whose name says it all. Ginny Jolly shares her fascinating story of resilience. Read on to discover how she was able to stay jolly throughout the ups and downs of her life.

Chapter 7

RESILIENCE WITH A SMILE:
Ginny Jolly, India

Ginny Jolly is a proud mother and successful businesswoman in the Health and Nutrition industry. She holds a Masters degree in Nutrition and Child Development and is a professional Business Advisor. She is the President of The B Jolly Foundation where she empowers women to unleash their free spirit.

BE RESILIENT
Resilience With A Smile
Ginny Jolly - India

"The Birth of every child proves that God has not lost hope in humanity."

I was born in a very small town in India to loving parents and dominant male society. My name is Ginny Jolly, and this is my story of resilience. I was very fortunate to have a father who defied societal norms and celebrated me as his daughter as this was not the agreed-upon standard in my town or culture. My father, an aspiring Sikh, was a visionary, a champion for gender equality, and ahead of his time. It was very unusual at that time for a man to be a champion of women. So, I was very fortunate to have a dad who understood how important women were in society. He was a very successful engineer in the sugar mill industry.

My papa was my mentor, friend, and champion. He believed that we would have fewer wars if we had more women in leadership. He understood that women by nature are nurturers, supporters, and natural leaders who know how to make a beautiful home out of the house.

"A strong woman is needed for a good home.
A strong woman is needed for her community
and a strong woman is needed to be a good leader."

This is what my dad whispered in my ear almost daily. Everything I do and have done in my life is to honor his memory and legacy. My father's words have been the foundation of my resilience.

I grew up very wealthy because of my dad. That does not mean that I did not have my share of hardships. Imagine growing up in a culture where everyone wants, waits for, and cherishes a son. Yet here I was a daughter going against the grain of societal norms. My younger brother was born 2 years after me. My dad, however, always treated us both equally. Just to further highlight the societal disparity of girls vs boys, my friends who were girls did not have the same relationship with their dads as I did. I could run and hug my dad whereas they could not and did not. I was given educational opportunities that were privy to only males. They on the other hand were raised to be somebody's wife.

Like many women in our society. As you leave your teens (or often before that), the next step is marriage. My father allowed me to meet my various suitors formally. Arranged marriages were the accepted norm. Looking back, I think that he wanted to give me the experience of choosing. However, in the end, my Papa's opinion is what mattered to me. I was twenty-one at the time when I married Amarjit Jolly in 1979. We have been married for over forty-two years now. An arranged marriage, between two individuals who are opposite, yet have learned to respect and support each other.

As an IT consultant, my husband has had projects in many states of the U.S. We were visiting Canada at the time when I sensed that my Papa was in serious trouble. He had gone to Tanzania to help that country set up its sugar mills. Unbeknownst to me, he got into a car accident when his jeep flipped. He suffered severe injuries to his chest and nose.

Imagine him being in an underdeveloped country where healthcare is not at its optimum. Imagine him not being able to be transported to Canada, the U.S., or the UK because of his severe injuries? Imagine him lying there not being able to see his precious Ginny again? He was taken to a hospital in Tanzania which was run by nuns, where my mom joined him. They did everything that they knew to do including round-the-clock prayers

Have you ever had times when your heart is sinking, and you don't know why? The tears started rolling down my eyes and I started sobbing uncontrollably for no reason. As I was sobbing in Canada, my Papa was transitioning in Tanzania in that hospital on the top of the mountain with my mom at his side.

The day I officially got the news, was the day I lost my will to live as well. I thought that I would never be able to smile again. My Papa was my mentor, my best friend, and the bedrock of my resilience. Who will I be able to lean on to? Even though I was married, in the back of my mind, I knew that everything I needed was going to be taken care of. Hence his passing brought unspeakable grief and a void that still exists to this day. I probably would have completely fallen apart if it were not for those words he whispered daily in my ear as a little girl.

"A strong woman is needed for a good home.
A strong woman is needed for her community,
and a strong woman is needed to be a good leader."

All his belongings were flown back to India with his embalmed body in a box. My world was shattered, and I had no solace. Finally, after the funeral, going through his briefcase, I found a note that my dad had written, and a twenty-dollar U.S. bill in his wallet. The note simply read:

"The Birth of every child proves that God has not
lost hope in humanity."

Reading the note, I started crying profusely. My biggest regret at this point was not having any kids. Amar and I had planned to take time to get to know each other, travel, and build a life together before bringing another human being into this world. I believe that God and my dad had other plans.

Within a month I discovered that I was pregnant. I took the $20 bill as a sign that we would be going to the United States even though we had no plans to do so. However, within that same month, my husband got a job in Detroit, Michigan. A new chapter of hope was starting in my life. We were blessed by the birth of our first son on May 23, 1984, in Detroit.

My resilience and happiness returned the day I held my son in my arms. It was like my Papa had come back to me. I felt now I had a purpose to live and smile. I was feeling empowered again as I had a baby to raise, my son was the continuation of my dad's legacy. I also realized that I had to raise this kid to become what my dad envisioned all kids should be—a strong, loving gift to humanity. For any woman, the birth of a child is a defining moment in her life. You suddenly realize that the life you have been living is not for you but for the continuation of life itself in another.

I have been blessed. My husband's job has afforded us to live in many states in America. Every two years, he got a new project, so we moved a lot. Whether it was Ohio, Michigan, California, Virginia, or Tennessee, I always joked that I have probably seen more of America than most people who were born there. Six years later, our second son was born in Ohio in 1990.

Almost 30 years ago, I declared my desire to start my own business. With little money and no business know-how, it is still a miracle that we opened our first GNC store in the suburbs of Chicago. A mother's heart was asking the Universe for the ability to raise her kids and thus, the dream became a reality. The GNC brand was a perfect match for my degree in Education and Nutrition as I was able to expand my services in the areas of alternative medicine and healing for our many customers. GNC also gave me the flexibility to be with my boys. Homework was done at the store where they also learned about how to run a profitable business. Most of life's valuable lessons are not in books. I still had not given up on the adoption of our daughter.

Part of my dad's legacy was the celebration of women, I had two boys but for me, that feminine side was missing. My papa would always say,

> **"Any household that doesn't have a girl or daughter is missing the laughter in life."**

About nineteen years ago, I sat with my Jolly and discussed the possibility of adopting a little girl. That would make our little family complete. We had two sons and with my luck, if we tried again, we might have another son. I was also older and did not want to deal with pregnancy, childbirth, and all that accompanies that process. Amar is an amazingly wonderful husband and a phenomenal dad. He is also very logical. Jolly (Our last name, but he is known by that instead of his first name, Amar) is an IT guy who doesn't make decisions until he has thoroughly thought them through. He was adamantly against the idea. He said,

"Ginny, we have two children already. We don't have the money or the resources for adoption right now. Plus, this would be a huge commitment to raise another child."

I could only share with him to trust the Universe and reassured him that the resources would come. They always did because I have a mindset of abundance. It is one of the cornerstones of my resilience. After bringing the topic of adoption in our discussions, I waited patiently for the right moment, gently held his hand, and said,

"Jolly, somewhere there is a little girl sitting in an orphanage who needs to be lifted up from there. Why? Because you are the best person in the world who treats your kids and me so well. She needs to experience what a real dad should be. Jolly, you are the only one who can give her that experience because you are a phenomenal husband and dad."

I lovingly watched as his hard core melted. My husband never said a word. He only nodded. I took his nod as a yes and immediately started the adoption process.

We agreed that she should be a toddler as that would be closer to our son's age who was nine at the time. Initially, we wanted to adopt from India but were refused since we had two biological sons. It is all the bureaucracy and red tape and rules that defy any logic. We finally chose Vietnam because we wanted to adopt someone from Asia and the adoption process was also easier. Although we met the financial and other requirements for adopting a foreign baby, the actual process took about a year to complete.

My days were filled with dreaming about this little girl and about being her mom. I was beyond excited when the time finally came to go meet our daughter. You can only imagine how we felt at the thought that what I had dreamed of was finally coming to pass. As the days grew closer, nervousness and happiness overtook me as we packed our bags, checked our tickets several times, ensured that the staff in our stores knew what to do in our absence, and alerted our neighbors and friends of this glorious day. Jolly and I were finally going to Vietnam to pick up our daughter and bring her home. We took our younger son for this trip to Vietnam with us.

About two weeks before we were to board the plane, I experienced the worst day of my life. We got a call from the agency stating that the child we had dreamed of, prayed for, selected, and waited for had been adopted by another family. In other words, sold to the highest bidder. My heart sank at the gravity of what we were walking into, the impact of my decision to adopt, and the reality of the adoption process itself. As a very successful businesswoman, I was not ignorant of the business side of adoption. Truth be told, adoption particularly in the foreign market is a multi-billion-dollar business where children are bought and sold. The cost and acquisition of a product (i.e., child), can come with a hefty financial and emotional price tag. For any person wanting to adopt a child from another culture they should be prepared for all the financial, emotional, and psychological spaces that one experiences before, after, and during the process. We Jolly(s) were determined to give a little girl a chance to experience a loving caring family.

We accepted the reassurance of the agency that they had another child who would be perfect for us. My dream was to raise a child to be an exemplary woman who would one day return to Vietnam and impact her society and country. I am a big believer that there are no accidents in the Universe and thus this change of plans was what was meant to be.

In March 2001, Jolly, I, and our younger son flew to Vietnam. The next day we were in Hanoi at a courthouse signing the papers for a toddler girl, who would be officially our daughter.

Almost 19 months old, a tiny little Hoan Thi Huang was clinging onto me from the time she was placed in my lap. I was feeling overwhelmed and kept asking the interpreter about the Vietnamese words this child spoke. I wanted her to feel comfortable with strangers. To my surprise they said, there were no words to share.

We rode in silence back to the hotel on what seemed to be the longest drive of my life. At the hotel, Jolly noticed that something was wrong with the baby. She did not talk, kept on crying, and was afraid to even watch the TV. As her crying continued coupled with her inability to speak, we realized that our new daughter probably had some special needs that the agency failed to mention. Our desperate cry for answers and help took us to a doctor in Hanoi. The doctor confirmed that there were developmental delays with our newly adopted daughter. The doctor's comment to us was not to worry. After all, we were taking her back to the U.S. which had all the resources to help her.

My heart literally sank again as I realized that we had been duped for a second time. I had always imagined my daughter to have long beautiful hair just like the little girl in the picture. Instead, what we got was a malnourished toddler with literally no hair—a far cry from the picture previously shown. Standing there, looking at this child who was looking back at me, my very soul went on an emotional roller coaster of shock, anger, guilt, betrayal, frustration with a slight glimmer of hope, only to cycle back beginning at shock several times over.

I didn't even know how to face my husband at this point since adopting a little girl was my idea. However, as an eternal optimist. I realized that something was happening in the spiritual realm. A huge part of my being resilient is being connected to my feelings and understanding the bigger purpose for life in general, and specifically my life. I trusted that God / Waheguru (the word means wondrous God) must have a plan for myself and this child. It is said that people enter your life for a season, reason, or lifetime.

It is also said that your children are your teachers. What then was the purpose of this child in our life, and what lessons were we supposed to learn from her?

At this point, we were given two options. We could either undo the adoption and leave the child or bring her home. I don't think that I have prayed and cried more than I cried that night. It did not help my decision at all when this little girl held on to my leg and wailed, miserably. We were both torn at this point because this little girl had bonded with us. In discussing the decision with Jolly, he said

> *"Ginny, the final decision is yours. You are the mom. You are the one who initiated the whole process. I will support you with whatever you decide. Keep in mind that there may be more challenges because we do not know the extent of her special needs. Whatever you decide, just know that by tomorrow morning, we must decide. Keep in mind also Ginny that you always say that you have no right to judge anybody because everybody is God's child and creation."*

Send her back or keep her? That was the decision that weighed heavily on my heart. I was now deciding the present and the future of a little child. This was not one of my GNC products that I could return if damaged or even some inanimate object. This was a living, breathing, human being who was at the mercy of my moral and ethical decision. That night was the longest night of my life as I struggled with everything that had happened around the adoption. I agonized over this little girl who needed a mom and a future. I seriously examined my ability to let go of my dream and embrace mothering a special needs child. I also strongly considered the impact that raising her would have on my family and my life. I also wondered how many times she had been sent back by others for being less than perfect. What did God really want me to do? After praying and crying out to God during the night, I finally made peace with my decision.

After a long talk with Jolly, we called the agency and informed them of our decision. We boarded the plane and took the long journey home with our daughter in our arms. The effects of malnutrition and neglect on our little one were more devastating than we imagined. Our daughter has hearing loss, speech impediments, and was diagnosed on the autism spectrum. Her logical thinking is missing, and she has a lot of challenges. She is twenty-two now and she has come a long way. Even with her challenges, she has proven herself to be resilient.

Patience, love, joy, and peace were the gifts that this little girl brought to our family. I learned these gifts on a deeper level and the true meaning of resilience through the many challenges that our family faced over the years with her. I feel that her presence in our life brought us closer together and taught all of us how to appreciate the little things in life. I see our daughter as the best gift. She is the angel in our house. My daughter knows how to live life. She finds happiness and joy in the smallest things. She is attached yet detached, as she can be very loving one minute and in a split second, become aloof. We have learned not to take her behaviors personally because all I see in her is a beautiful soul. She helps me to serve people better. Even with her cognitive issues, she is self-sufficient in her self-care and simple matters.

In retrospect, my journey of resilience has been a long one which began with the death of my Papa. It continued via the challenges of being a dutiful wife to my Amar, mother to three beautiful children, running three businesses, and dealing with a myriad of life's disappointments and betrayals. Through it all, I have learned that the only thing in your control is your thoughts and actions. Nothing belongs to you because everything is a gift, and we need to be caretakers of that gift.

I am always willing to keep learning and being resilient. Having a flourishing GNC business, it was lack of time freedom that made me look at a new flexible business. Our oldest son convinced me to investigate an online business so that I could devote more time to taking care of our daughter. For the last 9+ years, I have been on a mission to share the LegalShield advantage with every family and business. My best friend, who happens to be my supportive husband, is my rock and the reason I can be resilient and 'Jolly' all the time.

Here are some of life's lessons that have helped me to be resilient

- Money is a great servant and an important resource. Never let it be your master.
- Lead your life with gratitude in your heart.
- Be positive and you will create the world that you want.
- Do your BEST always and leave the rest.
- Being Jolly all the time is a choice and the ONLY way to live.

I don't waste my energy and time on futile things. My purpose in life is to inspire women and encourage others to be financially, spiritually, and mentally free. My goal is to serve millions through my NP B Jolly Foundation. I love life and live in the moment in peace, joy, abundance, and happiness. I am Ginny Jolly, wife, mother, business owner, spiritual and abundance advocate, and I am resilient.

To learn more about Ginny and her resilient journey contact Ginny at:

Website: https://ginnyjolly.com/ Email Address: GinnyJolly@AJollyLife.com Ph: 818-GINNY-4U or 818-446-6948

So, what's your takeaway from Ginny Jolly's story?

#PhoenixesRising

https://bit.ly/phoenixesrising

Question: What kind of Phoenix do you want to be?

Ginny's story was inspiring to say the least. We will need to return to the US for a moment but just bear with me. I promise you this stop will be worth your while because we are going to visit with centenarian Charlotte Blumstein. I cannot even fathom what it is like to live to 100. However, Charlotte is one of the sweetest Phoenixes I know, so her resilient story needed to be told. I am so profoundly grateful to Charlotte, her son David and her family for allowing me the honor and privilege to share her resilient story.

ON RESILIENCE

"Life doesn't get easier or more forgiving, we get stronger and more resilient."—**Steve Maraboli, author of "Life, the Truth, and Being Free"**

Chapter 8

NAVIGATING THE WATERS THROUGH TIME
Centenarian Charlotte Blumstein

Charlotte Blumstein was a beautiful soul who practiced what she preached. Loads of fun to be with, Charlotte was always up for an adventure. Her greatest joy was assisting in the transformation of children, and being the matriarch of her family.

BE RESILIENT

Navigating The Waters Of Time

Centenarian Charlotte Blumstein

"My mother always used to say, "The older you get, the better you get. Unless you're a banana."—Betty White**

By 1919, the year of my birth, the last horse and buggy had rolled down the street heralding the genesis of the Ford automobile and streetcar that would change the trajectory of transportation in America forever. The memories of my childhood and a bygone era are just a few of the things that have sustained me over the years. My memory dims a little sometimes but looking back on my childhood, and more recently, it seems that it was just yesterday that I celebrated my 100th birthday. Yes, you heard me correctly—my 100th birthday. My name is Charlotte and thanks to the good Lord, great genes, a loving family, a positive attitude, and my "occasional" trips to the casino, I have survived the great depression, outlived two husbands, a son, countless friends, and stood the test of time.

On my way to celebrating my 101st birthday, I can say that I have been blessed as I never expected to live this long. Growing up in Williamsburg, New York as an Orthodox Jew in the 1900s was the best of times and the beginning of a new life for my family. My father immigrated to America from Romania while my mother did the same from Poland.

Both of my parents were escaping hard times, war, and poverty in their respective countries and believed that a life in America would be far better than the impoverished existence in their homelands. I could not have imagined what it must have been like for my mother to escape Romania after being pursued by the Germans.

By the time she had arrived by boat and landed on Ellis Island, luck would have her meet my father who had already settled in America. You never know where you will find your life partner, but sharing similar values, my parents fell in love and later had my two sisters and me.

As a window cleaner, I often admired how my dad hung ever so gently yet sturdily from harnesses or scaffolding all the while ensuring that each window shone with the pride of his craft. My mother also brought that same level of integrity and care to the homes that she cleaned. In Williamsburg, we shared our neighborhood with the Italians. Living side by side, we were two different cultures bound together by a common goal of creating a better life for ourselves and our families.

Our home reflected the spirit of humility, generosity, kindness, traditional religious and Orthodox values. Life was therefore orderly and predictable. Our life was also far from materialistically luxurious, instead what we did have was a lot of priceless love and respect for each other. Our family's guiding principle was that we must help and care for those who are sick and less fortunate. Hence, if we had two nickels, we should not be afraid to give one away to someone who was in need. These were the values that our parents and especially my mother instilled in her girls.

In the 1900s, a nickel and dime went a long way to providing for our family. My early life was uneventful and consisted of going to school, keeping a kosher home with my mother and sisters, and following the laws of Orthodox Judaism. We did not venture out much from our neighborhood as Williamsburg provided everything we needed. The 1900s was also the era of silent and black and white movies. Admission was a dime. We were lucky to get a dime to see the latest movie on the big screen. Expensive dresses cost five dollars. We made our bread but the cost of a loaf of bread was between four and eight cents. Today, that same nickel and dime cannot even buy you a decent candy bar and ten dollars does not go far. The butcher was our source of meat and the dairy store sold bottles of kosher milk, eggs, and cheese. We could feed our family on a tight budget of $10.

During the great depression, life got tough for everyone. There were often stories of men who lost their fortunes and hurled themselves to the ground perhaps from some of the very windows that my father cleaned. I have watched history repeat itself in wars and financial crises as life seems to have sped up, and become more complicated with the advent of technology. How I miss those simpler times!

Graduating from high school was embraced with a sense of pride by my family. My college journey was thwarted due to my father's crippling accident which significantly decreased our family's income. Despite his misfortune, we survived thanks to my mother's ingenuity. Nineteen years old, and the elder sister, meant that I had to go to work. I was, after all, daddy's little girl. Wrapped around his finger like a tightly woven piece of wool, my soft, gentle, yet persistent nature got me virtually anything I wanted. A sad face coupled with a few tears worked every time. It did not however work on the love of my life and husband, Milton, who gave me my first job at his electrical store.

My first job, can you believe it? I remember arriving on time for my interview. With five dollars in hand, my mother had sprung for a new outfit from Macy's that would surely land me the position. I did not expect that my life was about to change in ways that I could never imagine. Fiddling nervously as I waited for the manager to appear, he finally emerged from his office. One look at the most handsome specimen of manhood had me declare to myself that he was not only going to be my boss, but my husband. When his blue eyes met my brown ones, I knew that I had hit the jackpot. Milton and I were married a year later, and we spent the rest of our lives making the electrical store the most successful in Williamsburg. We were like two peas in a pod. We did everything together, traveled the world together, and had three beautiful boys together. We traveled all over Europe, Jerusalem, and multiple places in America. By plane, boat, or train, Milton, his brother, sister-in-law, and I were a regular traveling foursome.

Seeing the world opened my eyes to a life and lifestyle far beyond Williamsburg. Meeting different people and cultures had me understand that they are good and bad people in all cultures, you just must find the ones that resonate with you. Slowly, I became less and less Orthodox, but held on to some of the major traditions which I have passed on to my children. One tradition which Milton introduced to me, but one which I did not pass on to my boys, was that of visiting the casinos.

People really underestimate the power of playing the slots. You just must play responsibly. Playing the slots has kept me from being 'Alzheimeric' and kept my brain active. It is not for everybody, but it certainly helped me to be mentally resilient. I remember the first time I entered a casino. With a twinkle in his eye, Milton told me that we were going to an exciting place that we had never been before. Life was always a bag of thrills with my Milton!

Leaving the kids with mom, we headed to the Jersey shore where the Italians had opened a slew of casinos. Back in the day, the Jersey shore was the place to be. It was the late 1960s and the Italians who had made their money in the "entertainment" industry had added legitimate gambling opportunities for those who wanted to try their luck. Building on the casino concept of the first gambling house in Venezia and other successful houses, gambling was legitimized because a portion of the proceeds would go to help the disabled and those less fortunate,

Hey! My mother's mantra was that I should always take care of the sick and less fortunate. How then could I not support this organization? If I made a few pennies for myself, then that would be swell.

Overwhelmed, excited, and bedazzled by the bright lights, glitz, and glamor of the towering edifices of The Sands, Caesars, The Golden Nugget, The Tropicana, and Playboy, to name a few, I couldn't wait to visit them all. I still was not sure where Milton was taking me but knowing him, wherever we were heading was going to be an adventure.

Then, as if from out of nowhere, there it was—a very, very large bunny on one of the buildings. I mean, who puts a bunny on their building? As my curiosity peaked, my face became increasingly flushed as Milton, tongue in cheek quietly whispered in my ear as to why Playboy was not on our list of casinos to visit. We then entered one of his listed casinos where the bleeps, bells, and whistles pulled me right over to a seat in front of their slot machines. Slots were a nickel back then. Milton had given me a handful of nickels.

"Try your luck sweetie."

He said encouragingly.

One nickel pull—nothing, two nickels pull —nothing, after the tenth nickel and pull, I looked at my palm. Only two nickels left.

"Here goes nothing."

I said to myself.

My heart raced with anticipation, "please, please. please, please" became my not-so-silent prayer. Eleventh nickel pull, then three 7s lined up, bells rang, excitement ensued, My Milton hugged me in utter delight, while our friends and others loudly cheered. It was a no-brainer—casinos would be part of my life forever.

Visiting the casinos became a regular thing for me. In part, it was fun but more than that, it provided me with a welcome distraction to life's problems. I revisited other gaming establishments on our travels, but when Milton became sick, and even afterward, I went with my friends. I became a responsible gambler taking only a specific amount that I could afford to lose. Most of the time the clinging and clanging of bells signaled the cascade of coins which doubled or tripled my initial investment. Truth be told, playing the slots saved my life and sanity, particularly during Milton's illness and final demise.

Milton's death was the last thing that I expected. His passing left me feeling like a rock in the bottom of the ocean. I felt like I could not go on and did not want to. As I held his hand for the last time,

I desperately wondered how could he leave me? Why just forty years? Together, we were supposed to live the rest of our golden years well into our eighties. There was so much more to see and do with my Milton—and what about watching our boys grow up with children of their own? Life was not supposed to go this way. Yet here I was, a widow in my late fifties with three boys and no visible means of income.

My emotional and physical support came from my mother. An ever-present tower of strength, she basically told me to get up and to get on with my life. After all, I had three boys to raise.

After Milton's death, life became exceedingly difficult. However, as time passed life became easier. Being good with numbers, I found a job as a bookkeeper and volunteered at the hospital. Giving to others less fortunate than myself helped me to heal and has become a major key to my resilience.

I very much needed to heal from the emotional baggage and scars that I didn't even know were impacting the quality of my life. At one point, someone introduced me to a personal development course called the Landmark Forum. This was the greatest course ever, because, for the first time in my mid-sixties, I discovered Charlotte.

I was able to forgive Milton for dying, forgive the many women who thought that I was after their husbands—as if I did not have enough problems of my own. I even let go of hurts and disappointments that I had no idea existed in my psyche. The bonus, ahh the bonus, was finding love again in my early seventies. Yes, ladies, it is possible to meet and remarry. Bernie was an extremely kind and generous man. I had to learn that although he was not my Milton, Bernie was someone who loved me and was willing to take great care of myself and be supportive of my three sons until he passed fifteen years later.

My greatest joy came during the many times assisting the young people and teens who took their Landmark Forum. I could not believe how many children between the ages of eight to twelve years old had tried to commit suicide. What has happened to our families in America? Seeing these beautiful children in so much pain had me work harder to make sure that my boys and grandchildren lived their best lives possible.

My boys—grown men now, are the pride and joys of my life. We are truly close. This has caused some rifts with their wives as my sons are very protective of their mother. For my 100th birthday the bank of all places threw me a birthday party. The boys, along with a celebratory party and a plethora of gifts and well wishes, had brought me a jar of Smuckers' Strawberry Jam.

"What kind of birthday gift is this for your mother?"

I muttered.

There was dead silence in the room as they watched me slowly turn the jar around. Surprise! There I was on the label of a Smuckers' Strawberry Jam jar that was designed just for me. The card read "To the sweetest mother I know." I later discovered that the Smuckers' Corporation pays tribute to centenarians by giving them their personalized jar of jam on their 100th birthday. You just must love my boys!

That is why losing one of them was the worst day of my life next to losing Milton. It felt like I had lost my Milton all over again. However, despite the long battle with my son's illness, I found peace through it all as my other two sons' countless grandchildren and great-grandchildren were there for me. We are a resilient family, and, despite our ups, downs, hardships, and joys of life, we protect and support each other.

Like my husband and son who passed, most of my friends have also gone now. My last friend moved away a couple of years ago to be with her family. At 100, I have slowed down a bit and do not physically visit the casinos anymore. However, the casinos come to me.

I am proud to say that I play the slots and other games on my iPad. Yes at 100, I consider myself tech-savvy and love it. At one point, I won six million dollars (in theory). I am still waiting on the check.

Folks, part of being resilient is keeping up with the times. People often ask me how I managed to live this long and look so good. Well, I have a routine. I do not drink or smoke. Upon awakening, I am grateful for another day. Then I grab my iPad and play a few slots and games. A simple breakfast gets my day started. A simple lunch and a hearty dinner keep me going. Then around two in the afternoon, I go to my comfy chair on the patio, watch some TV, and marvel at the wonders of nature expressed in the varied flowers, plants, and animals. I make it a point never to watch television before two in the afternoon. I heard somewhere that it does something to your brain. I am in bed by eleven/eleven-thirty. I also volunteer a few times a week at the senior citizen center. On weekends and sometimes during the week, my sons take me to see the grandkids or out to dinner. I love spending time with my children as my peers have all gone.

Do I get lonely? Yes, I do, but I try not to let myself get too depressed. Every day I work on maintaining a positive attitude and being grateful that I can live to see another day. My family also surrounds me with love and care. Of course, I am saddened when I think of my Milton, Bernie, son, or the many friends who have gone before me. Being 100 seems cool from the outside looking in, but in my quiet moments, I often wonder if today is going to be my last day, and, if not now, when. It probably is more difficult for me because I stay active. Recently, I got that I am old. What keeps me going, however, is following my mother's advice to be in some way of service to others. When I can, I volunteer and give back to those less fortunate. I find this gives me a purpose to keep going until … So, there you have it. This is my story. I am Charlotte Blumstein, a feisty, blessed centenarian, and I am resilient!

As of the writing of this story, Charlotte transitioned at 102 on 7/11/2021. We dedicate this story to her family and the many children and families whom she touched in her lifetime.

To learn more about Phoenix Charlotte Blumstein, contact David Blumstein at https://www.beeextraordinary.com/https:/ or /www.linkedin.com/in/david-blumstein-76abb35

So, what's your takeaway from Charlotte Blumstein's story?

#PhoenixesRising

https://bit.ly/phoenixesrising

Question: What kind of Phoenix do you want to be?

Wow! At 102, Charlotte was an amazing lady who never lost her zest for life. For those who had the privilege to know her, she was an inspiration for how to live life. As we leave the US, our next stop is France. Here we meet poetess, Colleen Dupont. As you read her I AM poem, see if you can identify what has made her resilient.

I AM POEM

Colleen Dupont, USA/France

I am from the sun-drenched shores of South Florida where barefoot children play.

I am from avocado and coconut trees and kumquats.
From spices of the islands simmering through open windows.

I am from God never gives us too much, but always
enough. From family is everything and love thy
neighbor as yourself.

I am from the Horkan and O'Dowd clans with the grace
and elegance of the south. And the Johnson's with
the grounded earthiness of Kentucky farms.

I am a blend of what's best in humanity.

I am Colleen Dupont

As a Transformational Coach, Colleen Dupont is a catalyst for change. As a workshop and vision board facilitator, she guides groups through context-changing exercises in self-awareness and clarity to shift unconscious blocks to making the imagined future accessible and real. Contact: colleen@colleendupont.com 305-741-0406. She stands for World Peace Through Individual Fulfillment.

So, what's your takeaway from Phoenix Colleen's poem?

#PhoenixesRising

Share your thoughts in our FB Group

https://bit.ly/phoenixesrising

As we say goodbye to Colleen in France and continue our journey of resilience, we head back to the US to Brooklyn, New York. Now at this point, you might be asking yourself, from France, why did we not travel to Germany or stay in Europe. Consider that in the world of resilience life does not occur in a neat and orderly manner all wrapped up with a beautiful bow. On the contrary, what builds our resilience is our ability to navigate our nonlinear lives until we reach our goals. As we mentioned in our book's preface, it helps if you have a goal or purpose that you want to fulfill. Knowledge through education is certainly a viable avenue and supportive tenet of your resilience. It gives me great pleasure to introduce you to our next Phoenix and quintessential educator Dr. Marguerite Cassanave Thompson.

ON RESILIENCE

"One child, one teacher, one pen and one book can change the world."—Malala Yousafzai

Chapter 9

WEATHERING THE CHANGING FACE OF EDUCATION:
Dr. Marguerite Thompson, USA

Dr. Marguerite Cassanave Thompson is a pioneer and passionate champion of Early Childhood Education. A world traveler, and life-long learner, she has educated and continues to educate, several generations of children and adults.

BE RESILIENT

WEATHERING THE CHANGING FACE OF EDUCATION:

Dr. Marguerite Thompson, USA

"Give to the world the message that you have,
and the best will come back to you."
—My Mother Fannie Richards Cassanave

I am 91 years of age. I have lived through the great depression, the Civil Rights Movement, published several books, dabbled in the arts, traveled the world, mentored fellow educators, educated countless children, lost both of my natural children and, I am still here. Hello, my name is Dr. Marguerite Thompson, and this is my story of resilience.

Before I begin, I will share with our readers that a significant part of being resilient is knowing your history, being clear on where you are going in life, and committed to leaving a legacy for the next generation. Resilience is a subconscious and conscious choice that one makes every, single, day.

I was born in 1930 to a multicultural community and family that spanned three states—Louisiana, Georgia, and New York. I am extremely proud of my heritage because, since the 1800s, my family has been making history in the field of education, theology, law, and the arts. Although I was born in French-speaking Louisiana, I spent many of my formative years with my grandparents in Georgia. My maternal grandparents were from Griffin and Vaughan, whereas my paternal grandparents were from Louisiana. As a child, we would take the train from Louisiana to Georgia to see them. Both grandparents were freed slaves and well educated. My maternal grandmother was a nurse and one of the oldest graduates of Spelman College.

My grandfather who spoke Creole and French graduated from Gammon Theological Seminary which is now under the Interdenominational Theological Center as the United Methodist Church in Atlanta. In the 1800s, Grandpa was a renowned United Methodist Minister at Gammon.

My mother married a man of Creole ancestry, and had my sister and me. My father was an insurance agent, and so I was born in Louisiana. The depression wreaked havoc on our family and so my parents decided for me to be raised by my grandparents in Georgia. Living at the parsonage and going to school in Georgia was amazing. All the best treats were delivered to the parsonage by the community.

As their granddaughter, I found myself enjoying the experience of being thoroughly spoiled. In the summers my cousin Sherrill David Luke, who is a judge in California, would visit. Subsequently, I would visit my mom, sister, and family who lived in New Orleans and rural Louisiana where Creole was the language of choice. Eventually, my parents separated, and my mom would visit us at the parsonage in Atlanta.

My mother did not like the segregated South, so periodically we would pack up and go someplace else. This gave all of us a chance to escape the harsh reality of segregation and deep racism pervading Louisiana at that time.

My mother also had a travel club for black women. She took women throughout the U.S. and different countries in the world. When she traveled throughout the U.S. sometimes she would take me along, to carry the suitcases. In summer we would always go to unfamiliar places. We would never stay in any one place but delighted in every new place that we explored. I got a chance to be with the Tuskegee Airmen in Tuskegee, Alabama because we had a relative that was part of that history. Similarly, Chicago, Los Angeles, and other cities in California presented me with their own charm and educational opportunities. Attending Quaker camps in the Sierra Nevada Hills was another experience that I treasured.

Every travel experience provided an opportunity to gain experience in the country through my mother. As a family, we never had to depend on anybody else. We depended upon ourselves. It is called a family support group. Our family support group provided my first lesson in resilience.

School in Georgia at the Parsonage also proved to be interesting. One day upon returning home, Grandfather, as he always did, questioned what I learned that day. Well, I could not wait to share. However, what I proudly shared was a bunch of cuss words. I thought that Grandpa would pass out, hearing my newfound vocabulary.

"What in the world? Where did you get that?"
He spoke.

Well, Grandpa promptly marched right up to the school and reprimanded the students and teacher. I chuckled to myself at the thought that I learned to cuss at a United Methodist school before I learned real words. It is interesting that as an educator, times have not changed. Children can readily recant all the cuss words and degrading verbiage in Rap and other songs, but struggle with reading and speaking the vernacular that will advance them in life. I made it my life's mission and purpose to change that. I knew the value of a great education from my parents and grandparents, and wanted every child to experience what I had been privy to.

My journey as an educator started with a two-year scholarship to Dillard University in New Orleans. At Dillard, I joined the Young Methodist Exchange Program and was privileged to, not only be one of their ambassadors, but to also travel throughout Europe. This program opened the world for me and further fueled my love of travel. For a black youngster, it was unusual at that time because people did not have the money or the time to travel. But the Methodist Church would send me to speak at their conferences, so I always could speak and deliver monologues. So here I was, out there doing speeches and winning prizes. I always had a way and means to get money because people would finance my speaking engagements. Note to selves, financial resilience is necessary if you are going to survive and thrive in life.

After Dillard, I moved on to Wiley College in Texas. Founded in 1873 by the Methodist Episcopal Church, Wiley is one of our country's oldest historically Black colleges (HBCU). The then-president of Wiley was a family friend, and he was anxious to get me to his school. I once again excelled in my studies. This also opened the door for me to travel but this time with an escort named Dr. Thomas Thompson who eventually became my husband.

Tommy was from the country of Guyana. I had never heard of Guyana, South America but learned quite a lot about his country over the years. Throughout our marriage, we spent quite a bit of time traveling back and forth to Guyana where we, along with our friends and Guyanese empaths, founded an organization that provided supplies and clothing to the rural areas of Guyana. Like my grandpa, Tommy also spoke several languages including Hebrew. He was a character. Smart, funny, and shrewd, throughout his lifetime, we were the educational tag-team duo of Brooklyn, New York.

When we had our two girls, they traveled with us as well. However, I am getting ahead of myself. I successfully pledged for my AKA sorority. Yes, I am a proud Senior soror (sister) of Alpha Kappa Alpha. I completed my degree at Wiley, and moved on to the next phase of my life. I was accepted to New York University (NYU) and moved from Texas to New York to begin my graduate studies in education.

New York, New York, what a hell of a town! The view from my window was spectacular. I lived in an elite apartment at 938 Saint Nicholas Avenue at the top of the hill, in Sugar Hill. Sugar Hill, located in Harlem, was where all the up-and-coming Black people and celebrities lived back in the day. From my window, you had a panoramic view of the city, and you could almost see Central Park's polo grounds. I did not know then of the historic significance of Sugar Hill. However, my friends often teased me by saying,

"Girl, all the celebrities in the world live right up there where you live."

I realized in hindsight that a lot of show business people did live there. My days were spent traveling from Sugar Hill to Manhattan on the subway, which was an experience within itself.

I shared earlier that the South was segregated. Well, so was New York at the time. Regardless of what people said about the North, segregation was also prevalent in the North. I entered the field of education when Jews primarily ran it. Being a black woman and particularly a well-traveled and cultured black woman proved to be a challenge for my colleagues. I had to overcome all the stepping-stones to make sure I got to the top of the mountain and to fulfill what God had called me to do.

I always pushed myself to step and go higher because I wanted to make sure that my children and those around me were getting the best of everything. This was something that I not only had to do but was compelled to do. I did not let anybody step on my back but made sure that I stood straight and tall throughout my adversities.

I received my Masters and Doctorate degrees from NYU in Early Childhood Education—a new and wonderful field that I was advised to pursue. I always loved children and literature. At NYU I got to work under and was mentored by Dr. Howard A. Lane. Dr. Lane was one of the top early childhood educators of his time. I was also fortunate to also have Elizabeth Gilkeson, founder of Bank Street College in New York City, as my mentor. Under the Bureau of Educational Experiments in Washington DC, Bank Street became and still is the premier institution for researching and developing innovative programs for young children. These mentors along with a multicultural team of rabbinical, Afro-American, and other pundits helped me to craft my dissertation and studies on *"Developing Positive Self-image in the Inner-City Minority Child Through Use of the Community as a Classroom/Weeksville."*

It truly takes a village to raise a child. At the beginning of my story, I shared that a part of being resilient was knowing your history. As a descendant of a freed slave in the South, and now living in the North, I deeply appreciated the joys and price that comes with attaining one's freedom. Who would have guessed that there was an Afro-American community right here in Brooklyn that somehow the history books forgot to write about?

In 1820, a freed slave named James Weeks had the fortitude and vision to purchase a12,400 sq ft plot of land in Brooklyn's Crown heights. James was a stevedore who bought the land from a wealthy landowner. Many Black people coming out of slavery saw land as a pathway to financial freedom and status. On this plot of land, Weeks built a row of houses known as Hunterfly Houses. It is estimated that over five hundred freed slaves and their families lived in Weeksville. Weeksville grew to become a thriving town. People came from all distinct parts of the world, and they developed a cultural center, school—colored school number two, P.S. 243, where I happened to have been teaching at the time.

Through Weeksville I saw an opportunity to create a change in thinking as to how we could educate young children. Instead of reading about history, why not have the children experience history for themselves. My children at P.S. 243 engaged in an urban archeological and timeline dig. This was the only one of its kind ever done by children. During the dig, we made history when we found a part of Harriet Tubman's Underground Railway right here in urban Brooklyn. Everything began to make sense as Weeksville became known for providing a haven for freed slaves particularly those who wanted to escape the draft.

In 1960, historian Joseph Hurley, Eugene Ambruester, and colleague Joseph Haynes, lobbied to have the four remaining Hunterfly Houses declared a historic site. Director Joan Maynard, along with James Hurley, Dewey Harley, Dolores McCullough, Patricia Johnson, and I have been sharing the history and marvel of Weeksville with thousands of inner-city children and educators. Our purpose is to encourage the youth to not only know their history, but to dream big, and like James Weeks and their Weeksville ancestors empower them to go higher in life. Twenty-five years later, Weeksville Heritage Center serves as an educational hub for the promotion and preservation of black culture, education, social justice, and the arts.

It remains amazing what can be possible when a community comes together.

As an extension of Weeksville, I created the Weeksville Young Ambassadors. This was an international exchange program that brought children from all over the world to America to experience Weeksville. Similarly, I took children from America to communities in different countries, so that they would know that the world was their oyster.

The community was also vital to my survival as an educator in a hostile environment. The most challenging time of my career was when I pursued my doctorate. I remember when I was working on my dissertation, and I was going through very tough times. I had to fly from New York to Albany a few times a year to meet with my advisor. When you are pursuing a doctorate, you must be prepared mentally to deal with rejection as well as other psychological challenges. That degree will test every ounce of resilience created by God and man.

On the home front, I had a superintendent who did not understand that black women needed doctorates. So, everything that I would attempt to do, he would put his foot down and say,

"Oh no, you don't."

To which I would say,

"Oh yes, I will."

Don't ever let anybody tell you that you can't do everything, because everything they say you can't do, you can do.

To survive in the educational jungle of New York, I had to adopt that resilient attitude. I also developed my distinctive style; I always left the house well put together. I quickly learned that having a distinctive ensemble, coupled with the right hat, jewelry, and a briefcase from either Europe or Africa was a conversation starter.

Conversation starters helped to neutralize my enemies who felt that I should not be an educator.

Hence, to balance the toxicity, I started jewelry making, painting, sketching, and autoharp. Yes, I played the autoharp. Truth be told, as I made my pieces or sketched my way through boring lectures, I was processing my thoughts, challenges, and upsets. I would just work through the day, in my mind and tell myself,

"Oh well, it could have been worse. Tomorrow will be a better day."

I had to laugh because often I would show up at various schools the following day to start an early childhood program. Sometimes people did not even want to talk to me. Often, I received strange looks followed by,

"What are you here for?"

To which I would reply,

"Well, let's just wait and see. I think we'll all have a wonderful day together."

Which we did.

This was the way I was taught to always remember that I was a lady first, regardless of how many times people wanted to slam doors in my face or crush my fingers. There is an old and true saying of

"What goes around comes around."

I learned how to cope, and how to make it out there, for two reasons. The first was because I knew that I had the ability; the second was because I was determined to fulfill my mission to help and empower as many children as possible to succeed. Over my lifetime, I have mothered and mentored several children, fellow teachers, and colleagues. I am pleased to say that most of them have become successful. One of my mentees, Dr. Evelyn Castro is now president of Medgar Evers College, right here in Brooklyn.

As I reflect on my life, like everyone else there have been good times and bad, tragedies, and triumphs. Although bronchitis and respiratory issues have plagued me most of my life, they have not stopped me from living. However, what has kept me resilient is my faith and my prayers. I pray and meditate quite a bit. Meditation and prayer make the difference. And I continue with that. I also have my nuns in New Orleans; if I have a problem, I call them, and they pray around the problem. Their prayers helped me to cope with the loss of my two daughters which as a mother, was exceedingly difficult. So, it is prayer and meditation that make the difference and help me to stay resilient.

Recently, for my 91st birthday, I was able to return to Georgia. Along with my grandchildren and about fifty-five family members, we took a tour bus from Georgia to Louisiana where we visited with relatives. My grandchildren got to meet our relatives in Georgia and Louisiana. In Georgia, we followed the African tradition of call and recall. This is where everybody takes a turn in leading, following, and answering you back. What a thrill to have so many family members say,

"Welcome to Georgia."

At 91, I have come full circle in my life. I was so happy to have had my grandchildren with me on our recent trip to Georgia and for them to experience the love of family and learn their history. I am profoundly grateful for my life, heritage, my relationship with God, family, and good friends throughout the years. As an educator, author, and artist, I have lived an amazing life. I do not see myself slowing down, (well maybe a little), but with the help of my physical therapist, I keep going. I will continue to make my jewelry, mentor others when I can, teach a course or two at our community college, and continue to nurture the next generation. I am Dr. Marguerite Thompson, wife, mother, grandmother, and a recent great grand-mother, early childhood educator, artist, and influencer, and yes, I am resilient.

> *"Don't ever let anybody tell you that you can't do everything, because everything they say you can't do, you can do."*
> *—Dr. Marguerite Cassanave Thompson*

To learn more about Weeksville go to https://weeksvillesociety.org.or contact Dr. Thompson at 718-253-1842

So, what's your takeaway from Dr. Marguerite Cassanave Thompson's story?

#PhoenixesRising

Question: What kind of Phoenix do you want to be?

ON RESILIENCE

> *"We are not a product of what happened to us in our past. We have the power of choice."*
> *—Stephen Covey*

Knowledge is power and there is power in knowledge. Dr. Thompson discovered this from an early age. In keeping with the theme of gaining knowledge, we leave Brooklyn, New York, and head over to Pakistan. Here we will meet another fabulous Phoenix Nasim Bhatti who shares a very different story of resilience

Chapter 10

HOW I LOST MY RESILIENCE
Nasim Bhatti, Pakistan

As Matriarch of her family, Nasim Bhatti is a gentle
soul who is committed to empowering humanity to
be the best that it can be.

HOW I LOST MY RESILIENCE

Nasim Bhatti, Pakistan

*"Indeed, this life is a test. It is a test of many things –
of our convictions and priorities, our faith and our
faithfulness, our patience and our resilience, and in
the end, our ultimate desires.*—**Sheri L. Dew**

I lost my ability to be resilient the day my husband died. On November 3, 2019, he took his last breath and transitioned to his new beginning, ending our forty-five-year-old lifetime together. I gave up after he died because my core identity as a wife had been shattered. I asked myself,

"What was the point of continuing?"

Since his passing, my life has been void of purpose, which along with my reason for living was buried with him. My name is Nasim Bhatti. I am originally from Pakistan, and I am learning how to be resilient again.

My resilience is, and has been intricately woven, dependent on, and defined by my husband and children. I have failed over the years to include myself in this equation. I am sixty-eight now. I am not sure if anyone reading my story can relate, but when you have been indoctrinated into a culture that reinforces from birth that your only role in life as a woman is to be an invisible servant to your husband, and mother of his children, it is hard to see what your future holds when those roles have ended.

In my husband's later years, he became terribly ill. I did not know how to help him and so I lost my confidence as a wife and caretaker. This sense of helplessness chipped away slowly at my resilience. Additionally, my children grew up in America—a culture that is vastly different from our traditional Pakistani culture. They are now remarkably successful adults with busy lives and families of their own.

My husband's demise, coupled with my children growing up and independence from me, was another blow to my ability to be resilient that until now, was not distinguished. My role as a mother as I know it, and my purpose for living is yet to be defined. Truth be told, for the past three years, and perhaps even before that, I have been surviving my life by going through the motions. Countless times I have asked myself,

"Why am I here?"

Born and raised in Pakistan, my life's journey has been one of quiet suffering and rebellion against the status quo of a male-dominated society into which I was born. Yet I find myself trapped between my familiar traditional culture and a non-traditional American culture. How am I supposed to be resilient when I feel so trapped?

My children tell me that I must find a new purpose. However, they are speaking to someone born to parents who fled India after the religious Indo-Pakistani war of 1947. This was a religious war between Muslims and Hindus that broke out after the British had given the governance of India back to its people. The dissent between these two religions severed a once united country causing my parents and eight of my siblings to take refuge in the southern region now known as Pakistan.

Unlike my eight siblings, my younger brother and I were born in Pakistan. Like my husband, he has since transitioned to his new life. As a family, we chose to be Pakistani and to continue to follow the Muslim faith. This distinction between being Pakistani and Indian is an important one as outsiders tend to still label us as Indian. Even though our customs and foods may be similar, it is our faith that defines us as separate but of equal value. I am not sure if you have noticed, but if you have ever met anyone from our region, and you refer to them as Indian they may quickly correct you that they are from Pakistan. Subsequently, the same goes for people from India who are referred to as Pakistani.

Whether Indian or Pakistani, both cultures are male-dominated and gender suppressed. My father was a teacher who championed my brothers' education but not so much the girls. English was introduced after 5th grade. After 5th grade, my formal education stopped so I never got the chance to learn or speak English. As a woman, I was in preparation to be someone's wife. It was made clear on so many levels, that females, like children, were supposed to be seen and not heard. As women, we did not have a voice, but our value was and still is, seen as child-bearers, homemakers, and servers of our husbands.

I remember when my older sisters visited my parents. They busied themselves with cooking, cleaning, and sewing comforters. I truly hated that. I just did not understand why they would consume themselves with those menial tasks. This was how deeply rooted in our culture, the role that women played.

Perhaps their busying themselves with housework was a painful reminder that no matter how smart we were, the opportunity for us to be anything other than subservient, would never be allowed in our culture.

As one of ten children, I learned to be selfless. I always thought of others and put others first before myself. To this day I still have trouble thinking and doing for myself. For me, it is all about giving to others –especially to my children and family. This selfless giving to others reinforced that I did not matter.

When I was in my late teens/the early twenties, I succumbed to an arranged marriage to a man whom I barely knew. He had an eye for business and my parents thought that we would be a good match. That is how it was in the old days. Through good, bad, and ugly times, I stayed the course with him for forty-five years and gave him three beautiful children. My children are my pride and joy and in part have been the bedrock of my resilience. In addition, we are a tightly knitted and successful family who have embraced the American dream and tremendously benefited from it. We are fondly known as "The Firm."

In 1980 my husband, I, and two of our children came to America in hopes of a better life. Our third child was born two years later. My siblings were already here so they helped us to migrate from Pakistan to America. Although grateful for a fresh start, my biggest challenge was not knowing English and having to quickly learn the language. America offered me the freedom I had longed for and a new lease on life. After five or six years of being a housewife, I decided that I needed to get out there, learn the language, learn how to drive, and embrace my independence. This is what I had always wanted to do. America was the holy grail for me as I was determined not to depend on anyone but myself.

My transition from the role of housewife and child-bearer to working mom began as a front desk clerk at the Scottish Inn Motel. I remember being terrified to shake hands with people and to look them in the eye—particularly the men. I was shy and awkward. However, my first boost of confidence came when I was asked to train a male attorney from India. He too had transitioned to his new life here in America. I could not believe that I knew more than a degreed man.

Little by little, I got my confidence to be with people, learn the language, and hold my own as a working woman in this brand-new paradigm. My husband supported me working as he quickly understood that one salary would not be enough to take care of three children. In retrospect, I realized that this must have been difficult for him to accept, as this was a departure from our cultural norm. My non-traditional role as a working woman bucked the traditional female role of our Pakistani culture. The opportunity to work outside of the home and get paid well for doing so was huge for me.

With my newfound confidence and driver's license, I moved on from the Scottish Motel to land a better job at Service Merchandise, Dillards, and eventually at Walmart. Walmart gave me the freedom I needed and the opportunity to feel valued and appreciated. Here I was helping people with their purchases and to negotiate this Super Store which I found to be rewarding. As strange as it might seem, I loved working at Walmart. I had a manager who encouraged me to be my best and to try new things. She believed that this is how you learned and improved your skills and self-confidence.

She would often tell me that no question was a stupid one and if I need anything to reach out to her.

At this point in my life, it is difficult to know where I fit in. With my husband gone, I am painfully aware that my children have adopted more of the American than our traditional Pakistani values. Since my children are the bedrock of my resilience, I find myself not being able to advise or make a difference in their lives. In our traditional culture, divorce is not an option, living together is frowned upon, as is marrying outside of our ethnicity. The reason for arranged marriages is to keep our culture, values, and traditions alive throughout the generations. I firmly believe that if we were still living in Pakistan, our tradition would have been preserved. My children may not have been as happy, but like everyone else, they would have learned to live within the boundaries of our Pakistani heritage.

America offers the kind of freedom that I could have only dreamed about. I have longed for, experienced, and received that level of freedom. While it has been beneficial, at my very core is the traditional Nasim Naseem who struggles with fully embracing that freedom for herself. My children have chosen their own path which I find difficult to accept. How do I embrace the fact that as the matriarch of our family, my role is in name only? Even if I do advise my children, I find that they will do what they want in the end. I am experiencing a resiliency crisis of sorts because my very existence as an elder and family adviser has been thwarted.

The question that I find myself asking is "Where do I go from here?" In our tradition, when your spouse dies, your male child becomes your caretaker and provider. If we were still in Pakistan, I believe that our family would have been more cohesive. However, in America, given that there is freedom, my family has broken apart, and therefore, I have shattered as well. At this point in my life, I do not wish to live alone. I worry that I am a burden to my son and his new life. A bright spot in my life right now are my grandchildren. I love and am so immensely proud of them. My eldest grandchild just gradu-ated from her military training. I think that I would enjoy passing on our traditions to them. This is one of my roles as our family matriarch. However, I do not wish to be intrusive in my children's lives. Although I have an awfully hard time agreeing with their choices, I am learning to do so. Being resilient involves the ability to "roll with the punches," and life's disappointments which I am learning to do.

Financially I am in a good place because of my husband. Emotion-ally, I am not as resilient. When I reflect on my life, the happiest time was when I was working at Walmart while being a wife and mother, I felt fulfilled and confident. Unfortunately, that level of confidence has not been enough to override the early cultural indoctrination that has defined my identity spoken of earlier. At sixty-eight, I thought about returning to Walmart but quickly dismissed that idea as I do not feel called to be there at this time of my life. Sometimes your "glory days" are not as glorious the second time around.

So, I find myself at the crossroads of my life and learning to be resilient again. As of the writing of this story, I was able to visit my husband's grave with my three children. We had not been able to do so before because of COVID 19. We had a picnic, laughed, and reminisced about old times, traditions, and our life together. Un-beknownst to me, this was the closure that I had been looking for and could not voice since his passing. I have the confidence now to move on with my life. In a few months, my youngest daughter will be bringing a new life into this world. She and her husband have graciously asked me to come to help her with the new baby as they both work. She is an entrepreneur who owns several health clinics and spas.

I have now found my purpose and resilience. I can nurture my grandchildren from the soul of Pakistan, and be the matriarchal mentor for the next generation. It just does not get better than that. I promise to make my culture, heritage, and children proud.

My name is Nasim Bhatti, and I am resilient. To learn more about or to contact Nasim. Contact Naveed Bhatti at 321-948-6828.

So, what's your takeaway from Nasim Bhatti's story?

#PhoenixesRising

https://bit.ly/phoenixesrising

Question: What kind of Phoenix do you want to be?

Chapter 11

PLAYING THE GLOBAL GAME:
Dr. Caroline Makaka, Zimbabwe/United Kingdom

Multi Award Winner Dr. Caroline Makaka is the Founder/CEO of Ladies of All Nations International also known as LOANI which compromises of Beautiful Survivors World of Honors, United in Diversity Special Recognition Awards and Galaxy of Stars Young Inspirational Awards and LOANI Magazine.

ON RESILIENCE

"My grandfather once told me that there were two kinds of people: those who do the work and those who take the credit. He told me to try to be in the first group; there was much less competition."
Indira Gandhi

Playing The Global Game
Dr. Caroline Makaka, Zimbabwe/United Kingdom

*"The greatest glory in living lies not in never falling,
but in rising every time we fall"—Nelson Mandela*

Death, like a grim reaper, claimed the lives of both of my parents. Just like a malevolent thief in the night, death crept into my mother's bedroom and sucked the life out of her leaving me motherless and profoundly devastated. As if that wasn't cruel enough, it came back a year later and claimed my father. It was no surprise then that of all the days in my life so far, the darkest came after the death of my parents. For my mother, I can only surmise that the stress and strain of being a laborer and raising eight children had finally taken its toll. My name is Caroline Makaka, and this is my story of resilience.

They say that some men don't survive after the death of their spouse. This was true for my father. How do you go on when the love of your life and mother of your children has left so heartlessly? For me, losing one parent was bad enough. but losing two—one right after the other—was truly devastating. What was there to do now? What would become of us? With no choice left but for us to survive, I along with my sister and my eldest brother worked menial jobs to feed our family. There were so many times that I felt despondent and overwhelmed, but my brother's uplifting words of comfort and his resilient spirit increased my capacity to be fearless when I felt anything but.

As the three eldest siblings, we were lucky to find work where we could. However, there was never a time that we didn't fear for our lives as situations worsened daily in Zimbabwe and particularly in Harare. We went to school by day, followed by work into the night. Drugged with exhaustion, further heartbreak came with the realization that the money was never enough and the struggle to survive posed a harsh reality that teetered on the borderline of overwhelming poverty. Coupled with military unrest and an ever-declining economy, living in Zimbabwe was becoming increasingly dangerous. Although help came from our community, we knew in our heart of hearts that we could no longer continue to live this marginal, life-threatening existence. I have learned that survival and the key to resilience is being part book smart, part street-smart, with a huge dollop of feistiness—wrapped in a smile. Facing our dim reality, we made a plan. Since education was our pathway out, we decided on England as the best option for deliverance from our hellish experience.

England—I knew very little about that place except it was cold, damp, and the people didn't look like us. Furthermore, they talked funny. Zimbabwe had once been under the rule of the British but none of us had ever had the privilege to visit their country. Nevertheless, I was chosen as the brave, pioneering soul to fulfill our family plan. Truth be told, getting out of Harare was beneficial for anyone who could escape as the harsh political tidal wave had begun to further threaten our people's existence. As the leadership of our country changed, so did the ideology and regime which made it increasingly hard to live, much less survive. The plan was for me to be the first one to emigrate to England, and then have my siblings join me one by one in this new world that we now call our home.

Every adventure begins with a decision to have one. Adventures depend on one's creative resilience. What I mean by that is that to fulfill on any venture, the spirit of resilience is the catalyst that fuels your persistence, despite the hardships and guaranteed pitfalls. I had a goal. We had a goal, and that goal was freedom for myself and my family. I believe that a person cannot truly understand and appreciate freedom unless they have been in bondage. In Zimbabwe, we continued in bondage, as widespread corruption and violence engulfed our country. Rebels took over, killing innocent people. Those who opposed or were perceived to go against their ideology were hacked by the blades of machetes or felled by bullets. Our human rights were repeatedly violated. At one point it was estimated that over 700,000 people were homeless and wandering in Zimbabwe's barren lands.

Simultaneously, the rebels seemed to take delight in tanking the economy. Employment was next to nothing. Zimbabweans starved, as the dollar had been devalued several times, making it more difficult to purchase food and goods. Remembering our goal and plan, we pooled our money and survived on one meal a day. Soon, there was enough money to purchase my visa to England through Zimbabwe's underground network. The next step—secure a plane ticket to freedom.

As days turned into weeks and months, the sweet smell and taste of freedom continued to titillate my senses, making me hungrier for the day when I could board that plane and fly away from our hell-hole existence. I remember how nervous I felt approaching the ticket agent as I pulled the cash out of the tightly- secured spot in my handbag. Nervously unwrapping the wad of hard-earned dollars from my father's handkerchief, I eagerly handed it to the travel agent who processed my documents and finally handed me my ticket. Ever so slowly my water-welled eyes spilled over, sending a cascade of joyful tears mixed with relief and unbelief. As I held our first ticket to freedom in my trembling hands, I could hardly believe it. Like my brothers, sisters, and I leapt for joy and hugged each other, no words could express how we felt about the success of finally getting one step closer to our freedom. Our hard work, ingenuity, persistence, and teamwork had paid off.

The night before my early flight to Heathrow, no one slept. Between packing, unpacking, and repacking, we excitedly disputed which clothes to take. Then there were the native foods that our friends wanted. They had to go into the suitcase—where I didn't know. Eventually, everything found its place in the nooks and crannies of our luggage. All that was needed was for my brother to sit on the case and sit he did, while we ceremoniously zipped it shut. The final closure of the suitcases signaled the reality of the ending of one life and the beginning of another. It also marked the bitter-sweet reality that I probably would not return to Zimbabwe for a very, very, long time.

"Be strong,"

were a few of my parting words said to my tearful brothers and sisters as the plane taxied down the runway and eventually up, up, up, and into the fluffy clouds. I had officially taken my first plane ride to England where who knew what adventures lay ahead!

Needless to say, England was nothing like Zimbabwe and London was very different from Harare. Fast-paced and forward-thinking, I marveled as races from every nation scurried to and fro while boarding crowded trains that would eventually take them to their destination. As I settled into my new home, my thoughts and prayers for my family's safety were ever-present on my mind.

"A taxi! A real British taxi!"

I yelled loudly with excitement into the fresh summer's air at the site of this luxurious vehicle which I had seen as a young child in the movies. That was a different Zimbabwe of yesteryear. A Zimbabwe where going to the movies was normal. I briefly wondered if those days could ever return for our people. I was unaware that my exuberance over this vehicle had garnered curious stares from equally curious bypassers. If the taxis were exciting, my first ride on a red double-decker bus and the Tube was the experience of being at a theme park. Using my inner voice so as not to be glared at again, I continued to be quietly amazed at the towering marble buildings, London Bridge, the churches, the Gothic statues, the Tower of London, and of course, Buckingham Palace. I am sure that you will relate to my level of delight as you mentally watch what you have read or heard about unfold before your eyes. My excitement and awe were short-lived as I reminded myself why I migrated to England. Sight-seeing jaunts had their place, but as news of increasing unrest and violence in Zimbabwe reached me, my true purpose for being in England jolted me back to reality. I could only hope and pray that my siblings back home were safe.

Having settled in my new environment with my host family, I quickly sought employment, landing my first job in Social Services with our local government. A master of multitasking I also juggled several jobs at once and soon earned enough to fund my family's survival back in their Zimbabwe home in a soon-to-be short-lived, toxic terrain. Every time I sent funds through the network I whispered,

"Hold on! Not too much longer."

As always, we kept education at the forefront. Even though mummy and daddy were not with us, the least I could do was to make them proud. What an awesome legacy and tribute to my parents if all their children were educated and successful. Tears welled in my eyes and spilled down my cheeks at the thought of what it would be like once that reality was fulfilled. There was no turning back now as the pathway to the completion of our legacy became crystal clear. More certain to secure a better paying job, I enrolled at The University of North Hampton and within four years, I had reached a significant milestone by graduating with my first degree. Another milestone was the migration of three of my siblings, also accomplished, within those four years. We were on our way! Four more siblings to go and we would all be together. How I longed for that day. Family is everything to me.

As weeks turned into months and winter reared its head in full force, my summer's excitement waned. 2002 was going to be my first test of resilience as it was recorded as one of the coldest winters in Britain's history. Record temperatures clocked in at a bone-chilling -15 degrees Fahrenheit. I had heard of the British winters but had yet to experience their full effect. I was told to prepare myself, as I had to endure a somewhat long walk to the tube (train) station. My grey wool coat, layered over two sweaters, matching scarf, woolen hat, and warm gloves, two pairs of socks, matching leggings, and boots, were no match for the blustery winds of a bone-chilling winter. Looking like Nanook from the North Pole, my multiple layers of clothing proved to be powerless against the blustery winds that sneakily crept under my coat, attacking every part of my body.

"What the bloody hell!" "Why is it so cold?"

I shouted as if that would have made a difference. I could swear that the elements heard but ignored my thoughts as another cruel gust of icy wind attacked me, once again from what felt like multiple directions. By the time I got to the station, I felt like a frozen popsicle. With teeth chattering I swiftly made my way down the steep stairs and into the train's very crowded car. The warmth of the tube car was a welcome relief even though the person's elbow that dug into my side was not. With nowhere to go, I stood still and allowed the tube's and people's warmth to penetrate my ice-cold bones.

Despite braving the elements, I arrived at my job on time. A giant smile crept onto my face, stretching itself from ear to ear as it hit me that I was a working woman in London. Given where I came from, I could not believe that part of my dream had been manifested. Here I was, with a degree in Global Leadership, making a difference in the lives of others. A glutton for punishment, I returned to the university—this time the University of North Hampton where I earned my Masters's and Doctorate in International Global Studies. Along the way, I met Mr. Makaka—a kind and generous man. As my life partner, we have been married for 15 years now with one set of twins. My husband is a tower of support for all my projects. He is also my shield and rock particularly during times when I am double-teamed by our sometimes-mischievous children.

Persevering despite distractions, I now had an innate passion and drive to empower and celebrate those less fortunate. It took all the resilience and tenacity in the world to complete my studies, hold down a full-time job in the social service industry, and be a wife and mother to a set of darling twins. There were many times I wanted to quit but Mr. Makaka, my siblings, and my children would not let me. They became my accountability and resilience partners. One of the keys to being resilient is having genuine support. This journey was not easy by any means but somehow as a family, we made it work so a greater purpose could be fulfilled. As I thought about my parents and siblings, I also pondered my legacy. What mark did I want to leave on this planet? Whose life was I called to impact? After praying about which direction was the right one, I finally settled on making a positive impact on women around the world. I had no idea how this was going to be accomplished but I just knew that I wanted to celebrate the lives of ordinary and extraordinary women on a global scale. This mission would take great effort and planning but no matter what, the mission was going to be fulfilled.

Another four years passed and within that time, there were so many great milestones to celebrate. We repeated the process of sending money back, securing visas and tickets for each sibling, and ensuring that they had gainful employment and education. It would take just shy of eight years before all of us were united again. We had accomplished in part what our parents had hoped we would.

"Now what?" I wondered.

We had fulfilled our goal of leaving Zimbabwe behind and embracing a brand-new world and culture. I say that we left Zimbabwe behind, but the truth was that Zimbabwe was always in our hearts.

Having achieved our migration milestone, it was now time for me to focus on some goals of my own. As mentioned before, my passion is celebrating the accomplishments of women around the world. Mummy became the impetus for LOANI or "Ladies of All Nations International." Gone too soon, she had taken care of us without complaints, loved us unconditionally, and given us her resilient spirit. I am forever grateful. Her essence was enough to have her spirit live on in the lives of amazing women around the world. Hence, being a philanthropist became my passion and the driving force of LOANI. When we created LOANI, part of our vision was to inspire people of all backgrounds, religions, and cultures and to spread peace, unity, and understanding.

I quickly discovered that being a philanthropist is hard work. At times, it's not as glamourous as it sounds. Maintaining great relationships with wealthy donors as well as corporations means that you must be a hypervigilant networker. Then you need d to duplicate yourself in 85 countries. Teamwork, win/win opportunities, being clear and intentional are all part of the process. A healthy dose of passion and knowing your why is also essential. What I am also conscious of is that I carve out time to spend with my family. In my heart and soul, my primary mission as a philanthropist is to promote the welfare of others through partnering with organizations that have a global focus.

As a philanthropist, I manage and oversee LOANI As a not-for-profit international organization, we bring women of all nations together to support, help, and learn from each other. LOANI is a champion of diversity. We bring nations together under the umbrella of humanity with the ultimate goal of supporting and uplifting the underprivileged in various communities. One of the many projects birthed from my travels are the celebratory dinners, fashion shows, and award ceremonies. These events celebrate, for example, widows and those with disabilities. These are women who tend to be forgotten by society. LOANI finds these women through varied organizations and networks and celebrates their uniqueness. The return on our investment cannot be measured.

When a woman whose spirit is downtrodden either because of her disability or circumstance walks onto our stage to thunderous applause, you cannot imagine the overwhelming feeling of being recognized for their uniqueness. Finally, someone sees and appreciates me for who I am. This is the sentiment that we hear from women at our global events. I have the honor and privilege to travel to virtually every nation in the world and celebrate the accomplishments of ordinary and extraordinary women. The ladies are referred to me through word of mouth. The criteria to be invited to join LOANI are that someone sees you and wants to lift your spirits. We unite for greater causes and collaborate on different projects to improve the lives of the underprivileged and have an impact on the world because suffering in silence is not an option. LOANI now covers 85 countries worldwide promoting diversity and inclusiveness in age, race, gender, sexuality, religion, disability.

People often ask me how I do so much. Most people do not understand that when you come from a country where suffering and poverty are all that you see when you finally break free from that miserable existence, you want to free others. My parents died in that horrible environment. There was no choice for us but to become resilient. What keeps me resilient is my passion to help others. I am blessed to have an amazing husband, my siblings, and a set of beautiful twins who keep me going. They as well as my faith are the wind beneath my wings. Their support allows me to be the wind beneath the wings of our LOANI ladies. Mother, entrepreneur, global warrior, philanthropist, and humanitarian crusader, my name is Dr. Caroline Makaka, and I am resilient.

To learn more about LOANI or Dr. Makaka contact Dr Caroline Makaka | WEF https://uk.linkedin.com/in/dr-caroline-makaka-441073179

"Resilience is based on compassion for ourselves as well as compassion for others."—Sharon Salzberg

So, what's your takeaway from Dr. Caroline Makaka's story?

#PhoenixesRising

https://bit.ly/phoenixesrising
Question: What kind of Phoenix do you want to be?

Wow, more and more we are hearing that some African countries are doing well while others are not. Dr. Caroline Makaka's story demonstrates the beauty of "paying it forward." Like a Phoenix, she has not forgotten her humble beginnings and has chosen to elevate others as she has been elevated in life.

I AM POEM—Artist
Brenda Richards, Guyana

I am from the Land of many waters
Born into a family of four sons and seven daughters
In a country on the Continent of South America
Nestled between Brazil and Venezuela

I am from the diverse flavors of black cake, curry chicken, garlic
pork, pepperpot, and ginger beer

With tropical fruits like sapodilla, star apple, mangoes,
and cashew pears

I am Bellisima, Chutzpah, and Bataam Kunjo too with a curious
mind always eager to learn something different and new

I am from a legacy of the indentured and the enslaved
Which is part of the blessing to my DNA

What is my blessing that was once seen as a curse?
Has strengthened me to handle the worst

To you much Love from Brenda R

I am a Child of God; to the Most High
With the heart and soul of a giver
I will continue to grow until I die
they call me Brenda Richards

Brenda Richards, is a Guyanese American poet and writer. Her poetry is featured in several anthologies, namely the International Society of Poets Coffee Table Book (2003); Caribbean Erotic, which represents the works of writers and poets from the different regions of the Anglophone, Francophone, and Hispanophone Caribbean worked as a travel writer for Revista Esposito Santo, Brazilian magazine for many years. She was awarded a Summer Program scholarship to Oxford University, Oxfordshire, England, where she obtained certifications in Creative Writing; and Poetry. To learn more about or contact Brenda at: brichards7195@yahoo.com, or 954-643-1586

So, what's your takeaway from Phoenix, Poetess Brenda's poem?

#PhoenixesRising

https://bit.ly/phoenixesrising

As we leave Guyana, we head back to New York to visit with our next Phoenix, Mary Symmonds at the United Nations. To date, our Phoenixes have shared their individual resilient journey. Mary's story explores the concept of cultural resilience. This kind of resilience occurs when a country is committed to its success. Beginning with its leaders, the first shift would be in their mindset and commitment to choose a new path for the greater good of its people. The second shift would be to take the necessary action steps to have a country and its people thrive. Read on as Mary shares a fascinating tale of cultural resilience at the level of both herself, and the countries she was privileged to serve.

ON RESILIENCE

"Do not judge me by my successes. Judge me by how many times I fell down and got back up again."—**Nelson Mandela**

Chapter 12

CULTURAL RESILIENCE:
Mary Symmonds, United Nations

Mary Symmonds is a retired United Nations Executive and International Economic and Social Development Practitioner. She is also the founder of The Global Leadership Coalition which builds socially responsible, ethical, entrepreneurial leaders.

ON RESILIENCE

"Give people substantive power in their own affairs, encourage and support them in taking responsibility for ourselves, offer them assistance as they design tools for the exercise of that power – and chances are good that they will do remarkable things."—**Unknown**

. . . .

Cultural Resilience
Mary Symmonds, United Nations

"Dear Ms. Symmonds, the Executive Office of the Secretary General is pleased to inform you that you have been selected for a summer placement at the United Nations beginning..."

I did not have to read any further to realize that my declaration at age eleven had come to pass. My name is Mary Symmonds and my story of resilience is shared from a personal and global perspective. As individuals are called to be resilient, so too are countries. This is one of the major lessons I learned over my professional career of more than 35 years with the United Nations.

Resilience was the bedrock of our family because we understood that there was a higher calling and purpose for our lives. A native of Barbados, I, along with my five siblings, enjoyed a privileged life. My grandfather was a successful entrepreneur who instilled the value of education in all of us. Grandfather ran a grocery in Bridgetown, Barbados, starting in the late 19th century. This was no small achievement in those days, coming out of a history of slavery.

My father, born in 1904, was entrepreneurial. He began his career as a teacher and was renowned for his teaching excellence. He started off his career as a teacher and was highly renowned and sought after. Later, like my grandfather, he made his foray into entrepreneurship creating several businesses. My father had great compassion for those less fortunate than himself. He started the first bank, owned and run by people of color. This afforded individuals and businesses to save and invest, in housing and education. Growing up, I also observed how my father successfully weathered the storms of business, politics, and his personal life. I learned that life often handed you challenges that being privileged could not solve.

One of those challenges was an illness that ultimately led to the death of my mother. I was 12 at the time. A few months earlier, I had accompanied her on a trip to the United States. I did not realize it at the time, but this was a last-ditch effort to save her life. My father's work demands did not permit him to go, and my eldest sister was studying abroad. My mother was too ill to travel alone, so I was, therefore, the chosen one. She was traveling there for medical treatment; I was unaware of the seriousness of her illness but was certain that whatever it was, "America" would fix it.

Buoyed with a sense of hope and surrounded by caring relatives, I spent my Easter vacation visiting my mother at the shiny hospital with its wide corridors and smartly dressed nurses. My aunt, with whom I stayed, was also a nurse. She as well as her peers inspired confidence and ease around my mother's condition. This gave me the freedom to engage in the many activities my aunt planned for me which lessened my worry about my mother. My itinerary included visits to the Empire State Building, Radio City Hall, with its amazing Rockettes, the Statue of Liberty, and of course the United Nations. Upon seeing the UN, I declared that someday, I was going to work there. Unfortunately, my mother transitioned shortly after my return from America. Her passing had an indelible impact on my psyche and changed my life forever.

A gifted nurse, my mother loved the field of nursing as it gave her an opportunity to do what she truly loved—make a difference in the lives of her patients. However, in the early 20th century, the "Marriage Bar" prevented married women in certain professions from working. My mother gave up her career to become a mother, housewife, and socialite. The message to women during her era was that once married, your role was to "suck it up and smile," no matter how unhappy you were. I wanted more than that!

My mother influenced the trajectory of my life in many ways. One of the most important was the awareness of gender inequality and suppression. While she was unable to pursue her career as a married woman, the sisters of my father and mother who remained unmarried, were entrepreneurial. They were able to pursue professional careers as teachers, or accountants. I admired my mother's resilience to still pursue her passion to care for others through her volunteer work and service of others who were less fortunate. I can only surmise that she found her fulfillment through her role as a wife, mother, and benevolent soul. Though I could not articulate it at eleven years old, seeing the disparity between women who were forced to give up their careers for family, and those who were unmarried, had me commit to gender equality as a global leader.

Aside from the loss of my mother at an early age, another struggle of growing up privileged involved battling the guilt that comes along with having a leg up. This guilt emerged somewhere in my childhood as I realized that being privileged set me apart from others. It was the kind of guilt that was never spoken about, but was felt, when I saw, interacted, or tried to embrace those peers who were less fortunate than me. My experiences were a mixture of the concerns around privilege and also one of mixed feelings when my father faced business challenges. Retaining a privileged social position while dealing with my father's misfortunes was a challenge. I was never sure who my true friends were and were not. Thank God for my brothers and sisters. One thing I got from this was grit. Life goes on no matter what happens.

Being the fifth of six children has its advantages. Top of the list was having playmates. My fraternal twin brothers, two years my senior, were truly my best friends. I had to be resilient if I wanted to keep up with them. My elder siblings were a decade older and served as my guides and role models. I was an early walker, thanks to the twins. A year later came the best gift I could ever have asked for, a little sister. On Saturdays, my sister, Fran and I went for piano lessons and afterward. to the library to read for a bit and (then to) choose our new books. I loved reading. It was the gateway to my discovery about the world and adventures beyond my island home. Needless to say, I spent hours lost in my books.

Life is never a straight path. I found that mastery of the ups and downs of life takes courage, grit, and resilience. I determined that the path for me as a female was to have it all—education, career, and yes, a family of my own. I also knew that anything was possible as my parents, and their peers who served as my mentors encouraged me to pursue my dreams. To counteract my insecurities and uncertainties of life, I followed the moral and spiritual compasses that they bequeathed to me. These compasses served as roadmaps and mandates for my success. Couched within these edicts were the familial dreams and the expectations of others, my country, and my heritage. In addition, it was instilled in me that it was my duty to be a contributor and to have a purpose in life. It was also made clear to me by my family and others, that I needed to achieve three non-negotiables. First, I must be educated. Second, I must be successful. Third, I must make a difference in the lives of others less fortunate than myself.

These directives had their own challenges, with the greatest challenge being that of managing not only the pressure that accompanied these mandates but my mindset. Since I was subconsciously reminded that my success was their success, I *had no choice but to develop the spirit of resilience to keep going and to manage those challenging times when I wanted to quit.

In a small but powerful society, in case you ever forgot who you were, people from the community were quick to remind you. You were often referred to as your parents' child and not yourself. For example, on the street people asked,

"You're Mr. Symmonds's daughter?"

When I positively responded, they would recant all the good (or sometimes not so good) experiences of my father. I learned to listen, smile, but not respond, except to wish the person a good day.

A technique that helped me overcome my challenges and grow my resilience was to focus on the bigger picture, for example, my purpose. My purpose, and dare I say duty, is to make a difference for others. Every day, I examine ways to fulfill on that. This is what keeps me resilient.

Memories of my trip to New York and to the United Nations also reminded me of my childhood declaration that someday, I would work for that organization. I was totally mesmerized by the story of how the United Nations was created. Formed by a small group of countries, post-World War II in 1945, its overarching purpose is to guarantee world peace with a commitment to never have a third World War. Said another way, the United Nations is the peacekeeper of the world. I will never forget the story, the guide who led my tour told, of Nikita Khrushchev taking off his shoe and banging it on the table. This left me with an impression of how difficult it was to reach an agreement among a diverse group of world leaders. It also awakened in me an even deeper interest in Caribbean politics, which at the tender age of eleven, I had been following closely.

Due to my father's involvement in politics, dinner table conversation covered current affairs which I loved. I was deeply disappointed about the dissolution of the short-lived West Indies Federation in 1962. This Federation involved a group of eight islands that wanted to break away from their dependency on Great Britain. They would unite to form a coalition similar to the African and European Unions but timing is everything. This was not their time.

Years later as a college student, I toyed with becoming a teacher. I was following in the path of my father, aunts, and two cousins who were both principals of prominent girls' secondary schools (high schools) on the island. However, my undying curiosity about the

United Nations drove me to apply for a summer position as a Dean's List student.

One day I wrote a heartfelt letter to the United Nations expressing my childhood desire to work there and to be a part of their organization. To my surprise, they responded. I had not long celebrated my 21st birthday and thought that this would be my gift of freedom, to explore all those countries which I had only experienced through my books. Often, when opportunities of a lifetime appear, you just have to bite the bullet and go for it!

My career of over thirty-five years with the UN began as a clerk in the United Nation's External Board of Auditors where I typed the reports for the Department. This opened my eyes in a practical way to the importance of accountability. It also gave me a perspective of how the UN was organized. My performance, as well as my thirst to know more, and my passion to help those less fortunate, impressed the head of the Department.

Towards the end of my summer stint Congressman Bradford Morse, was appointed as Under-Secretary-General for Political and General Assembly Affairs and transferred from Washington, D.C. Who could have guessed that The Executive Office of the Secretary-General was looking for a person of color to join the team of the new Under-Secretary-General for Political and General Assembly Affairs? He had specifically requested a person of color to be on his team as a personal assistant, joining a team of two others in that role. The head of the audit unit recommended me to the EOSG and encouraged me to apply for the job. I was shortlisted for an interview and tagged; I was it! I was given an offer of appointment.

At first, though tempted, I turned down the offer as I wanted to complete my degree. However, after discussions with my superiors and family, coupled with the prospect and prestige of working in a department focusing on political affairs, accepting the position was a no-brainer.

In addition to the personal assistant team, the members of the Under-Secretary General's team included three grad students. The students had worked with Mr. Morse in his congressional office in Washington, D.C., and were completing their degrees, part-time. Two of them were at different stages of law school and another was studying international affairs. They had joined the D.C. team as interns and could not turn down the offer to join the congressman and later, the Under Secretary General's team at the UN. In part, just observing how they were able to handle working and going to school part-time, inspired me to achieve my dreams.

Determined to finish my degree, I resumed college part-time, and earned my Bachelor's in Political Science, focusing on Latin America and the Caribbean. It is not surprising that I subsequently took the decision to pursue graduate studies in International Affairs, graduating Magna Cum Laude.

Working for the Under-Secretary-General rekindled my interest in studying world politics, and opened my eyes to the inner workings of the UN. I was also exposed to the foundations of respecting, guaranteeing, and monitoring human rights in developing countries, and to the decolonization process of countries that were breaking away from colonialism. The United Nations gave these countries a platform to realize their dream, and the support to build their much-needed infrastructure. I was also exposed to the workings of the Economic and Social Council (ECOSOC) and gained an appreciation of the importance of the indispensable contribution, economic and social development made to guaranteeing world peace.

I was firmly committed to a career with the UN. It is, therefore, not surprising that when my boss was subsequently appointed as Administrator of the United Nations Development Program (UNDP), I eagerly accepted the offer to transfer to UNDP on promotion as his personal assistant.

For those of you who may not be aware, the UNDP was established by the UN General Assembly in 1965 and is based on a merger between two predecessor UN bodies, the United Nations Expanded Program for Technical Assistance which was created in 1949, and the United Nations Special Fund, established in 1958. One mandate was to help countries to be resilient by eliminating poverty and achieving sustainable human development. Another mandate was to foster economic growth that emphasized improving the quality of life of all citizens while conserving the environment and natural resources.

The UNDP today consists of a network of 170 country offices in the least developed countries and territories. The focus of its work, which has been adjusted over time to respond to changing world development conditions, is to eradicate poverty and reduce inequality. As a resilient warrior for equality and sustainability of nations, I was proud to be part of an organization that helps countries develop policies for good governance, improve key stakeholders' leadership skills, partnering abilities, and build resilience to achieve sustainable development goals. The UNDP currently focuses on sustainable development, democratic governance, peacebuilding, climate, and disaster recovery.

Before entering the UNDP's Management Training Programme, I was promoted to the position of Executive Officer where my duties included monitoring and facilitating the UNDP's country offices securing finalization of basic cooperation agreements, signed between the UNDP and host country governments, as the UNDP was expanding its country office presence. My duties also included supporting strategic preparations of the executive team for directing the UNDP's business. This gave me a bird's eye view of the organization, both at the headquarters and the country level.

I developed a growing interest in Africa, having noted that most African countries were among the least-developed countries. At the time I started working with the UNDP in the mid-1970s, it was still in its relative infancy as a merged organization. Its presence at the country level was growing in a period when the post-World War II decolonization was nearing its end. Fifteen years after its creation, the UNDP determined that to achieve greater operational efficiency, it should introduce a competitive management training program. This program would equip a cadre of career professionals to serve in its country offices. During the second year of the program's operation, I was accepted as a participant and this started my country-level career with a focus on Africa. My first posting was to Kenya as a management trainee. After three months I was transferred to post-independence Zimbabwe.

It is important to recognize that history is replete with national liberation struggles. For instance, during the 16th century, the Swedes waged their liberation war. The Dutch War of Independence lasted for 80 years, between the 16th and 17th centuries, and in the 18th century, the Americans waged their liberation war.

The independence struggles in Africa were no different. African countries were tired of conditions of inequality and discrimination and sought independence. During the post-World War II period, the African continent saw most countries become independent peacefully between 1956 and 1977, although some gained their independence through bitter struggle.

Like the Europeans before them, after attaining independence, the countries had to embark on rearranging the way their countries were governed. The transition to self-rule came with challenges of state and nation-building and economic development. Challenges included the need for strengthening institutions, as well as instituting laws, schools, and administrative systems, and achieving post-conflict reconciliation. There was also the major challenge of economic development as colonial powers left behind great deprivation among most of the populations. The UNDP played an important capacity-building role in working with countries to address these challenges. These historical episodes attest to the resilience we have as human beings to claim our rights, in the face of conditions that did not serve our advancement.

In my work, I developed projects and programs that built capacities to help countries build resilience. I learned many lessons regarding the challenges of building and developing countries that are able to offer their citizenry a better life. I could also see the propensity we have as human beings to be resilient. While in Kenya there was an attempted coup d' état. While the coup failed, I observed levels of deprivation that I had never before witnessed, yet people continued to pursue their lives and survive. This opened my eyes to the meaning of accountability that I had seen discussed in meetings at UN headquarters. I saw that there was a need for accountable leaders who work towards making a better life for the people.

Other challenges and their impacts that I witnessed included the following: Post-independence Zimbabwe was both trying to rebuild their nation after a civil war and deal with the need to heal a postwar nation while redressing pre-independence inequalities. Lesotho had its challenge of being led by a military government that had laws in place that limited large public gatherings and as such, stymied the ability to build organizations and teams that worked, factors which slowed the African State's progress towards civilian governance.

I was also there at a time when the HIV and AIDS epidemic was setting roots in Africa, and I saw, real-time, how it spread geometrically; and I was able to discern the important role that Governments play in putting in place policies and prevailing resources to foster the resilience necessary to overcome epidemics. While working on developing our country's programs, we were required to advocate for integrating HIV and Aids mitigation strategies into the planning process.

Post-colonial Africa also faced other challenges that led to conflict, other than liberation struggles. These were also a consequence of foreign intrusion into domestic affairs, and historical colonial economic practices to gain control over natural resources. In the course of these incursions, some ethnic groups in an ethnically diverse continent were privileged. The colonial powers built on historic local conflicts, creating societies characterized by vast disparities in wealth and power. The confluence of colonial power interests, and the influx of weapons and money, fueled competition for wealth and power, rendering local conflicts, deadlier.

To make matters worse, at the end of the Cold War, unstable countries were flooded with arms, and this fueled new competition for wealth and power and prolonged periods of armed struggles that robbed democratic structures of development, such as political parties, leaving room for strong leaders, not democratically elected, to emerge. These scenarios created conditions where the UNDP had to deal, both with gearing its programs of support towards addressing developmental challenges, as well as conflict resolution, post-conflict rehabilitation, and reconstruction.

My experiences in Ethiopia and Sierra Leone, as well as to some extent Uganda, were other examples of the challenges of rebuilding countries, or parts of countries, after civil wars and years of deprivation. I served in Sierra Leone between the three military coups d'états, which destroyed the country's social, economic, and physical infrastructure. I worked with leaders to develop projects and programs that contributed to rebuilding the economy, even as conflicts continued to rage.

I continued to advance within the organization and was soon spearheading multi-million dollar projects that financed development programs, to assist war-torn countries recoveries from the disastrous effects of conflicts. Of the more important lessons

I learned, has been the limitless resilience of the people, in the countries I served.

In the course of my assignment in Ethiopia, I contributed to the development of its National resilience after the war in 1992. As an executive of the UNDP, my portfolio focused on disaster prevention, preparedness, and rehabilitation and reconstruction, in previously neglected, war-affected, and drought-impacted areas. I contributed to the development of, and managed the implementation of a $14 million dollar Reconstruction program, which rebuilt capacities in 4 northern regions of the country, focusing on the Amhara and Tigray regions; the South focused on the drought-affected areas of Boloso and Konso, which bordered Kenya. Additionally, integrated were the Somali regions of Gode and Kelafo in the East, and the Western region, Gambella, which bordered Sudan. I continued to advance within the UNDP, leading and providing oversight to teams that worked with governments to spearhead multimillion-dollar programs and projects that contributed both to redevelopment, as well as recovery, from the devastation of war.

In the 1990s the African continent experienced an increase in conflicts. At one stage, over twenty-two countries were either in or affected by, conflict. This placed a great strain on our country offices and indeed governments, which were designed to deal with normal developmental situations, and did not have the ability to pivot to changing conditions on the ground.

After Sierra Leone, I returned to New York as an integral part of an emergency response unit that addressed this institutional issue. My role focused raining programs that would contribute to resilience in times of crisis, at the level of the country office, as well as at the government institutional level. My work aimed to equip country office staff to be able to monitor indicators of a country's risk of declining into chaos, and set in place contingency plans in order to safely evacuate non-essential personnel, while leaving our offices intact and able to resume work when the opportunity arose, without loss of institutional memory. It also put in place measures to ensure the livelihoods of our staff were maintained, while our office operations were closed. I also worked on guiding how projects could be developed during periods of conflict, to ensure the quickest return to the development path. Furthermore, I worked with governments to ensure that they set up multi-sectoral disaster mitigation management teams that would monitor, and ensure actions to ensure the livelihoods of the population, were maintained in times of crisis. The key was to have developmental programs that could be implemented during the conflict, so that recovery time was shortened, post-conflict.

One of the highlights of my life was witnessing the resilience of Tanzania. I had the opportunity to return to Tanzania, twenty years after my first visit, and witness the results of seeds sown decades earlier, that resulted in the transformation from a dusty Dar es Salaam town to a thriving capital; it has since become a country where progress indicators have drastically improved. Ethiopia is also a very different country from when I was there in the 1990s. Despite its current challenges, it has drastically reduced poverty. To know that I was part of the institution and movement that contributed to the resilience of a country continues to be inspiring for me.

Government officials have egos! You must learn how to work with people and to advocate carefully and courageously. Some governments were easy to work with, while others are not. An important lesson I learned in my career is to learn about the culture in which you work and share your own culture. In addition, you need to have the ability to listen and to be respectful of different views while being continuing able to negotiate and advocate. Most importantly, one needs to develop good relationships and be reliable. These combine to create resilient relationships.

Among the things that make me most proud is one program in which I was involved, using participatory bottom-up planning for development, in a country that was very authoritarian. When an evaluation was done, 4–5 years later, we found that the program approach had built the community's capacity to come together, discuss and come up with solutions to solve new problems as they arose.

This capacity proved to be instrumental in stemming the HIV and Aids epidemic as communities could be called upon to work together to problem-solve. This led to giving up some of the traditional practices that contributed to the spread of the epidemic, and ultimately, reduced the incidence.

Throughout my career at the UNDP, the best opportunity I received was meeting my amazing husband Ben, a gifted economist and communicator. Ben's work ultimately overlapped with mine and was complementary. Ben initially worked in marketing in the private sector and moved into social marketing. Examples of where our careers converged included his productions of radio social dramas that addressed societal problems, and films that raised awareness about such challenges as the impact of corruption on development. We also collaborated on the importance of girl-child education, as well as contributing solutions to the management of the HIV and AIDs epidemic. He also undertook policy work that contributed to the management of the epidemic. Despite his busy career, he enjoyed being "Mr. Mom" to our two beautiful children who, as adults, are leading lives in which they display the resilience that we have demonstrated through our own lives together, managing busy careers and raising our children.

You will recall, I declared earlier in my story that I wanted it all. I worked hard at mothering, and my career. I made the layette, pillow covers, blanket, and crib bumpers, and decorated my children's rooms with curtains and stuffed toys, all of which I lovingly made despite my busy schedule. I organized the birthday parties, special occasions, and graduations, and made sure that I was present as much as I could. When I was not traveling, we had dinner as a family. Ben and I worked as a team. We were seamlessly dedicated to raising our children. For us, being the best mom meant having the best dad.

We agreed that it was important to establish a consistent routine for our two children in the midst of myriad inconsistencies. No matter where I was, we had dinner together as a family. After the children were in bed, I would then return to work for a couple of hours. The resilience of our marriage and raising our children was a team effort. The foundation of our successful marriage and family was great communication. As women, we have many challenges pursuing careers and raising families. Both my husband and I were career people, so we needed a team to make our lives work. Wherever we were, we employed a support staff of nannies, housekeepers, gardeners, chauffeurs, and others, to support traveling between countries for work and other pursuits.

Unfortunately, Ben became ill and transitioned a few years ago. There are no words to describe the enormous contribution that he made to our children, and to me. As I reflect on my life and resilience in general, like anyone else, I have had my challenges and losses. Life as a journey brings us hardships, heartaches, joys, celebrations, and special moments. We draw lessons from all these moments. As a friend has consistently reminded me. "No condition is permanent." Indeed, if life proceeded seamlessly to the same beat it would be boring. I have gained a profound appreciation of the similarities we share as human beings and our responsibility to make a difference for others. I also appreciate that, although we have many challenges for advancement in the Caribbean, conditions in other parts of the world are far worse. I remain eternally grateful to our

Caribbean leaders for the bold actions they have taken to transform our countries and region.

My greatest challenge was the loss of my mother just after I turned twelve. The loss of Ben was my second greatest challenge. Recently, I also lost my baby sister. In each case, I thought my world had ended. But I drew strength from the fact that I was not alone. Three of my friends had lost their mothers at an early age around the time that I lost mine. Three friends lost their husbands around the time I lost mine. I am able to see that despite life's hard knocks, we are able to survive. Although deeply saddened by the reality of death, I have come to realize that in the process, many doors have opened. I have supportive relatives, family friends, and peers. I learned in the two challenging years after death, that no matter what happens in life, we can pick up and move on. I learned not to judge others but to let them show their qualities. I learned to be kind to others, to be adaptable and to fit in all situations.

I have also learned to love the Caribbean and all that it has to offer. Life has a beginning, middle, and end. What has kept me resilient through the ups and downs of life is my family and my career.

After retirement, I have devoted my life now to making a difference through my involvement in activities that make a difference for others. I am involved in several organizations that make a difference, including the Global Leadership Coalition which I founded. It aims to foster a new brand of leader who is ethical, entrepreneurial, and connected to their society while taking actions to transform their societies. Through this program, I aim to develop leaders between the ages of 18 and 29 in underserved communities in the Caribbean and Africa who will be able to take transformational actions that contribute to the achievement of sustainable development goals.

So I started off my life of resilience with a commitment to being educated, being successful, and making a difference. I believe I have achieved this.

But as George Bernard Shaw said,

"This is the true joy of life. I want to be thoroughly used up when I die."

Overall, the highlight of my life has been my work at the United Nations and being strategically positioned to contribute to an organization that contributes to the world. In the coming ten years as a resilient woman, I would have written the three books on my bucket list, and handed over the thriving Global Leadership Coalition to young leaders who are committed to a purpose that is greater than themselves. Whether individual or country, being resilient entails a willingness to shift your mindset for the greater good. I am Mary Symmonds, wife, mother, policymaker, and global leader, and I am resilient!

"We may have different religions, different languages, different colored skin, but we all belong to one human race."
—Kofi Annan

To learn more about The Global Coalition, visit https://www.globalleadershipcoalition.org, email address globalleadershipcoalition@gmail.com Tel: (908) 485-7355

So, what's your takeaway from Phoenix Mary's story?

#PhoenixesRising

Share your answers in your FB group

Take a deep breath as we will stay in the US for the next leg of our resilient journey. We will head over to Florida where we will meet one of our extraordinary veterans Michelle Angelique Poitier. Her story about her life and time in the military is riveting to say the least. Read with caution as her story might be triggering for some.

WARNING TRIGGER

ON RESILIENCE

"God I just want to take a minute not to ask for anything from you, but simply to say thank you.
—Unknown Soldier

Chapter 13

SURVIVING AND THRIVING POST MILITARY:
Michelle Angelique Poitier (Perry), USA

A United States Veteran of the Navy Intelligence Community with 13 years of honorable service, mother, grandmother, and leader; Michelle is a force of nature and mouthpiece for recovery and reconciliation to the communities she serves. A graduate of the University of Phoenix, she earned a Bachelor of Science in Management. CEO of Michelle Speakz: If You Hide It You Can't Heal It, a Coaching & Mentoring Organization; Founder of Healing Women; Healing Nations, NE Florida Inc, a Social Service Organization; Trainer and advocate for National Alliance on Mental Illness. Michelle uses her voice of commitment as she advocates for survivors of domestic & sexual abuse, homelessness among female veterans, and those battling Post Traumatic Stress Disorder (PTSD) and Military Sexual Trauma (MST).

Surviving and Thriving Post Military
Michelle Angelique Poitier, USA

"Healing is truly a journey. It's not a destination."
—Michelle Angelique Poitier

Resilience is the ability to bounce back from your adversities, correct? Then let me ask you, how was it possible for me to bounce back from being sexually assaulted multiple times, and by different men over the course of my lifetime? Was it my fault? Was I really to blame for this repeated and unwelcomed violation of my body, mind, and soul? Was it? Sexual assault of any kind should never be tolerated, and although some people may differ, it is never the victim's fault. However, according to my grandmother I was definitely to blame for each and every incident. Hello, my name is Michelle Poitier—military to the core, and this is my story of resilience.

Although born in Memphis, Tennessee, I moved with my mother to live with my grandmother when I was a baby and was raised in a predominantly female-led household. I never knew my father. As the story goes, my mom was around seventeen when she fell in love with my dad. She trusted him when he told her,

"You know, Babe, that you won't get pregnant on
the first time, right?

Why do some of us always fall for that line? Nine months later, I appeared on the scene. As the story goes, I was around six months old when my dad told my mom that he was going to the store. He left, and never came back. If I saw my dad today on the street, I wouldn't know him. My mother's story is an all too familiar one, where the fantasy of love seldom matches the reality, particularly after a child enters the picture. Children change everything, and even under the best of circumstances they can tax the relationship between yourself and your mate.

My grandmother raised all of us to be very independent. However, as far as children were concerned, they were to be seen and not heard. I come from a family of six footers. I am the smallest one at 5'5". I say that I am small, but mighty. My mom at 5'11" was, and still is, an extremely strong woman. She did not want to go the traditional career path that other women chose for themselves. In addition, she had to consider that she was a single mom with a daughter for whom she had to provide for. She decided to break the mold and join the military. She wanted to experience something new and live a different aspect of life.

While she was away in Vietnam and getting herself established, I spent the first six years of my life with Grandma. I was an eclectic, free spirited child. I loved the arts, and would often sing and put on plays for the family. My grandmother took me to church. My mom made me go to vacation Bible School. I was not particularly religious, but at least we did the church thing. I did not develop a personal relationship with God until my thirties.

One day at a family gathering, I was being my free-spirited self when my uncle decided that I looked particularly cute. Why is it always an uncle or close relative? He lured me into the bedroom and molested me. I was seven years old. At seven, my child's brain could not even begin to process what had happened. Numb and ashamed, I could just crouch in a corner, hug my knees, and attempt to deal with my pain. At some point, my cousin endured the same torture from our uncles. This incident with my uncle was my first lesson of resilience. Pulling on the strength of God and my mother, I gathered myself together and "carried on."

In our family, we kept secrets. If we told, we were threatened. Furthermore, under the banner that children should be seen and not heard, we shouldn't do anything to hurt or embarrass other family members. No one in the family cared that my cousin and I were hurting the most.

By the way, did you know that according to The United States Department of Health and Human Services there are over 83,000 children who are sexually assaulted every year? Twenty-seven percent are females, and male relatives are the biggest perpetrators.

From an early age, I was told that no matter what happens, to put back on your big girl panties, suck it up, and keep it moving. So, I learned very early how to suppress bad stuff to survive. My cousin and I kept the secret of our assaults until we could no longer hold it in. Secrets can only be suppressed for so long before they manifest in different ways, shapes, or forms. A lot of things that went on in the family, honored the saying,

"What goes on in this house stays in this house."

This was just the first of multiple sexual violations that my cousin and I endured at the hands of our male family members. When I couldn't endure it anymore, I finally found the courage to say something to my grandmother. I was sure that she would stand up for me, beat my uncles into a pulp (as only grandmas can), perhaps, kill them. Instead, she said—like no kidding,

"Why did you wait so long?" "I don't know why you waited so long; you must have enjoyed it."

Like a razor-sharp knife her words inflicted more pain on my psyche than all the pain caused by the perpetrating pedophiles in my family. So, I'll ask the same question that I asked earlier in the beginning of my story. How is it possible to bounce back from being violated by multiple male family members over the course of my lifetime? Was it my fault? Was I really to blame for this repeated and unwelcomed violation of my body, mind, and soul? Could my grandmother be right? Void of answers and support, I built a wall around my heart and spirit and completely shut down as this was just too much for my seven-year-old soul to bear. When you find

yourself unable to cope with life, your brain will compartmentalize your experiences to deal with your reality. I could only pray for
justice.

Justice came, sort of, when my mother returned and took me to
live with her in California. I was eight at the time and more than
happy to escape my dysfunctional family in Tennessee. Come to
think of it, I don't remember if I ever told her about my assault. In
the seven years since her departure to the military, she had married,
divorced, and had my little brother. I became his second mom. Subsequently, she remarried again to a wonderful man. My mom had
finally found her happiness. My stepdad was also in the military.
Unlike my uncles, he was what a man should be,* and a wonderful
father. Together my mom and stepdad added three more boys to
our family.

Despite now having a loving and complete family, for so many
reasons, I found it hard to connect with people. Therefore, I created my own virtual reality. I viewed this as how I developed my
resilience to combat the loneliness and isolation that accompanies military life, and being disconnected from friendships formed
along the way. I did a lot of things that I could do by myself. I was
involved in the arts and became creative. I was in the choir and on
the dance team. I was on the drill team. I loved theater and would
put on shows for my mom and her friends. I'd get all dressed up and
pretend to be a famous singer. Natalie Cole was one of my favorite
artists. I rehearsed her songs and made my mom and her friends
watch me perform. That was so much fun. This is also how I buried
my pain and tarnished past.

We stayed in California for three years until we moved overseas
to the suburbs of Japan. Japan was my first experience in a different culture, and I absolutely loved it. I fell in love with the culture
of a people who embraced us. Each year, I participated in their Bon
Odori Festival. This is a street festival that is held in villages and cities

all over Japan. Dancing and the beating of the Taiko drums are a big part of the festival as it is designed to bring back honor to the dead. How appropriate this was for me as my spirit and honor died with my grandmother's words several years ago. I enjoyed dressing up in their traditional kimonos and participating in their traditional dances because I loved to dance. Perhaps subconsciously, I was trying to arouse my own dead spirit. I loved Japan and was able to graduate from high school on our Military base there.

My life was going well and on track for a career post-graduation when another predator struck. I was sixteen when I was once again assaulted. One of my mother's coworkers decided that I was ripe for the picking, and picked he did! Truth be told, I was someplace that I wasn't supposed to be. I didn't tell my mother about the incident because we all have dualities and different sides to our personalities. By this time, my mother had been in the military for several years since 1972. I had heard but later discovered for myself that combat does horrible things to your psyche. I just want the other side of my mom to come out and, I certainly did not want to get her in trouble. So I held it. Yes, once again, I buried another violation like all the others under built-up layers of shame, guilt, anger, and despair. As I shared earlier, one can only hold and bury your pain for so long.

One day, I don't remember the exact incident; maybe it was a touch, or an off-colored comment, but that day, and that moment was when all my emotions got triggered from my childhood trauma in Tennessee. It did not help that my grandmother's comments had been subconsciously and repeatedly playing in my head. I experienced an emotional meltdown and attempted the first out of five failed suicides. God, talk about feeling like a failure. I couldn't even kill myself.

My mother was beside herself as she struggled to understand what had happened to her little girl. Thank God my parents were supportive and got me into some therapy. I was just beginning to heal when we had to move again. This time Iowa was going to be our new home. Military life is nomadic. Orders are orders and you pretty much went where you were assigned. We were never in any one place longer than about three years because of my parent's military experience.

After graduating from high school, I followed in my parents' footsteps and joined the military in 1990 for two major reasons. I was seventeen at the time and decided on the Navy because it seemed like this branch of the military would offer me an opportunity to see the world. There were also two personal reasons why I chose the military. The first one being that I have always had a heart for advocacy, community, and serving. I was taught to serve others. I think that is a large part of leadership and what better way to learn how to lead and serve than to serve my country. The second, and I think the more important reason, was that I wanted to escape from and to separate myself from the dysfunction that I grew up in. Joining the military also gave me an opportunity to reinvent myself without anybody knowing what my past had been.

As a female, when you sign up for the military, very few people will share with you the truth about the journey that is guaranteed to change you for the rest of your life. People seem to delight in saying,

"Thank you for your service."

Most of us smile and agree. However, if people only knew what life as a female lioness in a male dominated lion's den was really like, then "thank you for your service" would adopt a completely different meaning. Of course, every story is unique, and there are always three sides to a story—your side, their side, and the truth. Like my family, I discovered to my dismay that the military had mastered the art of denying and hiding the truth.

I became one of the Navy's top codebreakers, and highest performing sailors. Codebreakers have existed since WWI. In layman's terms, I was on military assignment as a code breaker helping the military keep their secrets, a secret. I'm very analytical and love to analyze problems. As a child, one of my favorite activities was solving puzzles. My job was to intercept and decipher coded enemy correspondence. As a covert operator in Panama, decoding encrypted messages was right up my alley. Each message gave us intel and an advantage over the enemy as we unraveled and disrupted their plans. Having grown up in Japan, my first duty station was in Asia and more specifically, Korea. It was the first time that I was going to be overseas by myself and away from my family. I was beyond excited. So here I was in Korea, breaking enemy codes, excelling at my craft, and loving it. Finally, I had found something that I loved and could be good at, on my own terms. It turned out that I was one of their highest performing sailors

I was so proud to join a group of Navy code-breakers who were placed on an Army installation. I had no idea of the rivalry that existed between the Army and Navy. Surely, we were on the same team, right? Well, I discovered as the saying goes that,

"It ain't necessarily so."

Folks, the rivalry is real, as there was this ongoing competition between Army and Navy. Unbeknownst to me I crossed the line big time when I ended up dating an Army guy. Based on their reaction, you would have thought that I committed a high-level crime. My dating choice caused some friction with Navy colleagues. This seemed silly to me but my Navy folks did not share my point of view. I was genuinely unaware that fraternization between ranks was taboo. So many secrets, so many. My Navy colleague decided to teach me a lesson. One night I was cornered by him on the brig. This time, I fought back, but in the end he won and I was assaulted again.

According to the Department of Defense,

"Sexual assault is defined as intentional sexual contact, characterized by use of force, threats, intimidation, abuse of authority, or when the victim does not or cannot consent. Sexual assault can occur without regard to gender or spousal relationship, or age of the victim. Sexual assault must involve physical contact."

Our military motto is "to protect and to serve." Does that only apply to others? What about my protection? What about honoring my rights? I was not going to be silent. I was not going to sit this one out or be quiet about my assault. This caused a big shift in my unit as I was not honoring the "don't ask, don't tell" code of silence. We were told that no matter what happens, I needed to put back on my big girl panties, suck it up, and keep it moving. These military instructions supported what I was told and had been ingrained in me, by my family, since childhood. Little did they know that my knickers were just about worn out. Unlike civilian life, in the military, your first and main objective was and still is, to complete the mission.

So, if we had anything going on, we didn't address it. Any personal issues were pressed down, as the main objective and focus was on completing the mission.

Now while that may make sense, I quickly understood that in order to succeed, your person needs to go somewhere else in your brain. I call it my resilient happy place. This is where I went during my training. This is what had me rise up and win many battles during Navy Bootcamp. This place in my brain was where I found the courage to keep going. This is where I pulled on the strength of my faith and my amygdala. Your amygdala is a walnut shaped structure in your brain that gives you four choices in response to trauma (such as in the case of assault). These choices are to either fight, take flight, freeze, or appease. This time, I chose to fight the greatest battle of my life—the battle against my womanhood and all that it stood for. This was the final straw for me.

"ENOUGH WAS ENOUGH!"

I was trained to be a soldier damnit! How dare I fight for others, be willing to give my life for others and country, and not be willing to do that for myself? Michelle, the little girl had finally grown up. Oh yes honey, those big girl panties that I was told to put back on, they were back on and in full bloom. I declared to myself that, not one more time, was I going to play this assault game. Quite frankly, I had run out of emotional spaces to hide, and the compartments in my psyche were full. There was nothing else to do but to take a risk and to cause a big shift in the area of sexual assault in the military.

I took a risk, filed a report, and addressed the matter with my command. To no surprise, they kept telling me they were taking care of it. Whenever I inquired about the progress of my complaint, the answer was always the same.

"We're taking care of it."

or that they were '...going to take care of it'. Sad to say, nothing was ever done. Day after day, salt continued to be poured into my wounds as I watched that bastard who had violated me walk around with a smug smile on his face like nothing had occurred. I think that I solidly vowed to make things better for us women in the military, I just had not yet figured out how to do so. This incident gave me a different perspective and outlook of the military.

For our readers, know that military sexual assault is real. According to the Department of Defense, over 47% of women in the Armed Forces experience this violation, and 65% never report the crime. Most of the violations are done by superior officers in the person's chain of command. The act itself is connected to power vs. a need to relieve sexual tensions, or to be intimate. Let's face it. Our training is designed to prepare our psyche for conquering the enemy. Perhaps once this "conquering" switch is triggered in the brain, we women become targets for the lions in our pack. I stand corrected if I am incorrect in my assessment. Despite my setback, I still continued to serve because I wanted to. However, moving forward, I had a different outlook on the military. It would be a few years before I could realize my dream to help abused women in the military get free and stay free.

As chance would have it I met my husband at that first duty station. He too was in the Navy. At 6'4" and built like a brick wall, he was physically strong and represented safety. I felt that he could protect me, as people would have to get through him before they got to me. For the first time, I allowed myself to trust this person and fell deeply in love. It was also the first time that I had opened up my heart to anybody. I basked in the way that he catered and attended to my every need. What I was not aware of was that my sense of love was very misguided.

What was hidden from my view was that his 'love' was more like control. After we got married, we started having some challenges as things turned physically, emotionally, and sexually abusive. Yes folks, sexual abuse in a marriage does happen as "NO" for some men is often perceived as rejection. For someone who is controlling, the word "NO" is often not respected, and serves as a catalyst for behaviors that do not end well, for either of you.

For me, marriage is a three-cord covenant between God, yourself, and your spouse. So, here I was, dealing with my marital challenges, and trying to make everything work because failure was not an option for me. No matter what, I said,

"Okay, I made these vows, I'm going to stick through this for better or for worse."

Well, wouldn't you know that our relationship worsened. It got to the point where I was not functioning but only going through the motions.

Listen, married life can be challenging on a good day. However, being married and in the military is rough. It is like code-switching. When on a mission, your amygdala is in full throttle as you operate from your lower brain in a combination of fight, flight, or freeze mode. However, when you return home, you are expected to operate from your higher brain with compassion, logic, emotional control, and to do the critical thinking to override your amygdala and act "normal."

If your marital relationship didn't have a solid foundation before going in, it is almost impossible to sustain a marriage. In the Navy, you are on sea duty. That means you spend a lot of time at sea, couped up with other sailors, many of whom are single and experiencing the same loneliness and stress. The environment is a breeding ground for infidelity. You're married when you're home, but when you are out to sea, you are single. Every time that you return home, you have to adjust to this person that you said I do to. However, what people don't understand, and particularly your spouse, is that you have come back differently. Even if you are both in the military, when you return to each other your mindset will be different, because of what you experienced. You have changed because in the military, a mission-focused mindset is necessary to complete the task at hand. The mantra has, and will always be, to complete the mission.

However, what is your mission when you come home to your spouse and kids? Many are confused about that. For example, you return from your tour and accompany your spouse to the supermarket. As you walk down the aisles, let us say that your mind is still on the military mission that you have just completed. Yet, you and your brain are expected to code switch and to be attentive to your beloved. As you walk down the grocery aisles, with the military mission still playing in your head, you are expected to code switch to your spouse who has asked you to retrieve the cereal from the top shelf and place it in the basket. This requires you to turn off the military mission that is playing in your head and switch to husband or wife mode.

Now your mission at home gets complicated because of interference. Let's say in your single life on the ship you disavowed your marriage and crossed the line with one of your fellow sailors. You are expected to turn off not only the military mission but the thoughts about your girlfriend or boyfriend with whom you just spent time at sea "switch." You are to then focus on your spouse in the grocery store "switch," and retrieve the right cereal from the aisle's top shelf "switch." Little did you know that while you were at sea, your family had switched from Corn Flakes to Cocoa Puffs "switch." Hold on, it gets better! Let us not even mention the kids in the cart who are vying for your attention "switch, switch." Am I making sense so far? Further complications arise when you want to share about all you encountered at sea while on your military mission but can't because it is considered "classified" not to mention, taboo. So, you learn to compartmentalize those experiences as well— or not.

Every day, I prayed over my husband and our marriage. Unfortunately, we did not have that solid foundation spoken of earlier. This allowed our insecurities to mess with our psyches, which resulted in unbecoming behaviors. Over time, I discovered that my husband had also been emotionally traumatized by his childhood and military experiences. It was bad enough that we fought the enemy without. However, and even worse, our fight was with the individual and collective enemy, within. We were each other's triggers. We fought a lot, both verbally and physically. Love and control got collapsed in the murky waters of who would win. At times, we were not even sure what we were fighting about.

Adding fuel to the fire, I got pregnant quickly which seemed to piss him off even more. Our relationship was very combative and it only got worse after our daughter was born. Having our daughter did not help our relationship as this brought additional stress to both of us.

Ladies, please hear me when I tell you that children sometimes do not make a damaged relationship better because they add stress to an already fragile situation. I later discovered that many women like myself fall for men who are physically appealing, but do not realize that behind their looks and charm can lie a very dark side. This dark side seldom emerges in the dating process. If seen, sometimes our brain does not want to accept the reality because we are in love. In addition, for someone like myself where love had been elusive, my brain had routinely compartmentalized anything negative as I carried on with everyday living.

We divorced shortly after our daughter was born. My husband often told me that I didn't know when to give up or quit. Giving up or stopping was next to impossible when triggered because I had no emotional resolve to pull myself back from the abyss. When sparked, whatever trauma I had suppressed rose to the surface, was unleashed on him and myself, but stopped short of our daughter. It got to the point where we had to admit that our relationship was not working. I was starting to implode and explode simultaneously.

I was devastated that my marriage did not work out. I knew myself to be like my missions, and I was someone who did not fail. Furthermore, I had proven to be resilient. With God at my back, I compartmentalized my divorce, put my big girl panties back on, one more time, and kept it moving. I was now a single parent with a daughter to raise. Regardless of what her dad did, did not, or would do in the future, our child was now my responsibility.

We had just moved from Virginia to Florida and didn't know anyone. To make matters worse, I deployed three weeks after we got there. So, I needed to find a place to live, a babysitter, and get myself settled. I forced myself to do whatever was necessary because I had a daughter to take care of. She was only a baby at the time when I entrusted her to my cousin. Saying goodbye to her as I left for my tour was the hardest thing for me to do. However, since I worked for the Navy, I had to show up.

In addition, my modus operandus was to be the best at everything and to complete the mission. I picked a double shift which allowed me to work on land and at sea. This way, I could spend more time being a mom. God knows I tried to be the best mom. I was determined to keep a nice home and myself physically fit. I worked out five or six times a week for about two to three hours a day. I know that was excessive, but rigorous exercise kept me going until I became suicidal again. I made the fourth of the five failed suicide attempts about halfway through my military career. I realized that I needed help, particularly because my daughter was depending on me to see her through life.

What exacerbated this suicide attempt was when I was about to leave for my tour of duty at sea. I was just about to board the US Kennedy when I got a call from my distraught cousin. The call was the worst nightmare that any mother could get. In my case, it really was the worst call as my cousin tried to tell me as calmly as she could that my two-year-old daughter had been molested. I went ballistic and was truly ready to kill somebody. Having been in the military, I could do that with ease. It turned out that the perpetrator was the child care provider's husband who was also in the military. He and the provider felt that they could get away with the crime because my two-year-old daughter wouldn't be a credible witness. I appealed to the military and to the police but the case didn't go anywhere. There are not enough words in the dictionary to describe how I felt. You tell me, people, when did child molestation, and particularly of a baby, become normal in our country?

After the incident, I got help for myself and became very focused on our daughter. I made sure to tap into every resource that I could, to ensure that she got what she needed and the best of everything. My family was super-supportive. However, even with their support, I reached out to our military family support center. They provided the counseling and other support services that we needed. I wish more of us in the military would take advantage of what they have to offer. However, most people don't seek or participate in the counseling because of the fear. Nobody wants anything in their record, especially if you are in the military. It's crazy, because the resources are there, but you don't always use them because, for sailors, and I suspect other branches of the military as well, having a counseling record can impact your career and ability to advance. Any kind of mental health issue can get you black-balled. Perhaps that is why most veterans implode rather than talking about their experiences.

Other than counseling, what got me through the worst part of my life and furthered my resilience, was developing a personal relationship with God. Although my mother and grandmother took me to church when I was a child, I did not develop a personal relationship with Him until my thirties. For all that I had been through in my childhood and adult life, I knew I needed help beyond human intervention and what I could do. One day I found myself in a dark place and cried out to God for help, only to hear in my spirit,

"I sent you the help."

That same week, somebody invited me to church. I accepted their invitation, gave my life to Christ, and started my journey to healing.

The day I gave my life to Christ I felt this really warm, loving, indescribable feeling overtake me. Since then, I have had a few of those experiences, and each time, they have been miraculous and life altering. My life has never been the same since then. I tell you that there is nothing like feeling the unconditional love of God and His peace. As I reflect on my life, and as you can see, I have gone through a lot in my childhood and even in my adult life. After spending thirteen years in the military, I am grateful for the experience, but I am done with military life. I am resilient because I am a fighter. You can knock me down but I will get back up. If you ask me what has kept me going, it is my faith, my daughter, and my fighting spirit.

Currently, I am CEO of my company, Michelle Speakz, serving female veterans in their healing journey from life and military trauma. I am free of my traumatic past and now devote my time to helping women - particularly those in the military, to get free and stay free. In 2018, I was nominated as a "Game Changer" by former First Lady, Michelle Obama's United State of Women's Initiative. I have turned my tragedies into triumphs and have become an entrepreneur, author, and inspirational speaker. I also advocate for survivors of domestic and sexual abuse, homelessness among female veterans, and those battling with Post-Traumatic Stress Disorder (PTSD), and Military Sexual Trauma (MST).

My mission which I have willingly accepted is to take these survivors on their journey to healing and wholeness. My book *Healing Women Healing Nations* speaks of overcoming the trauma of sexual abuse and domestic violence. My name is Michelle Angelique Poitier (Perry). I am a mother, survivor, an advocate for female veterans who have endured abuse, a healer, and I'm resilient!

To Contact Michelle, visit https://www.michellespeakz.com 9043703549

Email: michellespeakz@gmail.com

BE RESILIENT

WOW! oh Wow!, after reading Michelle's story, I was speechless. This would be a good time if you have not already done so to join our

Facebook group, comment on what you are getting from the stories of these powerful Phoenixes and give them some encouragement and love. Just because they have experienced and accomplished a lot in their lives does not mean that they can't receive, welcome or appreciate your comments, positive vibes and encouragement. Consider that we are not strong or feel like being resilient all the time. Honey, let me tell you, being a Phoenix is hard work. Being a resilient Phoenix is next-level training and life-altering.

So, what's your takeaway from Michelle Poitier's story?

#PhoenixesRising
Share your thoughts in our FB Group

https://bit.ly/phoenixesrising

ON RESILIENCE

"Tell yourself this: I am a conqueror. I am a detour slayer, and my goals and dreams don't exist in a vacuum. Every bit of my life is preparing me for something better, something greater."—**Keisha Blair**

Reader are you still with us? Let's take a break and head to South Florida to meet our very gifted Phoenix, Poetess April Morrow. See if you can spot the essence of her resilience in her I AM Poem.

I AM POEM
April Morrow, Artist, USA

"Even our darkest times can bring us joy, love and connection."

I AM FROM laughter, music, my dad's stories of adventure, a family of nine, the beauty of many places, and freshly made German bread

I AM FROM German baked cookies, the smell of pancakes on Sunday morning, spicy crawfish, mouthwatering greens, butterball turkey and a to-die-for international cuisine.

I AM FROM Laissaez le bon ton rouler; (let the good times roll) Guten nacht, schlaf gut und susse traume (good night, sleep well, and sweet dreams) and I love you to the moon and back with all my heart.

I AM FROM Grandmas Hattie and Hester, Gene and Beth Morrow, two children, my eight grandchildren, and a collection of art, poetry and children's stories that are expressions of my heart and soul.

I AM April Morrow

April Morrow is an author who writes poetry and children's stories. She is also an artist who explores what is beyond the veil. To learn more about April's poetry and art contact her at Aprilmorrow99@gmail.com.

So, what's your takeaway from Phoenix, Poetess April's poem?

#PhoenixesRising
Share your thoughts in our FB Group

https://bit.ly/phoenixesrising

Florida was so great that we decided to stay here a little longer. Come with me to meet our next Phoenix, Marsha Feldman. I was looking for a lady who could represent Germany. Referred by our mutual friend Wilma Mulcare, Marsha accepted the invitation to share her story of resilience for the project. WOW! was I blown away. You will be too. I invite you to be amazed at what she has to share. I know I was.

Chapter 14

OWNING YOUR BEAUTY AT ANY AGE:
Marsha Feldman

Marsha Feldman is a former Ms. United States Ambassador Queen. She is a proud mother, community leader, model, published author, charity supporter and activist. She is a charity race runner in South Florida. Marsha is a brand ambassador and advertising specialist for several companies focusing on infomercials, testimonials, print and advertising. As President of the Aventura Chapter's Inter-national Association of Women (IAW), she empowers women and the local business community by creating opportunities for all to benefit.

ON RESILIENCE

"Resilience is based on compassion for ourselves as well as compassion for others."—**Sharon Salzberg**

Owning Your Beauty At Any Age
Marsha Feldman

"Ladies and Gentlemen, now for the moment that you've all been waiting for. Who will be the next 2016 Mrs. Florida Woman of Achievement? Can I have a drum roll please? Your new reigning Queen is none other than Marsha Feldman."

I could hardly believe what I was hearing. Did they really call my name? Am I really a beauty queen at my age? I mean who in their right mind enters beauty pageants in their mid-forties? Well, when you find yourself in a place where your self-esteem is in the toilet, and you are no longer desired by your husband, you either sink or swim. I decided to swim. Hello, my name is Marsha Feldman, and this is my story of resilience.

Believe it or not, beauty pageants for mature women have been around since 1854 when P. T. Barnum introduced the first of its kind for adult women. Barnum was ahead of his time as the masses were not ready for his creation. In a public outcry of immorality, Barnum was forced to close this aspect of his empire. My journey to enter a beauty pageant in my later years of life, stemmed from a profound need to rediscover, reaffirm, and celebrate who I was, as a woman. At the time that I entered my first pageant, I was at a very low point in my life. Although my husband and I dearly loved each other, we had not been intimate since our first child was born a decade ago. We had gone from being a loving couple, to being roommates.

My husband and I come from two different cultures but prior to, and up until our child was born, we shared the same mindset. I grew up in a German household in the Midwest in a suburb of Cleveland, Ohio. I have German roots on both sides of the family. Raised as a Christian Methodist, my mom, dad, brother, and I lived in Ohio for most of my childhood. Both working parents, my father was a dentist, and my mother was a dietician and nutritionist. My parents are still together today and have been married for over fifty years. I envisioned something similar for myself when I grew up and got married.

I was a latchkey kid who grew up pretty much on my own. Every day, when I came home from school, my brother and I would wait for our parents to join us around six o'clock in the evening. This gave my brother and me a little bit of freedom after school, to play and relax before our parents arrived. Mom and dad were always open to allowing us to be ourselves. We had the freedom and encouragement to be whomever we chose to be, and to do what made us happy. When I was in my late twenties, I moved to Florida to live on my own. I wanted to start a new life. Luck would have me hit the jackpot. Not only was I able to transfer my government job without difficulty, but Florida was where I met my future husband and soulmate. I'm a federal employee and have been since I graduated from Cleveland State University.

I've been with the government for about twenty-five years where I manage a large database for its legal system. I also fix computers for our judges. For the most part I love my job and excel at what I do. However, ladies, how many of us can be "dragon slayers" at our jobs, but may be failing miserably at home. Our families do not see us as often, and our mates may feel neglected. Worst of all, in our effort to be all things for all people, we neglect ourselves the most. Can any of you relate? In my case, I waited until I was in my mid-thirties to marry because I wanted to be established in my career before settling down and having children. I also wanted to make sure that I was marrying the right person for me.

My husband is Jewish and was raised in New York. We met at the courthouse and it was love at first sight. He had checked all my boxes, and I had checked all his. So here I was of German ancestry marrying into a Jewish family. It was amazing that given our history that two cultures—German and Jewish could come together and have a wonderful life. What made our union work was that we both believed in the importance of family values. I was accepted with open arms by his family, and so was he, by mine. We dated for a couple of years and even lived together before deciding to get married. We finally tied the knot and decided to start a family. Well, as with most marriages, things were great in the beginning. We decided to have our first child, and everything was swell until the point where I was giving birth to her.

This was the era where they allowed men into the labor and delivery room to witness and to be a part of the birth process. The thinking was to allow men to be part of the miracle of a life that they helped to create. This was a great concept in theory, but not in reality for my husband.

The birth of our daughter caused an unimaginable shift in my husband's psyche which left me undesirable in his eyes. She was born and at that point, and to my surprise, our love-life pretty much ended. What should have been a joyous happy time, where we welcomed a new life into this world, turned out to be an irreversible traumatic event for my husband, one that put a permanent scar on our marriage and relationship. It would be a decade before we could be intimate again. This time it was to plant the seed that would eventually result in the birth of our son.

Counseling did not help us. Therapy and religion also yielded few solutions to our sex and intimacy issue. Furthermore, he just did not want to talk about his dilemma with anyone. Little did we know that we were fighting an unknown male medical crisis that had yet to be discovered and far less spoken about in medical or social circles—Male Postnatal Depression/PTSD. When it comes to sex or openly speaking about the subject, there is still much shame, guilt, and embarrassment attached. I wanted to speak about sex and intimacy in my resilience story because we as women often take for granted and lack understanding as to how important this topic is to our male partners and their psyche.

After the birth of our daughter, my husband shared that he was traumatized by the experience, but he did not say he was out of here. The intimacy between us just stopped. Our physical expression of our love also stopped because of his experience of seeing our child coming out of the same place that was sexually sacred to him. Seeing the reality of childbirth—like no joke, profoundly traumatized my husband to the point where he didn't want to make love to me anymore. Utterly shocked by his behavior and at the words that had come out of his mouth, I thought,

> *"What does he have to be traumatized about?*
> *Are you kidding me? I was the one enduring nine*
> *months of pregnancy, seeing my body bent out*
> *of shape, leg cramps, nausea, out-of-control*
> *hormones and finally enduring the pain of*
> *childbirth. What trauma is he talking about?"*

Yet to my surprise, he was dead serious. I felt blindsided as his personality shift was very unexpected. I never thought something like that would happen to me or him, because we had such a healthy relationship in our sex and intimacy, before children. How could our loving intimate relationship just end so abruptly? I was beyond heartbroken.

Look, I knew that nine months was a long time to wait for either of us to be intimate again. Coupled with my raging hormones, cravings, mood swings, and anxiety about being a new mother, the poor guy must have had a rough time. The sad thing was that I was so focused on myself that I couldn't see if, and how much, he was suffering. Add to the fact that he never said a word to me about what he was feeling.

I remember him accompanying me into the labor and delivery room. As our daughter was about to enter this world, my husband helplessly watched me deal with the pain of childbirth. I believe what followed may have been too much for him to bear because, first her head and then the rest of her emerged followed by the placenta, and all the messiness that accompanies the birth. I never saw the messiness, but he did. As traumatic as giving birth to my daughter was for me, my husband who watched the event was overwhelmed, scared out of his mind, emotionally paralyzed, and may I dare say, disgusted at the grossness of it all. Readers would you agree that the fantasy seldom matches the reality?

Emotional paralysis in men post-childbirth is known as Male Postnatal PTSD. It is a bona fide diagnosis in the DSM-V manual. Updated every year, the DSM-V is a compilation of every psychological and psychiatric disorder known to man. The manual is used by clinicians to diagnose their patients. Male Postnatal PTSD has yet to be further studied, as the research has only been recently published within the last decade. According to *The Green Parent*—a publication focused on parenting and parenting issues, birth trauma in men affects about 5–10% of men who witness their child being born. Men who experience this syndrome will observe that they are unable to be emotionally available for their partners. They play the birth scene over and over in their heads, which causes them to be further traumatized.

There is also an undergirding helplessness and loss of power that men experience while observing the person they love in pain. They feel powerless to help. Post-birth, men may neglect their partners, display angry outbursts, and become emotionally unavailable. Some may turn to alcohol or drugs to deal with the trauma. Any underlying mental health or substance abuse issues can be exacerbated by the childbirth experience. Word to the wise—know your man!

Etheridge and Slade (2017) studied men between 25 and 45 years of age on their reactions to pregnancy and childbirth trauma. They found that these males, upon seeing the birth of their child experienced the birth on a very visceral level. They rode an emotional roller coaster of increased anxiety, fears of death, and inadequacy. Their feelings of hopelessness were further triggered by bustling staff, seeing blood spatters, and remembering the hospital's sights and smells. In addition, they reported feeling abandoned and belittled by hospital staff whose belief was that as men, they should "suck it up," and get on with taking care of their mates. What staff and others failed to realize was that these men had no idea what to do, or where to begin. Dr. Andrew Mayers—a noted British researcher of Male Postnatal PTSD concurs with Etheridge and Slade. He notes that depression in men, plus lack of support and follow up, only serve to increase their mental health issues. Furthermore, most men are reluctant to seek help; this information was not available to us at the time of our marital discord.

We continued to live like roommates with the forever looming "elephant in the room" which neither of us wanted to talk about. Ironically, everything else in our relationship worked beautifully except this one area of our lives. I was left angry, hurt, and frustrated. I was having a really hard time because truth be told, I needed a man. I begged him several times to get help, but he did not want to talk about those issues with a professional. Ladies, if you are reading my story, I hope I am not alone in this journey. Facing my dilemma, what else was this gal to do but to take care of herself. Neither of us cheated because at the very core of our relationship there was love, respect, and genuine friendship.

After several years, we decided to have another child. With the intimacy between us at zero, we reduced our lovemaking to checking ovulation charts and clinically performing for the sake of bringing our son into the world. After our son was born, we stayed together with the commitment to raise our children. He remains an amazing father and friend, who dearly loves his children and me.

I had done all I could do to help him. I realized that this was his battle to fight not mine. All there was left for me to do at this point was to work on myself. I started exercising and running again to get myself back in shape after having the babies. Running helped to free my mind of the negative thoughts and frustration built up over the years. It took about 9 or 10 months of being diligent with my exercise and diet routine before I returned to my former self. Miracles of miracles, I was over the moon with happiness, when I looked in the mirror and discovered a toned and gorgeous Marsha. I had reinvented, and rediscovered me!

My body was back. My mind was freed. Marsha, I said,

"It's time to write the next chapter of your life."

A huge part of being resilient is being willing to face your fears, ditch your worries and have the courage to write the next chapter of your life. One day, I decided to venture out, and signed up to run a mini marathon. Every month, corporations sponsored charity runs. I thought what a great idea to get my dose of exercise and to also support charitable organizations! Running for charity turned out to be a good hobby which got me out of the house and my negative thoughts. It also brought great joy and happiness back into my life. I ran early in the morning and returned home in time to take care of my family. Well wouldn't you know, over time, I started winning race after race, and medals—lots of medals. I was 'in like Flynn'. From that point (on), and after a couple years of winning races and collecting medals, I said,

"You know, Marsha, what else can you do from here? What can you do with these accomplishments and all these charities you have helped by staying in shape?"

Suddenly, the thought came into my head to enter a beauty pageant. I needed to feel viable, relevant. and fulfilled as a woman. I needed to get my feminine back. Can I tell you a secret? Ever since

I was a little girl, I wanted to be in a beauty pageant. Growing up I watched Ms. America, and marveled at the beautiful women their exquisite gowns, as they showcased the best of what God gave them. I just never had the opportunity to become one of them when I was younger. Guess what? Hot damn, I was going to be one of those women now!

The world of pageantry was what I chose. I didn't know if there were pageants for married women in their forties; however, when I researched the topic, sure enough, there were plenty of opportunities. Beauty pageants for mature women is a multi-million-dollar industry. There were senior beauty pageants, beauty pageants *for women with disabilities, and even pageants for grandmas. Who Knew? Honey, *let me tell you that you are beautiful at any stage of your life!

For each pageant, you need to have a platform/cause—that is, something you represent and want to showcase to the world. Examples of causes include global warming, breast cancer, human trafficking, education, or saving the whales. As this was my first time, my platform focused on utilizing my passion to help others. I chose that topic because of the many races I ran, and the thousands of dollars that I had helped to raise for any charity. I had officially moved from running to pageant street. I also got into modeling as well, because, with pageantry, you need headshots and bios for the program book and website content.

Pageantry led to photoshoots, and then into runway modeling. Runway modeling led to film work, which opened doors for other avenues and adventures. Although I still worked full-time for the government, Marsha was on her own reinvention and resilience journey. I didn't win my first pageant, but there was a lady in that competition that exposed me to another opportunity in California. It is called the Women of Achievement pageant. I entered and won the title, Mrs. Florida Woman of Achievement. My newfound title enabled me to board the Queen Mary ship and set sail for Long Beach California, where I entered and won "Miss United States Bachelor Queen" title.

I discovered that pageants—were in a good way, an opportunity to not only showcase your talents and skills but to tell your truth. I was on a roll! Suddenly, I was at the front and center of my life. When you go to functions, wearing your crown and sash, people come to you. They want to take pictures with you. They want to know your story. They want to know what you have to say and why you're there for those events. Pageantry brought so much joy and happiness into my life that I could hardly stand it. I was busier than I've ever been, so much so, that I forgot my troubles at home. My husband supported me 100% which made it easier for me to continue to rediscover a new life that worked for Marsha. I was able to put my bedroom woes on the back burner as I brought happiness into my life in another way. I was enjoying my life and discovering that as great as sex is, to be happy and fulfilled is what is truly important.

As I continued to enter competitions and to travel, I felt like I was going down the right path for me because life became effortless. From pageants to modeling to film work, everything was smooth sailing and fun. Here is the kicker; this was my side hustle. I became Marsha the Federal employee by day, and pageant queen celebrity on nights and weekends. My schedule was packed as I kept my life very busy. Thank God for my husband. Even though his issue remained, I believe that he was happy just seeing me blossom and become happier.

My work and popularity led me to become president of the International Association of Women. Originally known as the National Women's Organization under its founder Starr Jones, it has now become an international and global women's organization. As we move into the future and beyond, we must think on a global scale if we are to thrive in our professional and personal lives. The organization's mission is to provide women with an array of services, including networking, personal development, empowerment, and support as they travail through their life's journey. I was fortunate to have been president of this women's association for about seven years.

This year, I started my own organization within the last two months. I created Business Divas. At one point, we had about 350 women in the organization. We came together at various business locations to support and do business with each other. A local area business would host our meetings. Whether at a restaurant, clothing store or spa, we ensured that both the women and business host got an opportunity to connect with each other. It provided good networking connections for all. I always had a guest speaker come to share their expertise and knowledge about the topic of the day. It was helpful in so many ways. Our chapter received accolades in local newspapers. It was just a great way to expose women to not only other business owners, but to certain unknown areas of our city. I learned a lot about the different areas of my city and even the surrounding cities; from North Miami to Hollywood, we covered it all.

That is how I built myself up to what I have now. Looking back, my life just kind of evolved that way, and I now have this big social resume of all these accomplishments and achievements. In addition to working for the federal government, which I still work for right now. I just hit my 25 years with them as well. I was able to accomplish all that I have because of that agency. Hence, I owe a great depth of gratitude to all who have supported me over the years. I don't think that they knew all I was dealing with, and how they were instrumental in helping me build a life of happiness and fulfillment, which increased my job performance. I've been there for so long, that I had accumulated a lot of time. My accumulated time is what I would use to pursue what I call my "Marsha adventures." From pageants, modeling and film-work, I did it all.

Ladies this is what is meant to plan your work and work your plan. Once you have a plan, put it in motion, and don't stop until you have fulfilled your goal. That, for me, is what being resilient is all about. I am living, loving, and thriving in my life right now. My husband and I remain best friends and he is a great co-parent. I am also setting an example for my children that they can be anything they want to be, as long as they are happy. This is what my parents did for me, and so it is my duty to pass that onto the next generation; and to empower any woman who wants to take the first step on their resilience journey.

My advice to our readers is to not let anything stop you from reaching your goals. I am Marsha Feldman, wife, mother, government worker by day, pageant queen by night, influencer, and mentor to many, and I am resilient.

To learn more about Marsha or her charity work, contact: www .marshafeldman.com

To learn more about Male Postnatal PTSD, here are a few resources which you might find helpful.

PTSD and birth trauma | Mind, the mental health charity - help for mental health problems

One Man's Story Of Suffering From Male Postnatal Depression (elle.com)

NCS | Postnatal Depression In Men (nationalcounsellingsociety .org)

So, what's your takeaway from Phoenix Marsha's story?

#PhoenixesRising
Share your thoughts in our FB Group

https://bit.ly/phoenixesrising
Question: What kind of Phoenix do you want to be?

ON RESILIENCE

"Courage doesn't always roar. Sometimes courage is the quiet voice at the end of the day saying 'I will try again tomorrow." **Mary Anne Radmacher**

Wow! Who knew there was such a thing as Male Postnatal PTSD? As we change directions, we leave Marsha in South Florida and jetoff to none other than Kazakhstan. Here we will visit with Phoenix, Poetess Tatyana Sobolevsky who has remained resilient despite her triumphs and adversity. Let us see how she expresses her essence in her I AM Poem.

BE RESILIENT

I AM POEM

Tatyana Sobolevsky, Kazakhstan/Russia

I AM
From the priceless treasure of the Republic of Kazakhstan,
a country rich in oil, coal, and minerals,
a cultural and religious melting pot of 131 ethnicities

I AM

From a nomadic palette of titillating meats and cheeses,
like mouthwatering Beshbarmak, Chechil, savory Kazy,
sweet Chook-Chook, and Baursak

I AM

From the festival of Nauryz celebrating the new year and change
with song and dance

I AM

From a family of well-known educators who shaped our country
and its economy

I AM

The proud daughter of Larissa and Anatoliy and granddaughter of
Grandpa Viktor and Grandma Olympiada

I AM

Tatyana Sobolevsky

Tatyana Sobolevsky is a multicultural, experienced real estate professional with master's degrees from Russian and American universities. As a fully licensed realtor in the State of Florida, she specializes in the sales and rentals of Miami's Sunny Isles Beach apartments. She is a member of the Miami Association of Realtors and National Association of Realtors. As Mrs. Miami Beach, her Passion Project is using mass media and events as a platform to bring positive energy that bridges diverse cultures and fosters relationships with Russia and Kazakhstan cultures.

To learn more, contact Tatyana at tatyana2003@mac.com, Coastal-MiamiProperties.com

So, what's your takeaway from Phoenix, Poetess Tatyana's poem?

#PhoenixesRising
Share your thoughts in our FB Group

https://bit.ly/phoenixesrising

We say goodbye to Tatyana in Kazakhstan/Russia and head back to the Caribbean. This time we will visit the island of Jamaica. At this point, you might be asking yourself why didn't we just go to Jamaica when we were in Florida? Remember reader, this is a journey of resilience which requires you to roll with the punches. "Brave up" as they say in Jamaica and go with the flow. Life is not linear or neatly packaged with a big bow. Come on, let's go! You are going to enjoy meeting our next Phoenix G. Woodie Lesesne.

Chapter 15

STAYING POWER IN THE MEDIA INDUSTRY:
G. Woodie Lesesne, Jamaica

Yir
Sending Love & light

One Love
Woody

G. Woodie Lesesne is a multi-media entrepreneur whose career success spans more than two decades and who has led cutting edge innovations in both traditional, non-traditional and new media. As co-founder of Lesesne Media Group and publisher of IN FOCUS Magazine, she guided the print property to an unprecedented 19-year success in the South Florida region. Her passion is empowering women through her Women Power Caucus Network and Leadership Conferences.

ON RESILIENCE

"Don't bury your thoughts, put your vision to reality."—**Bob Marley**

Staying Power in the Media Industry
G. Woodie Lesesne, Jamaica

"As women, we make the world work."
—G. Woodie Lesesne

Jamaica is a beautiful, culturally diverse, lush, mineral-filled island and yes, the birthplace of Bob Marley, and me. Abundant in vegetation, surrounded by majestic mountains, and beautiful beaches, Jamaica cultivated the spirit of entrepreneurship and resiliency, that was woven into my DNA from an early age.

My name is G. "Woodie" Lesesne and this is my resilience story. I could not imagine being born anywhere else other than on my beautiful island of Jamaica. Jamaica is filled with beautiful, culturally diverse, ambitious, resilient people who work extremely hard. Growing up, in addition to their day job, many people had what we now call a side hustle.

If you had ambition and a desire to do better, a side hustle was just a way of life, as well as a deep sense of pride. For many people, in order to overcome, to be resilient, you had to put in extra effort and time (side hustle) to get beyond the basics and excel. This common characteristic and behavior contribute to the resilient nature of a people that have significantly impacted the world in music, agriculture, sports, became world icons, and so much more. I, too, am cut from this fabric of many cultures, and succulent flavors, as I am a child of overcomers.

My family lived in Trench Town where I was born. It is a rough neighborhood in Kingston, with mostly tenement housing, built on narrow deep lots often with multiple homes. I am the youngest of six children, three girls and three boys. I was about three years old, when I had a life-threatening injury that caused me to undergo emergency abdominal surgery on my tiny body, and to think we were just playing childhood games with makeshift equipment. This could have been the end of my story but thank God it wasn't. It was shortly after that, however, we moved to Washington Gardens, a neighborhood in St Andrews parish and a suburb of Kingston, where my parents built our family home. My brothers and sisters and I had to adjust to our new surroundings, the neighborhood, and kids.

Living outside of town meant it could take up to two hours each morning to get us all to our respective schools. I was the last one to get to school because my school was closest to Dad's office. This meant that I sometimes got to school late, and this didn't sit well with the Nuns. This was an important part of my resilience experience, even as a child. I learned a lot about resilience from my parents who were my first teachers. Let's start with my father. Growing up, he had his own independent dental practice.

I saw first-hand that working for himself provided for our family, and the flexibility to help people by providing dental services, sometimes in exchange for a basket of fruit, food, or even live animals, to people who could not always afford his needed services. He worked hard to build his practice, but political unrest and concerns for the safety of our family, to the point where he carried a gun in the car when taking us to school, became a major issue. Soon, our family would leave Jamaica to pursue greater opportunity, in the U.S.

My mother, I believe, was the true entrepreneur of our family. Though she only got through the 3rd grade she had a natural knack for business, and was a true salesman, earning top dollar for her manufactured products. I have early memories of her making a variety of decorated pillows and various ceramic art. When we were small children in Jamaica, Mama worked in a biscuit factory by day, and turned her talents for making tasty delights like coconut cakes, roasted peanuts, and a variety of other consumables, into another source of income for our family. She truly had the uncanny knack for making a dollar out of .15 cents.

Perhaps because she was a woman, I identified with my mother's style of business. I understood that she had unique responsibilities as a mother, wife and business owner. My mother exposed me to entrepreneurship, even before I knew what that was. It is my parents' resilient nature that I witnessed first-hand; I believe this trait runs in my veins. Partly intentionally, and part unwittingly, they taught me to be independent, strong, compassionate, and hard working. "If it's not working, adjust or try something different, as long as you keep moving something will give." She still says this today

"If you want something good, you have to put in the sweat."

All over the island and in my own neighborhood, we were blessed with an abundance of fruit, and ground provisions like yams, bananas, ackee, breadfruit, and so much more. After school, my days were filled with climbing fruit trees and eating my favorite, mangoes—until my belly was full to the max. That was all the food that I needed. That and dreaming about what life was like in other parts of the world. At the end of the day, we basked in the titillating smells of all the wonderful spices like curry, pimento, thyme, ginger, coconut, and a myriad of other aromas coming from kitchens around the neighborhood. My mouth watered in anticipation of thoroughly enjoying a plate of curry goat, jerk chicken, ground provisions, or whatever Mama was cooking for dinner.

As a child until age nine, I attended Catholic School in Kingston just blocks away from my father's dental office. At St Ann's Primary School, I would learn many lessons about life and myself, even as a small girl. Being the child of a Black man and an Indian woman came with its share of teasing and name calling. You know the story, '...too different to be just Black and too Black to just be Indian'. I learned early on to judge people by the way they treat me, not by their exterior appearance. An important discovery during those very formative years, was that I was going to be the person who stood up for others, and would defend their rights, even when they didn't themselves. A bit of a tomboy, I had my share of physical fights, usually with boys, and usually when defending someone else, or if they said anything bad about my Mama. I had a very low tolerance for anyone who even thought about saying anything bad about Mama. It didn't matter how much bigger they were than me. I can't stand idly by if I see someone being bullied.

Though I was a good student at St Ann's, I often found myself at the receiving end of bamboo cane 'swats' across my palms for being late or daydreaming about being a stewardess and life beyond my island paradise. I questioned the nuns and teachers, not to be disruptive, but simply to understand. I was a fighter for fairness and was never one to accept things just because the speaker said so. Unlike today, this was during a time when children were to be seen and not heard; so many questions went unanswered.

Because my father couldn't get work in his profession due to a lack of the proper U.S. credentials, he worked in construction by day. As a true Jamaican, he did dental work for friends and friends of friends in the Caribbean community, in the evenings and weekends at our kitchen table. This was now his side hustle and a clear example to me of his resolve and willingness to push through the challenges of starting over in a new country to care for his family. Mom once again found factory or housekeeping work and continued her entrepreneurial craft.

Once in America, I found camaraderie and friendship among other immigrant children. This gave me a perspective that in the U.S. everyone except the Native American people come from somewhere else in the world. We are a diverse mix that often have more in common than differences. This has stayed with me throughout my life, and my world today reflects a diverse mix of people and alliances.

In high school, although I was a music and theater major, I also had advanced studies classes. This kept me extremely busy. You see I was bused to school across town from where I lived. This meant I had to be up at 5:30am, to be on the school bus at 6:30 a.m. I was a lead actor in many of the school productions, which meant practice, then rehearsals and then evening rehearsals; in addition to my class load of homework and projects, there were also dance classes at least twice a week. I even sang in a local band when I was seventeen. Theater, music, and dance were my escape and where I found the most joy. I flourished under the comradery (Jamaican for camaraderie) among my closest friends at school.

I do remember when I was in the 9th or 10th grade my well-intended guidance counselor, Ms. Sandy, fervently tried to steer me towards a career as a secretary. I know she meant well but her suggestion didn't settle well with me, especially because she too, was a Woman of Color. The fact that her vision for me was so narrow and limiting to my own aspirations, was disheartening.

Don't misunderstand me, there is nothing wrong with being a secretary. In fact, my life experiences have taught me that many CEO's attribute a big part of their success to having excellent support from their secretaries. I guess I was a bit audacious at such a tender age to think that I would have my own company. I don't know where it came from, but I promptly told her that my intention was to be the boss of my own company, and I would have a secretary to help me. This confident posture was the impact that my family and culture imprinted on me, recognizing that ownership was important to one's success. I didn't have any idea what that business would be, when I said that to Ms. Sandy, but my future had possibilities.

Winters in the Northeast were brutal in the 70s and this island girl hated the cold weather, because I could never seem to warm up enough. I always enjoyed fashion and although I loved dressing in multiple layers every day, I longed for the warmer summer climate. I knew, even then, that I would eventually migrate to a warmer climate because the novelty of shoveling snow would surely get old.

Life was full and being busy made me happy, but it was tough at times, and I often felt alone as I barely saw my family as they were all busy anyway; so, I didn't feel missed. I took on lead roles in many of the music/drama productions throughout high school.

I started college but did not complete my degree. I was accepted on a probationary term into the music program on mostly natural talent. I had little formal training in the area of music theory which put me at a disadvantage. Though I did well in my performance courses, I had catching up to do, where my peers had been studying their instruments and theory for most of their lives. I was not accepted back for the following year, which was heart- crushing for me. I was so young and unsophisticated, I didn't have anyone in my life who could help me put that in perspective, so I sort of moved on, knowing I would find my way; I remained hopeful that it would somehow be in film, music, or business. The lesson here was hard to swallow. But to sum it up, you have to believe in yourself and work hard for what you want. Others may not always see the potential in you, but that doesn't mean you should give up. Put in the work and surround yourself with people who believe in you. If I could do this chapter in my life over again, I would have found another option to get back to school. I took what I saw as rejection and let it impact my confidence. After this period, I grew thicker skin and learned to trust and believe in myself more.

When I returned home from college, I found employment at Eastman Kodak's factory. Here, I became fascinated with the world of cameras and what they could do, beyond taking photographs. I never imagined that I was being prepared to stand in front of, and behind a camera, at my own company. Lesesne Media Group which

I co-own with my business partner and husband of twenty-eight years is a manifestation of my declaration to Ms. Sandy.

Prior to me becoming a business owner, the previous years were rough. Between 1984 and 1989 were the hardest years of my life. My parents had separated, and I wanted to spread my wings, so I moved from Rochester to Richmond, VA, knowing only my youngest brother and his family. I launched my real estate career in Richmond but only stayed for a few short years. It was a bit too southern for me, with too many rebel flags in the back of trucks. I worked mostly alone on the road in unfamiliar areas, and I was new to town on top of that. I was adventurous, but I didn't always feel safe there.

After a three-year stint in Richmond, VA, and just when my real estate business was taking hold, I moved to South Florida to help my dad open a furniture business to sell mahogany furniture that he manufactured in Jamaica. When I got to SoFL, I knew no one other than him, until one day I was at the DMV and ran into someone that grew up in my neighborhood in Jamaica. We didn't know each other well but our older siblings were friends. I am not sure what I was thinking at that time except that he was familiar, and it should be ok to share my contact information. Even though it had been more than fifteen years, I had no reason to not feel safe. I learned that he had been in the military and later settled in Miami. I was so naïve as I could not, and perhaps still don't, fully understand the impact of military service on the psyche. Over time and with pressure from him, we engaged in a relationship that would turn out to be emotionally, and later, physically abusive. Please note that like anyone else, not all military men, or men for that fact are abusive. I just happen to choose unwisely, in this case.

During the same time in 1988, my sister and nine-year-old niece got into a devastating car accident that almost took their lives. This changed my priorities for me and my family. We all needed to pull together so that we could be there to help my sister and niece. As if the near-death of my niece and sister were not enough for me to deal with, being in a new city with a new job brought challenges from all directions.

Then my boyfriend emotionally unraveled. I was so unequipped to handle, or face his emotional problems and the demons that raised their ugly heads. When he put a gun to my head and threatened that if I left him, he would take my life and then his own, I made up my mind to do whatever it took to flee from this man, or I could die. I tried to end it, but things turned violent and he did in fact attempt to take my life. In a desperate struggle for survival, I managed to dial 911 and the police arrived just in time.

With no family or friends to speak of nearby, I sunk into a dark place where I felt very much alone. It's an overwhelming and devastating experience that I will never forget because I wondered "How did I get here?" Always one to look at the bright side, I also wondered "What did God want me to learn from this situation?" I learned a lot about myself and the fight within me. I learned that never again would I ignore the warning signs and pretend that they don't exist. I also got crystal clear as to what I wanted and didn't want in a man, and what I was willing and not willing to live with. It took me months to heal physically and years to heal emotionally. Maybe I'm still healing.

Abuse of any kind is one of those character traits that is off the table for me– period. Sometimes as women, when we choose our men, we might see the warning signs, but because of pressure and/or being in love/lust, or even eager to please our loved ones, we ignore them. Sometimes, we blindly trust that things will get better. I'm not the only woman that has chosen unwisely. Recognize, forgive yourself and move on.

I continued to get stronger over time. I think as women, increasing our emotional resolve is a necessary life skill in today's complicated and demanding world. I've always known that life was not a rose garden. I also knew that I was a good person and I deserved to have the opportunity to live life victoriously. I was therefore not willing to let any one person or situation define the entirety of who I am and what gifts God had given me. I wanted to find my bigger purpose. That fueled me and kept me resilient.

I learned to love again but from a better place of strength and confidence.

Learning to love and trust again however was difficult. I credit my husband of twenty-eight years for his patience, commitment, and unconditional love for myself, our sons, and our extended families. I met my soulmate, Tony through a mutual acquaintance of ours who recognized that we had similar interests.

After our first date we both felt there was something special there and we have been together since. As a couple, we are 'ride-or-die' and enjoy many things together, especially our family. As business partners we make a phenomenal team, most of the time. I learned that just like life, there is resilience in business, love, and marriage as well. When I first met Tony, I was impressed by his easy-going nature; I felt a calmness in his presence and and true contentment in his arms. This was like nothing else I had experienced before. As our relationship grew, I slowly learned how to trust again as our love continued to flourish.

After about two years of dating Tony and I decided to get married, start a business and a family, all at the same time. We weren't going to wait but just do it all at once; you know, go for it. As I reflect on my life, this was the happiest time, but by no means the easiest at all. It was hard. Everything happened very quickly from wedding day to our business being launched, our first child, and second child; I was insanely busy, but in my heart, I was the happiest.

Everything was beginning to grow, my family, business, and me. This flurry of business brought good energy which kept me going. I was able to launch many of the ideas that I always wanted through a business that honored, lifted up, and celebrated other women. With an unbelievable partner by my side, we decided that we would go through life together no matter what. It takes some next-level resiliency to keep your marriage together, run a business, raise the kids, and take care of your aging mother. There were days when I couldn't tell you how I did it, but it got done with prayer, faith, hard work, a lot of energy, and a little touch of crazy.

At the end of each day, I would fall out in complete exhaustion, but because I was completely fulfilled, I happily got up the next day to do it all over again. I wasn't leaving anything on life's table except to just go for it. I flourished by keeping all the plates spinning simultaneously which I found fulfilling.

In 1993 we incorporated our first business, IN FOCUS Magazine. In 2001, the Lesesne Media Group (LMG) was incorporated as a viable business in Florida. Our company has grown from a tiny boutique production and entertainment shop to a highly respected, award-winning, multi-media group of experts, specializing in multi-cultural marketplace dominance. As a trend-setter in both business and entertainment, LMG has emerged as a formidable, multi-media focusing on publicity, web outreach, events, and creative content development. For more than twenty-eight years, our company has excelled in providing strategic brand positioning, while developing successful public relations, media relations, video and photographic services. This includes digital media to clients large and small.

Lesesne Media Group has been successful in bringing together talented, innovative, and creative professionals from a variety of disciplines to deliver guaranteed client satisfaction across the creative landscape. LMG is now a family affair that includes our sons and other family members. This is resiliency on a generational level and to which we are all committed.

Tony and I went into business with the hope of building a legacy, something that could grow over time. It has been our dream because we mostly saw multi-generational businesses in other communities, not in my our own. We understand that in the Black community in particular, it is especially challenging to start and grow a business, much less have your offspring take the mantle. So, we are grateful that my our sons are pursuing careers in entertainment.

When I reflect on my life, I can see how I have been born into a resilient culture and family. Couched in expectations that "you will succeed," my resiliency has come from my "never give up attitude." If I had to live my life over again, I don't really think I would change a whole lot because I believe that the sum of my experiences, good and bad, have brought me to the person that I am today.

What makes me resilient is my never-give-up attitude. I learned early on that this world is not for the faint-of-heart, and I approach my life, fearlessly. I believe as a mom you have to put your family at the top of your agenda. I know now that too many women, including myself, have that agenda stacked so high, with other people and responsibilities, too often there's very little left for yourself. Over the years I've been learning to say NO! when my plate is already full. Yes, I am still a work in progress.

True to my birth sign, I have the heart of a lioness, soft when I need to be and ferocious when necessary. I am not afraid to try, nor fail. As a younger woman I danced to the beat of my own drum, and today dancing is still one of my favorite things to do, and yes, I still hear that drumbeat! When I try something new, I am okay with whatever the results are, whether good or bad, as each experience is an opportunity for growth.

Daily, I lay it all on the line. I strive to make the absolute best of the talents and gifts that God has given me with no regrets. I seek and embrace what makes me happy. I also don't like to be told what to do as I have my own mind and thoughts. This has been a fine line to walk with my beloved Tony, and our business. Sometimes, you need to listen and embrace feedback from your loved ones.

When asked about what chapters in my life I would keep if given the opportunity to choose, I would keep the experiences with all the amazing and beautiful people that have been a part of my life's journey. Those that taught me so much about myself, about the world, humanity, kindness, joy, love, and so much more. I would keep all the experiences that have to do with being a mother to my sons, and those from other mothers, wife to a deserving partner, and friend to some amazing women who taught me what it means to be a friend and a sister. I would keep all of these angels of light that have enriched my life, because I know all these experiences helped to shape me.

As I continue my journey of resiliency, ten years from now, I would like our company to be operating as a successful multi-million-dollar, multi-faceted media company that makes films, documentaries, web programming, (one that)and produces signature events, much as we do today, but at a higher financial level than we currently operate. I would also like to take my Women's Power Caucus Leadership Conference to the National level, as the acknowledgement of the power women already possess is critical to us reaching our fullest potential. I believe this to my core and is perhaps tied to my purpose as a strong Black woman.

I started the WPC in 2001 to provide a place where two to three hundred women of all industries and cultural experiences could come together to network, share tips and strategies that lead to greater success and personal power; — A place where we could foster new relationships and work collaboratively while lifting each other up and celebrating all that we are as women. Undoubtedly, we may share tears and laughter, but without question, we will leave feeling motivated, inspired, and filled to the brim. The WPC is held once a year in Florida.

For me personally, as a resilient woman, I am almost ready to shed the day-to-day responsibilities of my business. My sons are adults now and life is taking on a different hue. The next chapters of my life will have more room for me. So, for now, I dream of operating remotely from some faraway place, greenlighting film projects that tell inspiring stories about strong resilient women and people around the world. I will continue to plant my garden and "Grow Things", basking in the joy of watching them flourish. Knowing that I put in the time and care to watch over, worry, feed, and pray over them as I do the people in my life, brings joy to my heart.

I am proud and grateful for the life I have as I know that I am extremely blessed. I am proud that the groundwork Tony and I put in, has manifested to where Lesesne Media Group is now a multi-generational, family-owned media company in South Florida. All four of our sons are working in entertainment and media to some degree. It's what they have known and experienced their whole life. In this case, '...the apple doesn't fall far from the tree', is appropriate. I see it no different than a family of lawyers, doctors, educators; it's what you are exposed to do that helps to open your realm of possibilities. What keeps me and my family resilient is our mutual love, respect, and vision that lives in our hearts and minds every day. I am G. "Woodie" Lesesne, wife, mother, daughter, sister, friend, and community leader. I am a resilient woman!

To learn more about Lesesne Media or The Women's Power Caucus Contact: emailwoodielmg@gmail.com https://www.linkedin.com/in/woodie-lesesne-57385a3 https://www.linkedin.com/in/in-focus-tv-online-71a5411b3 Women's Power Caucus | womenspowercaucus (wordpress.com)

So, what's your takeaway from Phoenix Woodie's story?

#PhoenixesRising
Share your thoughts in our FB Group

https://bit.ly/phoenixesrising

Question: What kind of Phoenix do you want to be?

From Jamaica, we will travel to Ecuador where Phoenix, Poetess Sally Villalba will share what has made her resilient through her I AM Poem. See if you can feel the rhythm of Ecuador as you read her poem.

I AM POEM—Sally Villalba, Ecuador

I AM from enchanting Caribbean beaches, white sands, and
tropical beats. Music that moves your body to the sound
of bass drums, accordions, and güiro. The land of
merengue, bachata, and song; the land of tobacco,
rum, green plantains, and sugar cane; most of all,
the land of warm, happy people.

I AM also from a land of ancestors, the land of the Incas where
the long tradition of the elders still prevail. I am from Middle
Earth, a place where you can be in two hemispheres at once.
I AM from the Andes Mountains where the beauty of its
active volcanoes is breathtaking; where the luscious hot water
pools from its womb can heal your body and soul; a land

that has beautiful beaches, a luscious rainforest, and an archipelago called Galápagos that is a treasure to the world.

So, you see, I AM a blend of music, foods, smells, beats, breathtaking landscapes, races, cultures, and traditions. I AM all of it because all of it is who I AM.

I AM from the land of sancocho. This is a powerful mixture of 7 meats, cassava, plantains, and other produce served with white rice and avocado. A meal that is usual for cold days or hangovers, where the expression "levanta muertos" (raise the dead) is very appropriate.

I AM from the land of many traditional plates. Among them is the one where celebrating holy week is an experience. The "fanesca" is a mixture of many types of grains, and cod, among other ingredients. This is prepared in all homes as gratitude of all the land offers and the fish to honor the greatest fisherman of all.

I AM from the land where Spanish has been altered and from the land that has the indigenous language embedded with its own. Where the native language, Quechua of the Incas still exists, and is mixed with the current Spanish.

I AM Tete Marcial's granddaughter who sang like the angels—a prominent and honored Dominican treasure.

I AM the granddaughter of José (Cheché) who embodied patience and was an example of many attributes in my life. Who showed me how a man who loves his woman, allows her to be herself and cheers her on? Who showed me what to look for in a true gentleman, for that and much more, I'm so grateful?

I AM the daughter of Miguel, a resilient man, a Jack of all trades, a fearless warrior in life, a man who started from nothing and build an empire. I AM the daughter of a fighter, a true hero that left his home at the age of 17 to seek a better future. A man who slept his first nights in New York under the train station in winter without knowing a soul or the language to later become a decorated military man who served this country honorably. I AM the daughter of a man who never gave up.

I AM Sally Villalba … a beautiful blend of wild Caribbean music and color while honoring the calm and respectful nature of my ancestors.

Sally Villalba is a single mother of two, entrepreneur, go-getter. She serves as the President/CEO of Sally V Enterprises, LLC., a company that facilitates business development & leadership transformational training for inspiring entrepreneurs and business executives. She is a weekly business radio co-host with

"Sally's Biz Tips," "Let's Talk SBA," and "Women in Business" on WZAB 880AM, The Biz in Miami FL. To learn more, visit Sally at www.sallyvillalba.com

So, what's your takeaway from Phoenix, Poetess Sally's poem?

#PhoenixesRising
Share your thoughts in our FB Group

https://bit.ly/phoenixesrising

ON RESILIENCE

"Jazz stands for freedom. It's supposed to be the voice of freedom: Get out there and improvise, and take chances, and don't be a perfectionist - leave that to the classical musicians."
Dave Brubeck

As Salsa is to Sally, Jazz is to Dr. Joan. As we read her story imagine Billie Holiday, Nina Simone, or any of the great women in Jazz playing softly in the background as you allow this diva to take you on her musical journey of resilience. Yes, folks the music industry has its ups and downs, but resilience is the glue that has you weather the storms of its sometimes tumultuous rhythms. Come let us see what Diva Dr. Joan is up to!

Chapter 16

LIFE AIN'T NOTHING BUT A SONG:
Dr. Joan Cartwright, USA/Bahamas

BE RESILIENT

Life Ain't Nothing But A Song

Dr. Joan Cartwright, USA/Bahamas

"Them that's got shall get. Them that's not shall loose. So the Bible says, and it still is news. Mama may have. Papa may have.

But God bless the child that's got its own
Billie Holiday

For as long as I can remember, Jazz has been the musical river that has run deep in my veins. Every doo wop, scat, and shoo-b-doo has shaped who I am today. My mother, if she were alive, would probably tell you that I came out of the womb singing. My love of Jazz runs deep, but the road to being a jazz aficionado and diva, well, it has taken something to get here. Although the journey has not been easy, the rewards have been worth the fight. Hello, my name is Dr. Joan Cartwright, and this is my story of resilience.

I was born on a very cold Sunday afternoon on December 7, 1947, in Kew Gardens, New York. My parents lived in the Bronx. My mother, Charlotte Galloway Cartwright was from Philadelphia, Pennsylvania, born in 1914. She was a graduate of Hunter College in Business Administration. She was an Army veteran who served in World War II in Belgium, and also the secretary to the Assistant Director of the Veteran's Administration in Manhattan. She had an older sister, June who lived in Philly with their mother Harriet Maude Logan Galloway. June had three sons—Robert, Hugh, and Auburn. My mother had me and my younger brother, Carlton Garfield Cartwright, who is a professional photographer and an Air Force veteran.

My father, Uriah Theophilus Cartwright was born on Long Island, Bahamas, in May 1919, but was brought to Vero Beach, Florida, at six months old. He was the middle son of five sons. The two older brothers, Garfield and Carl, were born in Florida. The two younger brothers, Christopher and Forest, were born on Long Island, Bahamas, but both of them died before puberty. Therefore, my father was the youngest son, while my mother was the youngest daughter. They were married for five years before I was born. I was the only child for nearly five years. I was their little princess and they treated me like gold.

I attended P.S. 123 across the street from our twin-family brick home in South Ozone Park, Jamaica, New York, until I was in the fifth grade, when I transferred to St. Clément's Catholic School, where I received a great education. I graduated in 1960, when I transferred to Bishop McDonnell Memorial High School, an all-girls parochial school in Brooklyn on Eastern Parkway, near the Botanic Gardens: there I would stroll on early, sunny mornings with my three school-mates Kathy, Theresa, and Joanie on our way to school. We lived quite a distance from the school and had to take two buses and two trains to get from Queens to Brooklyn, twice a day. The trek to school was wonderful in spring and fall, but winters could be brutally cold with temperatures dipping into the teens on many mornings. School started at 8:15 a.m. and it took about an hour and fifteen minutes to get there. So, we would begin our daily journey around 6:45 every morning. In winter, it would be dark by the time we arrived home.

My schooling was interrupted by an early pregnancy in my 15th year. That is a long story but the moral of it is "Never give up. Always push on. You are worth fighting for and there is life after teenage pregnancy." My son, Michael Joseph Serrano was born on January 22, 1965, six weeks after my 16th birthday on December 7, 1964. I was in the Angel Guardian Home for Unwed Mothers from October 1964 until his birth. Although the nuns approached me about giving Michael up for adoption because I was so young, my parents and I decided to keep him. Today, he is 55, with two beautiful daughters, Maëlle (21) and Sophia (11). Their mother, Regine Piqueon is from Petionville, Haiti. Michael's father, Peter Serrano was born in Catanio, Puerto Rico. We were married six months after Michael was born. We had Michele, better known as Mimi, 1 year, 11 months, 1 day, and 1 hour after Michael was born. She was a Christmas baby, born on December 23, 1965. Both of my children are gifts. They are extremely sociable, talented, and a joy to be around.

When my children were five and three, I began studying at Queens College. I majored in Communication which was in the English

Department at that time. After two years, I dropped out and married my second husband, Jesse White, who was a gourmet chef. We stayed together for nine years and moved from Queens to Florida in 1970. In 1976, I took my children and left Jesse, who became violent for reasons still unknown. Drugs. Alcohol. Who knows? Anyway, the children and I drove up to Cumberland, Virginia, where we stayed with my father and his second wife, Carrie, for one week, before driving on to Philadelphia. My aunt June passed away two weeks after we arrived, which was quite a shock to me.

Eventually, I enrolled at LaSalle University, which had been an all-male college only two years before. I studied Music and Communication there until graduation in 1981. The winters were brutal, and I really missed Florida sunshine. However, I moved back to New York in Harlem from 1982 to 1984, where I worked as a keypunch operator. In 1983, I had the fortune of learning word processing from a lady who was the supervisor at Ernst & Whinney accounting firm. I studied with her for about eight weeks. Once I got the hang of the machine, she referred me to human resources where I was employed as a temp. I worked for many different firms in advertising, accounting, and legal services for 18 months, until I decided to move back to Florida with my brother in Hypoluxo, FL, just south of Lake Worth, where my father grew up.

Before leaving Philly, I studied with one of the greatest jazz pianists, Gerald Price who accompanied Ella Fitzgerald, Sarah Vaughn, Gloria Lynne, and Dakota Staton. He taught me everything I know about music theory, piano, and songwriting. My first music lesson—resolving to a 13th chord—became a composition that I developed over four years, entitled "Sweet Return" that was recorded on Atlantic Records in New York in 1983 by Freddie Hubbard and the Kool Jazz All-Stars! That was a pivotal point in my musical career.

In New York, I studied with pianist Barry Harris, who had a vocal workshop attended by many of the jazz vocalists of the day, including Casandra Wilson. I performed at the Blue Note twice, at several clubs in Harlem including the St. Nicholas Pub with Danny Mixon, the young husband of Betty Carter, and at the jazz church, St. Peter's Episcopal Church. My last performance, before I moved back to Florida, was with an all-female quartet with Bertha Hope on piano, Carline Ray on bass, and Paula Hampton on drums.

Also, at that church, I was the only female speaker at the funeral of Budd Johnson, a notable tenor saxophonist and the husband of my dance teacher Bernice Johnson, with whom I had studied from the age of four to eight. Bernice also taught Ben Vereen and Michael Anderson, choreographer for Michael Jackson.

In New York from 1968 to 1970, I associated with all of the jazz musicians from Miles Davis, Dizzy Gillespie, and Freddie Hubbard to George Benson, Betty Carter, and Frank Foster, leader of the Count Basie Orchestra. Those two years shaped my jazz career in that I was steeped in the traditional, straight-ahead, jazz genre that enabled me to scat, sing standards, and write my own music. My two favorite jazz joints were Slug's in the Far East, down by the Bowery, where trumpeter Lee Morgan was shot by his common-law wife Helen, and the Harlem clubs, Small's Paradise, Red Rooster, Count Basie's, Well's Chicken and Waffles, Club Baron, and the Baby Grand. On Long Island, there was Joe Johnson's Bottle & Cork, Club Ruby, and Elegantes, where I first saw George Benson and The Village Door, known for good jazz and Chinese food. In Brooklyn, Jesse, a jazz promoter and chef, took me to the Blue Coronet, a tiny little club with an audience with a ferocious jazz appetite. Bobby Timmons and Paul Chambers played there, and I became friends with Bobby's wife Stella Timmons, who now lives in Plantation, FL.

After a failed 4th of July jazz show that Jesse and his partners Hilly Saunders and Jim Harrison of Jazz Spotlight Productions, spearheaded, we escaped to Tampa, Florida. For three months, we lived in the countryside at Jesse's father's farm. That was an eye-opening experience for this city girl. However, the week we left New York, Angela Davis fled with her companion, who looked a lot like Jesse, tall, dark, and handsome. Since I looked a lot like Angela, I ran into the police four times when they stopped me as her look-alike. The first time was a harrowing experience. They took me into the sheriff's office in Tarpon Springs, Florida, finger-printed me, and then, they had to let me go because I was not Angela. I was shaking in my boots. The other three times were on the east coast of Florida, in Miami and Fort Lauderdale. There was a big write-up in the *Fort Lauderdale News* about the woman who was mistaken for Angela Davis.

My notoriety in Florida continued when I moved back from New York, in July 1984. By 1985, I was singing in jazz clubs in Miami, Hollywood, and Fort Lauderdale. I worked at O'Hara's Jazz Club with trumpeter Bob Vandivort for three years. During the week, I was a legal secretary, and I sang almost every weekend. My first gig was at the History Hemingway House in Hollywood with a great pianist, Ernie Goldsmith, which that lasted six months. I performed at the top of Pier 66, on the Jungle Queen, for the Winter Boat Parade, and at the various jazz and blues festivals, until I began traveling to Europe in 1990. For four years, I flew back and forth to Switzerland, until I moved there, one week after I graduated from Florida Atlantic University with my master's degree in Communication, in 1994.

Living and working in Europe was the icing on the cake. I sang in eight countries and had the fortune of meeting a pianist, Giovanni Mazzarino who co-produced my debut CD "Feelin' Good" in 1995, in Sicily. We toured all over Italy for four years. Giovanni came to work with me for a month at the Montreux Palace in Harry's New York Bar. That was a blast because I knew many of the locals since my first trip to the Montreux Jazz Festival in 1990. I feel very fortunate to have had such a charmed life as a jazz singer and songwriter. I met so many wonderful musicians in my travels including

Quincy Jones, Chaka Khan, The Neville Brothers, Abbey Lincoln, Ray Charles, Dr. John, Linda Hopkins, Dorothy Donegan, Harry "Sweets" Edison, Jay McShann, and Roy Ayers, just to name a few.

I sang in Lausanne, Montreux, Bern, Zurich, Gstaad, Zermatt, Basil, and Fribourg, in Switzerland. Also, I worked in England, France, Austria, Germany, Italy, and Spain. Whew! Those eight years from 1990 to 1998 set the tone for all that came after, especially my first book, *"In Pursuit of a Melody"* and the other 13 books that I published. After 30 years of being a jazz vocalist, I realized that I had only performed with six women musicians: Kim Clarke and Carline Ray, bassists; Bertha Hope, Marianne Otten, and Tina Stein, pianists; and Paula Hampton, drummer. I began to wonder where all the female jazz musicians were.

In 1997, I developed the *Jazzwomen Directory*, online. I had started to learn hypertext markup language (HTML) and was creating websites. Few of my colleagues knew anything about the Internet and I became adept at building sites for artists, authors, and musicians. Today, the *Jazzwomen Directory* catalogs 100 notable and obscure women in jazz. In 2007, I incorporated Women in Jazz South Florida, Inc. as a non-profit organization. This came after a semi-successful production of *GaiaFest*, A Celebration of Mother Earth with Women in Jazz that I organized for the non-profit scholarship foundation of the *Westside Gazette*, Broward County's oldest African-American newspaper. This event featured women jazz artists from New York, California, and Florida, and honored jazz songstress Dakota Staton.

The attendance was poor. It was then that I realized that most people were not interested in women musicians. So, for the past 22 years, I devoted myself to the promotion of women musicians, globally. Today, WIJSF has 353 members with 213 musicians, and 61 men who support our mission. My activities included a weekly (now monthly) podcast on BlogTalkRadio entitled *Musicwoman*, that features women who compose and perform their own music. I publish a monthly newsletter featuring upcoming performances of our members from 14 countries and 22 states. Our board consists of an International President, President, Secretary, Treasurer, and I am the Executive Director.

I have crafted grant proposals and won several grants from Broward Schools, Broward Cultural Division, BankUnited, Miami Beach Cultural Division, and The Friends of the Library. The most ambitious program we did was with four composers, 35 middle school jazz band members, and 20 vocalists, performing original music at the Broward Center for the Performing Arts. Also, my 8-woman ensemble *Amazing Musicwomen,* performed at the Sunrise Civic Center, the Arts Garage in Delray Beach, and the Biennes Center for the Arts.

Reinvention has always been my forté. In 2010, when WIJSF was only three years old, I reached an impasse. I felt that this cause was not considered important. Few people really cared about women musicians, and I was putting my time, money, and soul into something that seemed like a lost cause. So, I enrolled at Northcentral University in Arizona to pursue my Doctorate in Business Administration/Marketing online. These were seven challenging years. I was not singing a lot. I had earned some money from grants, but they dried up in Florida. I was living on Social Security which was not a lot, and I was a full-time student.

I had not been in school since 1994. I had a lot of information stuffed in my long-term memory that needed to be revitalized. I was 63 when I began my studies and 70 when I graduated. The discipline of education teaches you to do what you need to do when you do not want to do it. From course to course, I questioned the sanity of my decision. Few of my friends had even a bachelor's degree. Even fewer had a master's degree, and only two women that I knew had a doctorate. I was in a world of my own creation, and I was determined to complete the task. Statistics made me doubt everything! But I managed to get a B! That's when I knew I was good to go.

I graduated with a 3.78 grade point average and was inducted into the Business Honor Society, Delta Mu Delta. I attended the graduation in Phoenix, Arizona in the hottest month of the year, graduating on July 8. It was so hot that tires were melting on the highway.

Once I got that Doctor before my name, I just knew I was a shoo-in for a six-figure salary. Little did I know that the world couldn't care less about a Black woman with a PhD. Of course, I was a Doctor of Business Administration (DBA) and not a PhD. Who knew there was a difference? I thought companies would be knocking my door down to use the knowledge I had stored up in my septuagenarian brain. However, that was not the case at all. I suffered from gender, race, and age discrimination while my student loans mounted from $101,000 to $116,000, including interest tacked on after two years of deferment.

I got one class to teach at Southeastern College in Speech Communication, which I was qualified to teach with my master's degree from FAU. I got a little more income because I was a doctor, but it was not that much, and I got nothing when I did not teach. After three years at Southeastern, I got a couple of classes at Keiser University. These two schools are owned by the same company, so the salary was the same. By 67, I had decided to retire from performing. I was just tired of being on stage, where I had been since I was four! So, my income came from teaching, only.

Finally, in August 2019, I got four classes at Palm Beach State College in Lake Worth and Palm Beach Gardens. At Southeastern and Keiser, I never had more than 16 students in a class which ran one month. At PBSC, I have up to 28 students per class, and 112 students in total. Some students withdrew, leaving me 108 students. The classroom is my new stage and I love teaching young people. I love watching the lights go on in their eyes. I love imparting knowledge that I've gathered over the decades from writing, traveling, and performing. Speech Communication entails how we communicate with others, the ethics of communication, and public speaking. Since I have never been shy or afraid of talking to people, this is the perfect subject for me to help others learn to do. I have found my niche and I am very happy in this station of my life.

I continue to lecture on *Women in Jazz*, *Blues Women: The First Civil Rights Workers*, and *Six Keys for Success in the Music Industry* at colleges and for community organizations. I am the founding member of the Association for the Study of African-American Life and History (ASALH) South Florida branch. Also, I am a music and letters member of the National League of American Pen Women (NLAPW) in the Boca Raton branch. Recently, I lectured on the ins and outs of the music business at PBSC in Lake Worth and Miami-Dade College in Kendall. Over the summer, I presented Blues Women for 30 Broward school teachers, and in Daytona Beach for the NLAPW semi-annual conference.

I am an advocate for women musicians, African-American History, and for Black PhDs in the academy. I joined the National Council on Black and African- American Affairs (NCBAA) at my college. In 2020, I will publish the second issue of *Musicwoman Magazine*, a 10-year effort, and will continue the work I do to promote women musicians globally! At the Miami Smooth Jazz Festival on November 10, an ASALH South Florida member introduced me to her friend as a Renaissance woman. I stay busy, keep my mind working, and look forward to a fruitful old age, and that is how I live!

If I had to live my life over again, I would do most of the same things. I might pursue architecture since I am always building something. But I learned that women architects are marginalized even more than women musicians, so maybe not! Music is what made me resilient. I can hear a song and be a young woman all over again, fall in love all over again, get up and shake my tailfeathers, and keep on trucking.

After visiting five continents and twenty-two countries, performing in some of the most exotic places on Earth, including China, Sicily, and Ghana, publishing 14 books, releasing nine CDs—two solo albums, and seven compilations of women's original music, teaching hundreds of students how to organize and present a speech, raising two beautiful children, five grands, and four great-grands, oh, and divorcing four husbands, I look forward to painting in my 80s until I decide to make that cakewalk into the heavens.

Until then, I will continue to be excited about living and working to improve the status of women in music. I have some of the best friends in the world, female and male. My male friends are mostly musicians or music lovers. My female friends are from all walks of life, and they keep me on my toes with suggestions as to how I can improve my services to women musicians and the audiences that they serve. I have girlfriends from my childhood, from my life as a musician, and from more current endeavors, who keep me lifted with their anecdotes, friendly gossip, and community and family events. I am a woman surrounded by bright, intelligent people who never cease to amaze me. Those people include my family, friends, professional colleagues, and students. I would say that life is good and getting better every day. My name is Dr. Joan Cartwright, mother, jazz diva, women advocate, professor, a lover of life, and I am resilient!

To learn more about Dr. Joan and Women In Jazz South Florida, contact: www.wijsf.org www.joancartwright.com www.fyicomminc.com Women in Jazz South Florida, Inc. 954-740-3398

So, what's your takeaway from Phoenix Dr. Joan's story?

#PhoenixesRising
Share your thoughts in our FB Group

https://bit.ly/phoenixesrising

Question: What kind of Phoenix do you want to be?

We leave Dr. Joan with the music still playing in our heads and bop over to Colombia where we will meet another fabulous Phoenix, Sandra Eichler, star of stage and screen. I can't wait to read about her resilient journey.

BE RESILIENT

Chapter 17

ALL THE WORLD'S A STAGE:
Sandra Eichler, Colombia

Sandra Eichler is a blend of German and Colombian ancestry and a formidable star of soap opera, stage, and screen. Her career as an actress began at the age of two, and she has won many awards for her portrayals of her varied characters. Sandra holds a degree in Social Communication with a Masters in Journalism. She is a proud mom and CEO of Saga11 – the award-winning music production company. As a philanthropist her passion is supporting several children's charities in Colombia and organizations that support the well-being of animals.

All The World's A Stage
Sandra Eichler, Colombia

**"*All the world's a stage,*
And all the men and women merely players;
They have their exits and their entrances,
And one man in his time plays many parts."**
William Shakespeare, As You Like It

In 1599, Shakespeare wrote this famous piece in his play *As You Like It*. How well do I know this statement because from birth, the ebb and flow of my life has mirrored a series of exits from stage right, stage left, and center-stage. As art imitates life, so do the lines between fiction, fantasy, and reality blur leaving you wondering what just happened here? As a star of stage and screen, the characters whom I have played over the last four decades have been a melting pot of varied cultures, roles, and experiences.

Trust me when I tell you that every single role that I have played, on and off stage, has required me to quickly pivot and shift my mindset to survive this journey called life. Hello, my name is Sandra Eichler and my story of resilience focuses on finding and embracing the true me, after decades of being adrift and lost amid a sea of fictional characters, who became my coping mechanism and resilient anchors.

I have met so many people who wish to be actors and actresses. However, fame and fortune have its price. When you are famous, people tend to be especially nice to you—at least to your face. Whatever negative comments they say when you are not around perhaps reflects more on their jealousy and inability to be as successful as you are. If you are to pursue a career in acting, you must develop a thick skin, be able to pivot, and bounce back quickly from your failures.

There are three questions that one should also ask themselves if you are going to pursue a career in stage and screen. Question number one is: "How badly do I want this career and all that comes with my choice? Question number two is: "Why do I want to be an actress or actor?" Finally, question number three is "What am I prepared to do to achieve success at my craft"? This last question needs careful thought as you may be required to engage in activities that can compromise your values. Had I been given an opportunity to ask and answer these questions, I am sure that I would have avoided much of the heartache experienced along the way.

I was born in Germany to two wild, crazy but completely lovable parents. My mother is Colombian and embodies the spirit of the Caribbean. Even in her darkest moments, she remained positive and happy. I learned how to be resilient from her because her mantra was no matter what, you must keep fighting. She recently passed away at the age of 85 leaving a legacy of kindness and resilience. Her extraordinary voice will be remembered by her students, audiences, and in many recordings. Her smile and kindness to others, as well as her teaching will transcend to other generations.

My mother was a gifted musical artist. When she sang, her voice filled the house, and wafted through the windows of her exquisite Colombian home only to stop those passing by in their tracks. She was that good. When she was around twenty years old, she got her first European scholarship to study music and voice in the prestigious Santa Cecilia Conservatorio in Rome. From there, she completed her master's degree in Music in Germany. Her life became interesting when she met and fell in love with a crazy, German guy who is my dad.

A gifted opera singer, my dad spent thirty-five years performing at the one of the oldest opera houses in Germany, Staatsoper Stuttgart or Opera Stuttgart. My dad is the total opposite of my mom. She was positive and bubbly. He was sarcastic, always with a taste of black humor, and didn't (liked) like to be around people or social meetings. Together they provided balance for each other and a rich upbringing in the arts for me. I am fluent in several languages including German and Spanish. We are a family of first born, and the only children of our parents. In my little family of three, neither of us have siblings. Imagine growing up with no uncles, aunts, or cousins to play with.

There is a funny story which my mother loved to tell. When I was born, my parents had a poodle named Lumpi. Everybody freaked out because they did not know if the dog would be jealous and how both of us would adjust. In my mom's social circles, there was even chatter about how the dog would adjust to sharing time and attention with me. Would the dog be jealous? How would it cope? My mom did not listen to anybody and decided to put the dog in my cradle from the first day I was born. Lumpi and I became best friends and inseparable. At this point if you are judging my parents, understand that eccentricity is the life blood of the opera world and the very wealthy. Today, because of Lumpi, I am an animal lover who supports and lobbies for animals, as well as human rights.

However, growing up, I spent the majority of my time backstage watching my parents perform from the theater's wings. Together, they were magnificent in their exquisitely rich costumes. I still remember my dad's baritone voice as he moved effortlessly across the stage belting out arias like *Papageno* from W. A. Mozart's the *Magic Flute*; or Gugliemo in *Cosi Fan Tutti* with such bravado that left me in awe of his performance. Dad came alive on stage. At home he was a different person.

From operas such as *La Traviata* by Verdi or Wagner's *Tannhauser*, I was exposed to the rich language and texture of opera and the operatic lifestyle. It was no surprise that I developed a love for the opera world. As a child I just enjoyed watching my parents perform. When I was not backstage, I hung out at home with Lumpi, the poodle.

It should come as no surprise that at the tender age of three, I made my debut in the role of Madam Butterfly's Little Boy. I remember when my mother carried me in her arms and sang the very famous aria. Ever so gently I opened my eyes to see the audience staring back at me, I think this was the very first moment that I wanted to be on stage. As I look back at that moment, it was so surreal. Here I was in my real-life mom's arms, playing her child as she played Madame Butterfly. We were two characters playing out our real life as two characters. As her soothing voice, and the music crescendoed, this moment with my mom, being her child, while simultaneously playing 'her child', is a moment that will be etched in my memory for the rest of my life.

In Germany, I even starred in The Magic Flute followed by more operas that required the participation of children. So, I developed this passion about acting, singing, and everything that had to do with the arts. My passion for my craft grew within me and became my primary motivator, because it was fun. Word to the wise, whatever you are pursuing, whether it be your career, marriage, or anything else, when you are unable to find the fun in what you are doing, consider pivoting and changing course. Life is too short to be miserable.

With regards to my being resilient and becoming who I am today, there are three noteworthy events in my life that served as catalyst for my ability to bounce back from my adversities. The first was when my parents separated, and life as I knew it ended. The second was managing the various aspects of my career. The third was having the courage to find the true Sandra. Each one of these incidents required a different level of resilience, undergirded by the greatest feat of character switching that should have won me an Oscar, or at least an Emmy. Now, while I will not go into detail on each of these incidents, I believe that an overview of each of these life-altering events will highlight why resilience is so important, to not only live but thrive. I believe that happiness and fulfillment is a gift that you give yourself.

Most people might have been devastated by their parents' divorce. I was actually relieved and never judged their decision. My parents were so different from each other. The most difficult part was leaving everything that I knew behind —the country, language, cultural behavior, and the many beautiful people. In Germany, I had finally found my stride. School was a blessing for me. Going to school in Germany was sublime. Germany is a safe place so since kindergarten and every morning, I walked to school without incident. My parents being both famous in the opera world were financially and professionally solvent. I, as their daughter, enjoyed all the rights and privileges that money could afford. When I was not in school, I performed on stage with my parents.

I remember the day that I waved goodbye to my dad as I boarded the plane with my mom and headed for Colombia. As far as I was concerned, I was off on an adventure. I was completely unaware of the big changes that I was about to face in Colombia.

The divorce however was devastating for my mother. She went from being a diva of the opera stage in Germany, to starting from zero in her home country. We left with just our clothes and a few mementoes. Gone were chauffeurs, fancy dinners. and lifestyle. Also gone were my dog Lumpi and my godmother. Gone were the pretentious attitudes of the opera world. My mom seemingly didn't miss a beat. As far as I was concerned, all was going well. She was still bubbly while papa was quiet. I am still not sure what happened between them that prompted them breaking up but neither of them remarried, and they continued to be friends until she took her last breath.

So, one minute I was living in luxury in Germany and the next minute we were beginning from nothing in Colombia. In the time that it took to fly from Germany to Colombia, we went from living in the lap of luxury, to the hard cold reality that we were poor and starting our lives from scratch. I shared earlier that my mother was a fighter. What was necessary now was that we changed costumes, scenery, acts, and take action to begin this new phase of our lives. My mom and I were now working with new scripts. This was my first lesson in reality, and resilience as I learned for the first time what it meant to be poor financially, but rich in all other aspects of life.

Colombia is a beautiful country, lush in vegetation and beautiful, positive people. We settled in our old family home and slowly began to rebuild our lives. Latins are warmer than other cultures and very welcoming to everybody. We are also very loud, and we love to dance. Family is also especially important to us as well. As Latinas, we celebrate everything with music, dancing, and a fun time. Even fighting is celebrated. In Colombia I learned that all the discipline I had learned from my dad was not that important. I could stay awake much longer, party a lot, people were never on time, and all was, just like freer. Colombia was also a harsh lesson of humility. For example, if I said,

"Mom, can I have a piece of bread?"

Her reply would be,

"Well, if you eat it all now, maybe you don't have this for tonight."

In my head, my response was,

"What is she talking about? I am used to being in five-star hotels in Europe where bread shortage is a non-issue."

As my riches to rags story unfolded, so did the reality that my life had changed forever. One of the biggest lessons learned was that material things are not the most important things in your life. You can be incredibly happy without having a lot. I learned that what really makes you happy are the things you cannot buy. What is especially important are the beautiful memories that you make with the people you love. I always say,

"It is not the richest person who has more, but the richest person who needs less."

Slowly, as the shock of my new normal sunk in, I often wondered what really happened between my parents to place us in this sorry state. How could my mom walk away with nothing, I mean no money, nothing? How did we enter this new production of our lives? Furthermore, how was this going to end? Some people find it difficult to bounce back after losing everything. What helped us to be resilient was our quick mindset shifts developed by decades of learning how to adapt to character changes, set designs, and scripts. All my mother's and my prior training had prepared us for the dress rehearsal of our lives and future.

Here is a hot tip, if you do not like how your life is going, do not suffer. Find the courage to change the script, scenery, and players. Then when you are ready, re-enter the next stage of your life. My mother still had her voice, we still had bread to eat, and she had me—her protégé. We were going to make it.

So here I was in a new country looking and acting different because of my blond hair, and German pedigree. I am like,

"Okay, where is my family? I don't have uncles; I don't have cousins."

It truly was just me and my mom on the stage of life, playing whatever roles we needed to play to survive. I learned very quickly how to never take things or people for granted, and to be grateful for something as simple as a piece of bread.

At school, I drove the teachers crazy. I questioned everything and every concept. When I was not in school, I was on the stage with my mom as her page turner. As she sang in that beautiful voice of hers, we worked together to make her performances the best per-formances ever. I never liked high school. I always was more into art. I was the weird kid because I was thinking about rehearsals, and everybody knew me at school, but not in a good way because I was a pain in the neck for the teachers.

In Colombia, I returned to the stage and at twelve years of age, I launched my first variety talk show for kids. Filled with music, kids' songs, and laughter, *Caracolito Magico* turned out to be highly suc-cessful. Can you believe that I was hosting my own show on televi-sion at twelve years old? My mother warned,

"Okay, you do that, and you're going to finish school, girl."

Little did I know that I was being prepared for a lucrative career in journalism and the soap opera world.

Entering these two fields was my second journey of resilience. With a successful child talk show under my belt and many theater performances, I made my mother proud by finishing high school and graduating from college with a degree in Social Communica-tion and a Master's in Journalism. The journalism world requires you to be tough, to be on, and to be perfect. You are in front of the camera which shows no mercy at times. I became the host of the most important news station in Colombia—Noticiero Nacional. This was one of the happiest times of my life as my performance as a TV anchor was stellar and got me noticed by the higher ups and media moguls. Being a reporter introduced me to a lot of interest-ing human beings, from politicians to prisoners, from celebrities to the homeless, I learned that everybody has a story to tell and that we can always learn something from those stories.

In this resilient journey of my life, know that others are always watching! Unbeknownst to me, the media executives who watched me deliver the news thought that I would be a good fit to play the key role of Daniela on the Colombian soap opera *LA Alternativa del Escorpión*. The funny thing was that this series was about a TV news anchor who was an awfully bad girl. When I told my boss about the opportunity, he encouraged me to go for it. However, he also cautioned me that I shouldn't speak about all the manipulation that goes on behind the scenes in the newsroom. He said,

> ***"Sandra, you cannot play a role where you are the worst journalist ever and you criticize the field of journalism, and then one hour later, you are nationwide giving the news. You have to choose."***

So, I chose to be a bad girl and that was the beginning of my career as a TV star in Colombia. I participated in *LA Alternativa del Escorpión*, *OKTV*, *Maria & Maria*, *Escandalo*, *Plamo*, *el Manantial*, *Tabu*, and many more. The show and I went on to win many awards and I won an award for Outstanding Soap Opera Actress.

Life in Colombia was good even though the country was in political upheaval under Pablo Escobar. When I was not acting, I supported my mother with her various charities. We supported many foundations. One of them was to educate and take kids from the street to offer them a better future. We worked very closely with them. On the weekends I would bring three or four children to my house. There I shared precious time with them, encouraged, mentored, and gave them hope for their future. I also fell in love and married my husband, Luis Guillermo Martin

As I was enjoying my success, Colombia was experiencing an awfully bad and scary time under Pablo Escobar. There were bombings, kidnappings, and political unrest. Wealthy people purchased kidnapping insurance policies just in case they or their children were kidnapped. Nevertheless, I enjoyed my fame and fortune as the bombs and political upsurgence continued. Sometimes, wealth has its privileges which gives you options, even in the bad times of life. You can escape a lot of catastrophes that other people cannot until those catastrophes land at your doorstep. As an actor, I enjoyed playing a variety of characters. However, being a political activist or refugee was not one of them. One day, my husband said,

"It's getting tough here. We should go."

I agreed even though I was at the top of my career. We left everything in Colombia and started one more time to create a new life in a new country with our baby son in tow. We did not have a lot of capital because we couldn't sell the properties. I sold everything else that we had accumulated in Colombia, which gave us the necessary capital to restart our lives in America.

Have you ever had the experience of knowing yourself as "hot stuff" until life gives you a rude awakening? Well, this was exactly what happened to me. In Colombia, I was readily recognized. For example, I did not have to wait in line at the bank. I also did not have a private life. One day I was having an ice cream with my brother-in-law, and immediately the next day it was in the news that ' … she has a new friend'. Of course, I was devastated more so at the reality that an innocent act could turn ugly because of the very industry of which I was a member.

As life would have it, our move to America would be my third lesson in resilience. This resilient journey of mine is every immigrant's journey. As immigrants, many of us are at the top of our game in our country. However, when you move to the United States, you find yourself as a nobody and having to begin from nothing.

Life in America, more than being difficult, was a new adventure for me. I could not readily secure a position as an actress. I went on casting calls only to be asked by the casting director,

"Who are you?"

Frustrated, I would give my name. However, in my head, I thought, but never said out loud,

"Like c'mon, you don't know who I am? Are you kidding me?
I'm Sandra Eichler"

"Sandra Who?"

they sometimes said after I repeated my name. They were not kidding. The casting directors really had no idea who I was. As they say, I was a little fish in a big pond. I also spoke no English so just negotiating simple tasks like grocery shopping was challenging. In addition, all my fame and success in Colombia seemed irrelevant in the United States. I was competing with better known actors and actresses. Those of Hispanic heritage became my toughest competition. My husband was working at a company and so he could not really help me with my career.

God would have it that I would meet a kind angel and her family—Colleen Dupont. She shared an opportunity to be a greeter with DMC, a company that provides event planning for American Field Scholars, corporate. and private clients. My job was to meet the students at Miami airport who were coming to America from different countries for their immersion experience in the United States. As their transition ambassador I ensured that they moved on to their next destination without incident.

Had I not been resilient and able to pivot into a new character of International Ambassador, I would have become quite depressed and given up. Most people living abroad view America as the go-to place for success. They judge what living must be like by what they see on TV and in the movies. Little do they know that life here is not like that. If you are somebody at home, you are nobody in America, until you find the courage to be somebody again. Success takes arduous work. Success requires you to do jobs that you would never do in your country. Success can be elusive. Success in America is a humbling journey of resilience.

I remember that I was at the airport to meet my AFS students. I was at work in Miami airport, dressed in khaki pants, the company t-shirt, and looking like crap. I also had this "Welcome to Miami" sign. Suddenly, I saw a famous guy and personal friend in Colombia coming through the gate. This guy worked with the likes of Sharon Stone and Disney. Unlike me, he was doing very well in his acting career. So, I looked at myself and I said,

"How can he see me like that?"

I found myself pulling down my cap and ducking behind a wall so that he would not see me. I was so ashamed of who I had become. Then it hit me that this was the role in which I was cast. I was playing an International Ambassador for International students whose families had sent them here to study and experience America. I had nothing to be ashamed about. Finding a new sense of courage and resilience, I worked as a Travel Ambassador and continued to go on casting calls.

Then God smiled on me again and I landed my dream role with Telemundo in a soap opera. I have been in nine soap operas with *Telemundo* and loved playing the characters in everyone. Our child cast me in the role of mother, and that is when things got very real for me.

Up until now I had played so many roles in my life and on the screen, that I had lost Sandra in a sea of characters. My son made me realize what was important and what was not. He was growing up so fast and I was missing most of it. This was an epiphany for me. I also did not realize my marriage was slowly falling apart. We had money. We had success in our careers. We had pulled ourselves back from the abyss of life. However, we had lost ourselves along the way until our son reminded us of what was important, and it had nothing to do with money. Instead, it included all the things that money cannot buy like love, patience, authenticity, compassion, and courage.

Somewhere, along the way I had disconnected from my humanity and perfected hiding behind my characters to cope with life's disappointments and pain. With professional help, I was able to find myself again as I realized that my first break with reality was when my parents got separated. They never got divorced and never married again. The second was when my mom became really sick which required me to fly back and forth to Colombia. My regret was that I was never able to bring her to the USA. I had to handle stuff from the distance and travel a lot to be able to be with her. The third break was my marriage which I took for granted.

Over the years and with professional help, I have become wonderfully comfortable in my own skin. I am remarried. My son is healthy and growing up to be a fine young man. I can tell you that it is so refreshing to just be yourself. Shakespeare told the truth when he said:

"All the world's a stage and all the men and women merely players."

In life we all play distinct roles. I have found that as an actor, you must learn how to unplug after each performance. As you exit stage right or left, you can exit towards peace, joy, happiness, and love. These are the qualities in which you need to ground yourself, so that you don't lose yourself along the way.

Many actors and actresses I know, have succumbed to drugs and alcohol addictions because they got lost in the glamor and glitz of stardom. Despite my challenges, I was blessed to have great parents and a strong resilient mother who was my greatest teacher. Today,

I continue to support the charities that she started in Colombia. In 2010 I opened my own company, Saga 11 Productions, where I can follow my passion even if it is from backstage. I also dedicate this story to her and my son. I am Sandra Eichler mother, actress, animal lover, entrepreneur, and philanthropist, and I am resilient.

To learn more about Sandra Eichler contact: sanda@sandrae-ichler.com sandraeichler@saga11.com www.sandraeichler.com

So, what's your takeaway from Phoenix Sandra's story?

#PhoenixesRising
Share your thoughts in our FB Group

https://bit.ly/phoenixesrising

Question: What kind of Phoenix do you want to be?

BE RESILIENT

We say goodbye to Sandra in Columbia and head to Haiti. It is my pleasure to introduce to you our youngest Phoenix, Poetess Kayla Eduord. Be inspired as she shares her I AM poem with you.

I AM POEM – Kayla Edouard, Haiti

I AM FROM walks at Champs de Mars after Sunday mass listening to the laughter erupt from every corner, the calming crash of clear waves on Wahoo Bay beach, and slow dancing to the jazz rhythm of Kompa music.

I AM FROM the savory taste of soup joumou on Haitian Independence Day, pate, and Cola Couronne burning my chest on a Saturday afternoon, and the sweet scent of chocolat and pain Ayisyen during Christmas celebrations.

I AM FROM "tout moun se moun," "lespwa è viv" and "wap konn Jòj."

I AM FROM Joseph Assad, Anne Hilaire, Nadine Hilaire, Abigail Hilaire, Dave Edouard, and hundreds more.
I am KayKay

Kayla Eduord is a 19-year-old student currently studying advertising and journalism at the University of Florida. She is a first generation Haitian American and is dedicated to storytelling and showing her creativity. Her Passion Project is supporting nurses from Haiti through The Haitian Nurses Network of South Florida

So, what's your takeaway from Phoenix, Poetess Kayla's story?

#PhoenixesRising
Share your thoughts in our FB Group

https://bit.ly/phoenixesrising

Readers, are you still with us. We are on the last leg of our resilient journey. From Haiti, we travel to the Philippines. Here we will meet Dr. Flora Satinover, a gifted alternative medicine practitioner in her community. Let us see what her resilient journey entails.

ON RESILIENCE

"Health is wholeness and balance, an inner resilience that allows you to meet the demands of living without being overwhelmed."—**Andrew Weil**

Andrew Weil's quote captures the essence of our next Phoenix Dr. Flora Satinover. Join her as she takes you on her incredible round-trip journey of resilience, from the Philippines, through her struggles and triumphs in America, only to finally return to the Philippines. Learn her one secret that sustained her through the good times and bad and why she is known as a resilient healer.

Chapter 18

MEDICINE FOR THE RESILEINT WARRIOR
Dr. Flora Satinover, Philippines

Dr. Flora Satinover is an Alternative Medicine Practitioner and Public Health Officer at the at the Municipal Health Office, Angono, Rizal in the Philippines. Dr. Satinover is a graduate of The Atlantic Institute of Oriental Medicine (ATOM) and Florida College of Natural Health. Throughout her career she has successfully treated those with both physical and mental health issues. Her passion project is ensuring that everyone in her community stays healthy.

Medicine for the Resilient Warrior
Dr. Flora Satinover, Philippines

"Physical well-being necessitates listening to what you already know, and then taking it seriously enough to act accordingly. When you wake up and feel the impulse to arch your back, stretch and exhale with a loud sigh, for God's sake, do it."
—Darrell Calkins

Many years ago, there lived an elderly Chinese woman. She was incredibly healthy for her age, never once having to be hospitalized, even in the later years of her notably long, one-hundred-twenty-five-year life. Much of this longevity could be credited to her dedication to natural medicine. She had always kept a garden, growing her own plants and herbs to make into natural remedies by which she swore. These remedies held incredible power, even restoring her vision in her old age. It wasn't until the final years of her life that the woman accepted help from others. By then her widowed grandson thought it would be pertinent to live close by. This woman was a pinnacle of resilience. I owe so much to her. She was my grandmother. Without her strength and determination, without her resourcefulness, and her belief in the healing power of the natural world, my life would have taken a drastically different course. Hello, my name is Dr. Flora Satinover and this is my story of resilience.

As it is, in my early years I never would have believed that it was possible to become what I am today, but somehow it still happened. It's a story that I believe needs to be told.

I grew up on the tiny island of Lao-ang in the Northern Samar province of the Philippines. This island was almost entirely covered by its mountains, which stood tall, flanking the Pacific Ocean. Where the mountains didn't dominate the landscape there lay a small sea-level town with a population of roughly 200,000 people.

It was about a fifteen-minute trip by outboard motorboat from the mainland island and in the past, it had functioned as the deep-water port through which all regional commerce traveled. Cargo boats would pull into our port and drop their loads. These loads were then transferred to boats small enough to port in the shallow bays of the main island. After this, the shipping vessels were filled with copra to deliver to their next port of call. So, life was, year after year, in the anything-but-modern port where I grew up.

My mother and father lived a privileged life. He was the market inspector. She had graduated from the University of Eastern Philippines and was a schoolteacher. Even more significant was her role as the medical authority in Lao-ang, despite her only undergraduate college education. My brother was two years older than me and bore my father's name. Not only did he have this honor, but he also had an advantage—he was male. I wasn't. This dictated our expected roles in life. My brother got to enjoy the privilege of higher education, while my family expected me to eventually relegate myself to the role of wife, regardless of my wishes. Two years of enviously watching him go off to the University of Eastern Philippines was more than enough impetus to make me realize I also had to go there.

Upon arriving, my mind was ravenous for all the new experiences. In contrast to the mundaneness of learning homemaking prior to university, attending school flooded me with new opportunities. I ate up the school's social life, and more importantly, mastered every academic challenge I was faced with. It didn't take long for people to notice me and in my third year of college, suitors began to make me offers of marriage. Though I was unwilling to consent, I had little say in the matter. Eventually, my mother accepted one of these dowries on my behalf—I was to marry the seventh son of a wealthy businessman who owned a large granary in Northern Samar. When the time came for our marriage, I unhappily found myself thrust into the role of second wife. The years passed unnotably, and

I bore my husband five children. Then, one day, the man I had so begrudgingly called my husband, disappeared. For a long while, life was hard. There were days that the burden of raising five children on my own felt impossible to bear. Even as I struggled to do so, I often found myself contemplating my mother. Though her circumstances had been drastically different from my own, I had seen her in countless situations that required her to be strong and diplomatic in order to care for her family. This gave me hope to muster the courage and conquer any obstacle that came my way. Seven years of waiting passed and with my husband's continued absence, I knew fate had smiled on me. By law I now no longer had any obligation to him.

With the excitement of my newfound freedom, I traveled to Manila where I acquired a job sewing for a local dress shop. It's hard to say whether it was the new job or the new climate that spurred the chain of events to follow, but shortly after I began, I fell sick, and had to be taken to the hospital. Upon examination, it became evident that I was in critical need of a gallbladder operation. The years after being abandoned by my husband had hardly been kind to my pockets, and left me nothing close to enough money to pay for my treatment. Once again, I was in the hands of fate.

I was not one to give up, however, so I sought out a better paying job to earn the money I needed. The gods were looking out for me, for on my search, I met a sweet lady named Gloria Banaag. She owned a local natural medicine clinic and needed someone to fill the role of caretaker. Generously, she extended the position to me. I gladly accepted and found myself doing everything from preparing lunch for the store's workers to aiding Mrs. Banaag in preparation of herbal remedies. In an act of thanks, Mrs. Banaag sent me to study reflexology. It was there that I fell in love with natural medicine. It was there that I was finally able to walk in my grandmother's footsteps.

After three years of tirelessly working under Gloria Banaag and accepting her treatment, the unexpected happened. I was cured. My gallbladder had been restored to complete health. Triumphant, Mrs. Banaag and I marched ourselves to the very hospital that had turned me away so many years ago. They had to know about the natural medicine that had saved my life. Receiving this good news felt like being reborn. I had never felt so alive and I had a distinct feeling that my purpose in life had shifted. I knew I had to become a health care provider. I knew that I wanted to care for the sick and needy people of my country. But first I needed to broaden my education.

Pulling together every bit of my funds, I traveled to Hong Kong to study reflexology diagnosis and treatment. Upon completion of my studies, I returned to the Philippines where I established a practice which provided me with sufficient funds for supporting my family. This health care practice did far more than sustain me, however. It introduced a strange opportunity into my life, for among my wide circle of patients were several who offered to pay me in Yamashita gold, a contraband currency.

During the Japanese occupation, in the final days of World War II, gold that had been plundered in Europe was shipped to Japan by way of the Suez Canal. Many of those traveling with the gold would stop on the islands along the way, and among those were the Philippines. As the war rapidly began to wind down, the Japanese were forced to speed their efforts at relocating the gold bars to Japan. They ran out of time, however, and many Japanese soldiers found themselves hopelessly burdened by their gold as they retreated from General MacArthur's troops. It was in this retreat that the ground beneath the soldiers' feet was pounded into mud. As valuable as the seventy-five-pound bars of gold were, they made escape almost impossible. Many Japanese soldiers, in their desperation, abandoned their treasure. These bars sunk into the mud trails and got covered over by the dense, jungle-like growth of our islands. In the following fifty plus years after the war, as residential development increased, gold bars began to turn up. Despite the fact that President Marcos had acquired some gold bars of his own, he forbade any citizens ownership of the so-called Yamashita gold. Under the threat of the law, many of the traders who possessed gold bars or had knowledge of their location made clandestine efforts to trade their contraband to European merchants. I was such a trader and found myself, yet again, in the hands of fate.

So it was that when the American sisters, Jacqueline Kennedy-Onassis and Princess Radziwill sent an agent to the Philippines to buy Yamashita gold, I found myself involved. I knew that because my various clients' claimed ownership of this gold, I had valuable connections. Armed with his verified, one-million-dollar bank account, this American agent agreed to meet with me to negotiate prices. For a full week, we fought to establish an acceptable commission split. Finally, we were able to peacefully settle terms, but it was without purpose. Contacting my clients left us empty handed. No gold was to be found. Even after I joined the buyer's team and we widened our search, we remained unsuccessful at locating any Yamashita gold among the alleged sellers.

Despite this frustrating scenario, something beautiful came of it all. That agent, the American man named David, finally found something worthy of his resources. It was me. We were married and he warmly welcomed my five children into his care. Before long, we found out we were expecting a sixth child. Nine months later, our son Louie was born. My husband is known to fondly say of this time, "I found gold in the Philippines." Sometimes the most valuable things can't be assigned a price tag.

When our son Louie was just about a year old, we decided to take him to the United States to meet his grandmother. In what was supposed to be a month-long trip, I learned that our family dynamic had changed. My American mother-in-law claimed me as her own child. She felt this new bond so strongly that me and my husband's labels shifted. She considered me her daughter and my husband, her true flesh-and-blood child, her son-in-law.

As time passed, Mom and I quickly became close, forming our bond over our mutual expertise and love for sewing, cooking, and storytelling. Then one day without warning, my mom suffered a stroke while sitting at the dinner table. Despite our best efforts, we couldn't contact her doctor. As the only person present at the time who had any medical knowledge, I burst into action. I used all my medical training to care for this beloved woman. When her doctor showed up the next day to perform an examination, he informed my husband that my intervention had saved her life. It was at that moment that we decided to stay in the United States until our mom fully recovered. It took a while, but when Mom finally started getting better, I ventured out into the workforce and landed a job in a coin laundry. It would have been a good job, but within the first few weeks, I uncovered some underhanded business—the manager had been stealing funds from the business' owner. I told my husband I needed to leave. I couldn't tolerate it any longer. Ever level-headed, my husband convinced me otherwise. Rather than closing the door on a perfectly good job, he suggested that we tell the owner what I had discovered. At first, the owner didn't believe our claims, but after a week of closely observing his manager, he was convinced. He fired his manager on grounds of theft and chose me to take his place.

A year passed and despite his increased earnings, the coin laundry owner decided to sell his business. The commute between that location, his other laundries, and his home had grown excessive. It wasn't worth it anymore. After a serious discussion, my husband and I decided to offer to buy the place. Quite generously, the owner gave us the business at no charge, we had only to complete the necessary paperwork. Under our ownership, the coin laundry became the biggest and most successful in our county. We eventually expanded our business by another three locations and by the time we sold it, we had virtually monopolized the industry—owning all but two of the coin laundries in our county.

In the midst of seeming success, rough times hit. In 2007 and 2008, the United States economy took a nosedive. It hammered our coin laundry business and under the mounting pressure of our family's financial duress, my husband experienced a devastating stroke that left half his body paralyzed. The doctors gave a grim prognosis. He was unlikely to recover. They believed the best course of action was to place David on home hospice until he died. Though I knew the situation was challenging, I wasn't about to give up so easily. When I consulted the doctors, they all agreed to let me treat him naturally. After all, he was my husband. Nothing could hurt him at that point. Determinedly, I set to work administering him treatment every morning and evening. Within ten days my care paid off and he was well again. His paralysis had left him, and David could walk without any evidence of the trauma his body had undergone. With his restoration to health, both he and my children prodded me towards finally furthering my pursuit of a medical career.

Letting myself be convinced, I returned to college and completed both a massage degree and a skin-care degree to get my associate's. Following that, I was accepted into a four-year postgraduate program at a school called the Atlantic Institute of Oriental Medicine. There I earned both a Bachelor of Science and Master of Herbology. After finally completing my masters, I studied acupuncture and earned the designation of Acupuncture Physician, or A.P.

When my American mom eventually passed away, my husband and I moved from the States back to the Philippines to care for my biological mother until she, too, had passed. We moved and finally settled in the town of Angono, Rizal where today, I have held the position of municipal Acupuncture Physician for three years. It's hard to say where fate might take me from here, but I find myself with no reason to worry. I am strong. I am determined. I am finally living out my purpose of helping the sick, needy, and helpless in my home country of the Philippines. Whatever circumstances may come my way, I know one thing—standing on the shoulders of my grandmother, my husband, my children, and my mothers, I will prevail. I am resilient.

"Pag may tiyaga, may nilaga."

"If you persevere, you will reap the fruits of your labor."

To learn more or connect with Dr. Flora Satinover, contact her via Facebook<u>Flora Satinover | Facebook</u>

So, what's your takeaway from Phoenix Flora's story?

#PhoenixesRising

Question: What kind of Phoenix do you want to be?

As we continue our journey of resilience around the world, our next stop will be China. Here we will meet another healer Dr. Dan Zhou. Her riveting story takes you behind the scenes of a culture that perhaps many of us do not understand. Here is an opportunity to learn about resilience through her eyes as she offers us a dose of resilient reality.

ON RESILIENCE

"Our greatest glory is not in never falling, but in rising every time we fall."
Confucius

Chapter 19

LIFE IS WHAT YOU MAKE IT
Dan Zhou, Ph.D.—The Resilient Healer

Dan Zhou is a healer and practitioner of Energy Medicine. She holds a Ph.D. in Computer Engineering from Syracuse University.

She volunteers her time with War Veterans suffering from PTSD, helping to restore their health and coming to terms with their trauma. This work not only helps these worthy souls, but has also helped her to continue her own healing.

ON RESILIENCE

"Health is wholeness and balance, an inner resilience that allows you to meet the demands of living without being overwhelmed."

Life Is What You Make It
Dan Zhou, Ph.D.—The Resilient Healer

***"As long as there is breath, there is life. Wherever
life exists, there is love."***
Dan Zhou, Ph.D.

To the Western world, China remains a mystery. Yet the resilience of one of the oldest civilizations in the world is steeped in ancient traditions, culture, discipline, and respect. Our understanding of spiritual laws, coupled with the ability to work with what we are given, fuels our drive to succeed regardless of our circumstance. For most of us, our resilience is cradled in the bosom of survival with a commitment to be the best at whatever we do. This is the culture into which I was born, and the foundation of who I am today. Hello, my name is Dan Zhou and this is my story of cultural resilience, born out of the will of the human spirit to first survive, and then thrive.

I was born in the middle of the Cultural Revolution in Zhou Village just outside Wuhan. Led by Chairman Mao Zedong, the Cultural Revolution was geared to replace capitalism with communism and to establish the People's Republic of China under a collectivist regime. My sister who was two years older than me, and I, were born to parents who were on the wrong side of the cultural revolution.

During the revolution, intellectuals like my father were considered enemies of the state. Hence, he endured persecution, detention, and was eventually incarcerated for his free thinking and writing. I must have been around eighteen months at the time of my dad's imprisonment. So, I grew up not knowing him. I did not really know that I had a father until I was about twelve or thirteen years of age.

With my dad in prison and with little certainty that he would make it out alive, we lost the primary source of our family income. Influenced by my mother's culture, I adopted whatever values and mores that she cultivated. After my dad's incarceration, we moved to the village where she grew up. My mother did not have much of an education, but she was hardworking and provided the best that she could for my older sister and I. Her main goal was to keep us alive; partly because there was little food to eat – one bowl of sparse rice porridge was all there was for the three of us to last an entire day, and partly because she had witnessed her grandmother starve to death at the age of eighty during the great famine in China.

The Great Famine was a man-made famine caused by Chairman Mao's attempt to move China from an agrarian to a communist society. This movement known as The Great Leap Forward was fraught with mistakes. These egregious errors caused the greatest famine of all times which lasted for three years. It is said to have caused the deaths of tens of millions of Chinese people, including my great grandmother.

Growing up with my mother was difficult to say the least. As a child she had chicken pox which left her face disfigured. Therefore, she lived with a lot of shame and the belief that she was not worth being alive. I am sure of the fact that the incarceration of her husband for being an enemy of the state also, did not help her self-perception, and caused further embarrassment, even though deep in her heart she believed in his innocence. Compounding my mother's estranged psyche was her perception of her parents. Her father loved her dearly. However, not only did her mother not like her, she was also beaten up regularly. These perceptions of her parents coupled with her disfigurement, and fall from grace led my mother to instill the practice of perfectionism in her children. Mother did whatever she could to make sure that her girls were perfect in everything. She felt that being perfect was how we earned the right to be here on this earth. Hence, my upbringing under my mother was quite challenging. There was no room for spontaneity or to be a child.

For her, survival was of utmost importance, so everything else became secondary. Looking back, I could see that her perfectionism and strong commitment to survive, kept my sister and I alive at a time when life itself was tenuous. I grew up with no running water, public toilets, or electricity as Mom's village had none of those amenities.

We relied on rain water for cooking and cleaning. I was about four or five when I, along with my sister and other children, started working in the rice fields. If we did not work, we did not eat. After the adults collected the bundles of rice, the children would pick up the leftovers because the adults always missed something. Whatever we collected, we turned in and weighed. There was no money involved for your work. Instead we got paid in rice portions based on our labor. We earned extra rice by the work we did and those portions had to last for a month or longer. Other than rice, I helped pick cotton, harvest sweet potatoes, water chestnuts and peanuts.

One of my other duties was to run after the cows that were plowing in the sweet potato or water chestnut fields. We got to keep the remaining sweet potatoes and water chestnuts after everything was collected by the adults. As children, although we worked long hours, we accepted that this was just the way life was.

Working in the fields gave me the grounding I needed to counteract the harsh reality of the daily doses of perfectionism administered by my mother. In hindsight these were all lessons of resilience taught to me by her, the land, and nature. Please keep in mind that my country was still in the throes of Communism, civil wars and destruction of the Chinese Bourgeoisie. Chairman Mao believed in the duality of love and struggle, and building his classless society.

"Love because it is love for the people which is integral to Mao's vision. In China, love is closely connected with the term unity for when combined with the decision to serve the people, love takes a

dynamic position. Struggle because society is marked by continual class struggle, which is reflected in each individual's thought. It is struggle that moves toward the final goal of love and unity — the classless society."
Alan S. Cajes, Whom Do I Serve

In a village filled with love and struggle, we survived. There was obviously a lot of hard work, but we survived. That was just the way it was. Ancient Chinese culture was built on harmony and balance. Mother Earth provided that for me. The earth provided the mud and blocks that built our houses.

The land fed and nurtured us; and as children we were free to roam that land dotted with rice fields and lotus ponds. The well and rain gave us the water necessary for cooking. Baths were a luxury that we looked forward to with great anticipation. If you don't know another way of life, then this is your norm for which you are profoundly grateful. You learned that even in the space of turmoil and hardship, you can find freedom in nature.

Another lesson was not to take anything for granted, because each day that you survive was a good day. So, what one might view as a life of hardship involving child labor, I saw as an opportunity to be one with nature which gave me the peace that I sought to deal with a life of perfectionistic bondage.

When I was not working in the fields or around the house, I went to school which was near our home. My school was situated between two villages, which was called a Team, that were side by side in proximity. It served many villages near and far. I left for school very early in the morning. After two sessions. I would come home for breakfast, and then return to school. So that was my mother's village, where I spent my first school semester.

I only spent a few years in her village. One day we received news that my grandfather was retiring from his job in the city and that there would be a position available. I was six years old when my mother left us behind with our grandparents and moved to the city to take grandfather's place at his company. Subsequently, he moved back to the country to help my grandmother raise us. Back then the policy of the country was that you couldn't move around easily. So there was no freedom to move from a village to a city, or from one city to another city. This is how the government kept control of its population migration. The only way that you could move from the land to the city was to replace a parent, or to be united with your spouse. Furthermore, to replace your parents, you had to be single, as the policy was that only single children could swap places with their parents.

My mother was divorced with two children. Without telling anyone that she had children, she entered the workforce in the city. I think that they actually knew that she had children, but in her mind they didn't know, and thought that she was single. This was where life got complicated for me in ways that you could never imagine. I had learned how to be resilient as a young farmer. However, the resilience training that I was about to receive as a six-year-old child exceeded human logic.

For reasons unbeknownst to me, my mother and grandparents decided that they would keep my older sister but not me. At age six, my mother took me to visit my father's sister and her husband. Well, my mother just took me there and left. I think that she actually sold or bartered me to those people. I didn't really know them, I may have met them once or twice before. A common denominator was that my aunt and uncle were farmers like me. Just for the sake of reference, the villages were not close so I was isolated there with my father's sister, her husband and their six daughters. What should have been a happy, welcoming time and a family reunion of sorts, turned out to be the worst nightmare, and an interesting life lesson that took my resilience to a completely different level.

My aunt was a cold, strict, disciplinarian who never smiled. In hindsight, I could see where raising six daughters and adopting a seventh might not be much to smile about. As the seventh and youngest child I became the Cinderella of the family. I was also the youngest pig farmer in the village. Trading in vegetables for pigs, my job in the family was not only to take care of the pigs but also to be the maid of the family. At six years of age, I became an indentured servant to my aunt's family. I learned to look after everyone, see what they needed, and volunteered to meet those needs. This included cleaning, emptying urinals, errand running and other duties too numerous to mention.

My oldest cousin had been married off but my second oldest cousin never got along with anyone. Ironically I got along well with her. She was sickly and had to take Chinese medicine. I would go to the field to collect the lotus flowers' stems and leaves for her. I did not know then but I later discovered that the leaves of the Lotus were used for improving liver functions, relieving headaches, nosebleeds, coughs and fatigue. The stem of the Lotus was a medicinal remedy for uterine bleeding, heart and kidney disease. I had no idea which of these ailments my cousin had. All I knew was that my job was to collect the Lotus leaves and stems, and to bring them back for her to burn and heat up for her medicine. That was what I did for her.

When I wasn't taking care of my oldest cousin, I fed the pigs to relieve my youngest cousin of that duty. When my aunt and uncle came back home after a day of working in the field, I would fan them to sleep with a handheld fan at night to keep them comfortable … Again, I was only 6 years old.

Similar to my mother's village, my aunt's village was also void of electricity, running water and modern amenities. There was a well on the property from which we got our water for cooking. One of the first lessons I learned from my youngest cousin was how to fetch water from the well. Of course the water supply came from the rain. Hence, if there was no rain, there was no water. I remember going with her to learn how to fetch water from the well that was a deep, round hole in the ground about one meter in diameter. To fetch water you had to tie a rope to a bucket and throw the bucket into the darkness, hoping it would catch water. For me that took many, many tries before the bucket eventually caught some water. And then you had to bring the bucket up from the well and back home without spilling too much of its contents. Please remember that I was still only six years old.

Speaking of holes in the ground, to be clear, the public restrooms were just three to four holes in the ground encased by stone and mud walls for privacy. Going to the bathroom in the middle of the night was a harrowing and very scary experience. The outhouse was in the back of the village. Picture it being pitch black at night and you have to poo. You wake up and have to make your way in the dark and past the barking dogs just to reach the outhouse. Gosh, there were so many dogs, all barking at the same time. So here you are running and trying to make it to the outhouse (to poo), and the dogs are barking, and you really can't see where you are going, and more dogs start barking. It is any wonder that I made it there without soiling myself. I was always super scared the dogs would get me. As if my nightly trek to the bathroom was not scary enough, I had to return home in the dark, tend to the family, feed the pigs, and get ready for school.

The school in my aunt's village was very far away. My cousin and I, along with other children, left the village way before the sun came up. We would walk with the stars for miles and miles to reach our destination. This school was much poorer than the one in my mother's village so we had to bring our own little stools to sit. We could only have class for half a day because another group of kids would come in the afternoon to use the same classroom. I remember thinking,

"Wow! This is different!,"

but so was everything else in my aunt and uncle's village. I spent one very long semester with my aunt, uncle and their daughters. This was my life as a six-year-old – a very young life driven by an internal mechanism of survival and learned resilience. I learned that just as the mind is resilient, so is the body.

February brought the Chinese New Year. My aunt and I walked an entire day to my mother's village. I walked her to her oldest daughter's house which was at the far end of the village before returning to my Mother's house, to be with my grandparents, my older sister, and Mom who returned to the village for the holiday. I remember my mother repeatedly telling me the same story. The story goes that at my grandparents' house, I got up earlier than anyone in the household, swept the house, and emptied the urinals. I also cleaned everything before the family woke up to my morning greeting. Horrified, my grandfather looked at me as the gravity as to what I had been dealing with at my aunt's house sunk in. This is when he said to my mother,

"She's not going back there, she's too young to be doing this."

"She's too young to even know how to do these things."

That day, my grandpa stood up for me. This changed the trajectory of my life as shortly after that, and at the age of seven, my sister and I moved with my mom to the city. They say that sometimes you don't really appreciate what you have until you lose it. This was how it was when we moved to the city.

The city was a culture shock for me. Living in the country, no matter how difficult life was, the one comfort that I could count on was earth and nature. Whether it was the land, rain, a humble home or friends made along the way, these were the simple things of life that made living in the country special. When we moved to the city, my connection with nature and friends was lost in a hostile environment that did not support our wellbeing. Looking back, I found it ironic that while my father was still imprisoned for being an enemy of the state, my mother found a bizarre sense of freedom working in a state-owned company, which was called a Unit.

I have to say that living in the city was more of a shock than going to live with my aunt. We traded our humble country home to live in a large room with thirty to forty other state employees and their families. There was no privacy. There was nothing -- no furniture, no dividers, just a big open room packed with people and beds. At least in the country our home had bedrooms. There was however, a public toilet down the hallway, still holes in the ground, but now with walls and doors.

Living in the city brought other challenges. In the country, the name of the game for us was physical and emotional survival. In the city, we dealt with surviving the stigma of social hierarchy and class structure. My sister and I were beaten up and bullied by Communist sympathizers as we were at the tail end of the cultural revolution. My mother, being the wife of a social outcast and uneducated, found herself ashamed and at the bottom of the hierarchy chain. Although I was educated, because she was my mother, and not, I was lumped into the same category as her. So as a victim of layers of my mother's shame – first with the chicken pox and then being uneducated, life was tough for all of us. Yet through it all, we stayed resilient as we adapted to each adversity life threw us.

I don't remember how long we lived in that one room with thirty to forty people. As the tentacles of Communism dug deeper into the Chinese psyche, all private companies became state owned companies. Gradually, I suppose as my Mom exhibited good behavior we moved from that horrible environment to a room shared simply with another family, a mother and a son of my age. Working for the state gave you no, or very little freedom.

We moved from one room to another, one apartment to another, all assigned by my mother's Unit. One of her jobs was distributing supplies to the people as well as keeping her company's supply inventory.When it came to food, unlike in the country where you lived off the land, we purchased food via a coupon system. If you were a resident of a city, you got a coupon for how much rice you could buy from the rice shop. Your coupons were not transferable from city to city. This was another way the government kept control of the populace.

From my negative experiences in the city, I became self-sufficient. I never expected that my life at my aunt and uncle's home in the village would prepare me to be mentally strong and independent. I was doing really well in school. People all said I was smart. I guess from that perspective I was, but nobody knew how hard I worked to achieve what I have achieved. There were subjects that were easy, like math. I also studied a lot, particularly those subjects that were not easy. For example, political science did not come naturally to me. So I actually used the brutal force method. I would recite the whole textbook over, and over again, until I memorized its contents. I think that's one of the nuances that people don't understand about Chinese culture. People might think that we are automatically brilliant. However, as a culture, we are willing to work extremely hard to achieve our goals. This is the collective consciousness of our culture fueled by the spirit of resilience.

As far back as my mother could remember, I was always the one person, the youngest one in the household, who got up earlier than anyone and studied. At a really young age, I made a vow to myself that I was going to do really well in school to make my mother proud, and that was the only thing I was going to give her.

I would say that my relationship with my mother was complicated. I am sure that I am not the only one who has a complicated mother-daughter relationship. Perhaps it was the unresolved anger of being abandoned at such an early age, coupled with being uprooted and disconnected from nature. I have suffered two major traumas in my life other than living in the city with my mother. The first was living with my aunt and uncle in their village that I previously discussed. The second was going to visit my father in prison.

If you recall, my father was imprisoned when I was just eighteen months old. Nobody ever talked about him to us. It was as if he never existed. The final insult was when my mother took me to visit him in prison. I believe that she went regularly but I was probably eight or nine years old when we made the day-long journey across the river in a boat to the other side. As we entered the prison's barbed-wire gates, and guards ready to discharge their weapons at a moment's notice, I experienced fear and numbness simultaneously. I briefly wondered how anyone could survive prison life in China, which I've been told was more like a concentration camp than anything else.

I remember how I felt when I saw my father. So thin he was, wearing an old stained, sweaty T-shirt which bared his shoulders, with a towel draping over one side of his body. I was disgusted. I felt so ashamed at the scene before me. This prisoner, with his bald, shaven, head and looking emaciated, was my father. Yet, through his gaunt face was a man who despite his circumstances, beheld me with love, grace and beauty in his eyes. As his daughter, whom he had not seen in eight years, that was quite a traumatic experience for me to see him in that light. I really despised seeing him disheveled like that. I couldn't even process that this was my father. As in the movies, the reality that he was one of the bad guys was overwhelming. From that experience, I got what was good and what was bad from a judgment perspective. This was a visit where I went to support my mother after my sister refused to go. I never visited my father in prison, nor in labor camp again.

After that, the tension between my mother and I reached unbearable proportions. From her perspective, I was the one who really understood everything, probably because of my experience with my aunt and uncle. Hence, I was her favorite daughter, as if one should say such a thing. In contrast, from my perspective, I hated every moment of my life and just wanted to get away. What my mother did not know, and what I could never tell her, was that I loathed my life and was just biding my time. I would have hated myself even more had I brought that up because she would not take any of that. Education became my ticket out of my personal jail.

In 1977, colleges and universities opened their doors after their twelve-year closure by Chairman Mao. If you recall, under Mao's model of a classless society, his ban of intellectualism and intellectuals like my father resulted in severe punishment. Many committed suicide. Yet here we were making history as the doors of higher education swung open, allowing me to be one of the first generation of partakers of a higher education degree at one of the top universities in China. Beginning in the 1980s, and thanks to Deng Xiaoping, China opened its gates to the West. Exchange students and scholars went to the United States to study at the top universities in America.

Only the people in the very top universities in China had any inkling of that. So you learned how to pursue and secure your freedom from your upperclassmen who learned it from someone else. When I was in my final year of university, many of my classmates were applying for scholarships to go to graduate school in the United States. After taking the TOEFL and GRE exams, I also applied and received a year-long fellowship to Syracuse University to study Solid State Science and Technology. This was an interdisciplinary area of study inside the College of Engineering. We took classes in chemistry, chemical engineering , physics and material science and engineering. A degree or study in these areas would prepare you for a career in Silicon Valley.

It wasn't straightforward to come to the States even after Syracuse University offered me fellowship, which was after the Chinese

Student Movement. After graduation I went back to Wuhan to work in a factory, not knowing if I could get the right papers to come to the States. My mother and I formed a team of resilience and we prevailed!

As great as I was academically, I was not great at managing the loneliness that came by being in America. The isolation from my culture, land, food, language and friends took its toll. In graduate school I met and married a fellow Chinese student, but the marriage was short-lived, probably because I really did not know how to have and sustain a relationship.

After graduate school I moved to Florida and joined the faculty of Department of Computer Science and Engineering in Florida Atlantic University, a state university. I had a wonderful time as a tenure-track, Computer Engineering Professor: interesting research, great colleagues, fulfilling career in teaching and guiding undergraduate and graduate students, in addition to the outstanding benefits offered by the state university system.

Have you ever woken up to realize that something is not quite right? This is exactly what happened to me after three years as a faculty member at the university. Having gone through so much, I had never taken the time to process all of the trauma experienced over the thirty years of my life. From the farm to both villages, then the city, followed by a new culture, each situation required me to be resilient. What I didn't realize was that resilience had a price tag.

Three years into teaching at the university, 9/11 happened. The ensuing large-scale turmoil and the emotional reaction of an entire society, reminded me of the trauma I had endured as a child in the midst of an unstable country. I was born when that society was most unstable. That instability caused the emotional death of my father and forced my family to make decisions that they might not have made under "normal" circumstances. When you are emotionally injured in the process, you don't really know the pain because your brain handles the trauma in the moment. It becomes problematic when you recover and your nervous system registers the pain of what you endured in a way that is raw and unbearable.

During my period of the dark night of the soul, what kept me resilient was hope. I never lost hope. I always had hope. Not the hope in the sense that I was hopeful, but the hope that one day the suffering would end. When I gave up hoping I was actually met with peace and serenity. So, I kept looking, kept seeking and everything I said to you so far, I would not consider it challenging. It was just honoring what had to be done at the moment in order to survive.

September 11, 911, jolted me and woke me up to examining the deeper meanings of life. I left the university and gave up everything to find enlightenment and peace in a Buddhist Monastery, training to become a nun. That path wasn't the answer, so I then went on to study with world-renowned Buddhist Masters, Thich Nhat Hanh and Master Sheng-Yen, on loving kindness, compassion, wisdom and mediation; I also studied with shamans from Andes and Himalayas on the esoteric teachings of antiquity, on the inner works of the mind, and the energies, in and around us.

There have been many other profound moments and epiphanies in my life that have all been part of my resilient journey. These periods of enlightenment caused me to return to my earlier days on the land where I pulled the energy from nature to find peace and to heal the wounds within. Joining a monastery provided me with the internal solitude, reflection and energy source I so desperately needed. As I began to heal, this shift in my focus opened the door to my becoming an energy healer for others.

For a number of years I lived close to the land and nature, before returning to be a part of modern society. With renewed confidence in myself and a combined sense of power and inner peace, I re-entered the modern world, taking on management and leadership positions in the IT field and personal development; I trained with master coaches and healers on how to work with body's energies to create joy, love, vitality, and performance.

What's the source of my resilience? You asked. I believe life itself is resilient. Human beings are created to be resilient. One only needs to look at what my father went through in his lifetime and how he bore his fate with such grace, love and beauty. Being nurtured by the land itself gave me extra strength. The strong bones that I inherited from my parents enabled me to be resilient.

Yes it took me years to find my way to love and joy, the resilience at the highest level. Along my spiritual journey and engineering training I acquired a vast amount of tools and practices to maintain and build resilience at physical, emotional, mental and spiritual levels. I have founded two businesses and a non-profit to support people with resilience and to take it to the next level.

My volunteer work supports war veterans to transform their emotional trauma from the war. My healing practice helps people with chronic health conditions to get their lives back on track. My newest venture, "Master Your Competitive Edge", supports entrepreneurs to create peak performance by optimizing energy, focus and mindset.

As I reflect again on my life, I think of the land and Mother Earth that gave me my foundation of resilience. This foundation helped me to deal with the hardships experienced while living with my aunt, uncle, and my mother, and the many challenges that life had in store for me. Through my own spiritual and healing journey, I have learned not only to keep going, but also take time out to appreciate the simple things of life.

Just as I did on the farm in my mother's village, I see love, beauty, and grace in everything. I even remarried and am continuing developing my capacity to love, transform, and contribute to the world. I have long shifted from surviving to thriving and it feels amazing to be of service to others. I have also come full circle as I now appreciate the courage, bravery and sacrifice made by my parents for love and freedom. Their sacrifice and love in part opened the door for me to live freely in the United States and to start my spiritual journey. Farmer, daughter, physicist, engineer, writer, healer, leader, and wife, my name is Dan Zhou and I am resilient.

"Life persists. Kindness persists. Inside incredibly trying circumstances, the human spirit still sings."
To learn more about Dr. Dan Zhou contact:
RadiantHealthAndWellbeing.comfb.me/RadiantHealthAndWellBeing333

So, what's your takeaway from Phoenix Dr. Dan's story?

#PhoenixesRising

https://bit.ly/phoenixesrising

Question: What kind of Phoenix do you want to be?

Dr. Dan Zhou's story gave you an inside glimpse not only of her individual resilience, but of an ancient culture whose DNA is resilient. As we leave China and continue our resilient journey, we head back to the Caribbean to visit with Poetess Tia Liburd, our spiritually gifted graphic artist, and our book's cover designer from the St. Thomas, Virgin Islands, shares her I AM Poem of resilience. Shall we see what keeps her resilient?

ON RESILIENCE

"I can do all things through Christ who strengthens me." Philippians 4:13

I AM POEM
Tia Liburd, St. Thomas, U.S. Virgin Islands

I AM FROM the steep mountains in the green hills of the U.S. Virgin Islands where the rooster crows every morning.

I AM FROM the sweet smell of cream of wheat my mom makes in the morning.

I AM FROM the island of St. Thomas where everyone greets each other by their unique dialect "Mawnin," "You ahright?" or "Wah you sayin?" depending on who you meet.

I AM FROM the Serrano, Rabsatt, George, Elskoe, James, and Freeman family from the British Virgin Islands to Culebra and throughout the Caribbean.

I AM Tia Serrano-Liburd

As a graphic artist, Tia Serrano-Liburd has always appreciated simplifying complicated issues into elegant, aesthetically pleasing, and straightforward designs. You can find me cooking, spending time with family, or spending time with the love of my life, God, when I'm not pushing pixels. Tia is The Art of Resilience: Phoenixes Rising as she especially created the cover design for this Phoenix anthology. To learn more contact Tia at: Empire Graphic Designs | home.

So, what's your takeaway from Poetess Tia's story?

#PhoenixesRising

https://bit.ly/phoenixesrising

We say goodbye to Tia in the U.S. Virgin Islands and set sail back to Barbados where I—Dr. Joy am waiting for you. As we come to the end of our resilient journey, I wanted to share on a topic that is near and dear to my heart. When we began our resilient journey around the world, I began by sharing my story of resilience. One never knows when or how you can be resilient. All one knows is that you must be willing to pick yourself up from the ground and carry on. As any of the Phoenixes will tell you, picking yourself up from your adversity is easier said than done. I dedicate this story particularly to any parent who has lost a child, or anyone who has suffered a loss.

Be encouraged as I share my very personal journey, in one of the hardest chapters of this book for me to write. Stay encouraged. You can and will get through your loss, and like all of us Phoenixes, you will rise again!

Chapter 20

FINDING GOD IN THE MIDDLE OF YOUR STORMS
Dr. Joy Vaughan

**"Weeping may come in the night but joy comes
in the MOURNING."**
Adapted from Psalm 30:5

In life we mourn many things—the loss of our first pet, first love, job loss, spouse, best friend and even the loss of our innocence. However, it has been said that no parent should have to mourn the death of their child. Children should not die before their parents. Yet on August 18th 2021, at approximately 6:30 pm, that is exactly what happened when my son Eric Hilton Vaughan Brown (AKA Professor Biz) transitioned to his heavenly home. He was my only son and child but, at 35, he had lived a full life, accomplished more than most people, gave us two beautiful heirs, and left a legacy. There is joy in that, and much to celebrate.

However, facing the devastating loss of my son, I asked myself: how was I supposed to bounce back after losing my only child? How was I going to ride the emotional rollercoaster that ensues after losing someone with whom you have shared a 35-year-old relationship and lifetime?

Could I now practice and be a demonstration of the very concepts of my Reinvention, Resilience and Sustainability curriculum? After I saw my son for the last time, and thanked him for the honor and privilege to be his mother for 35 years, these were the questions that ran through my mind.

If you ask people who know me well, they will tell you that my son and I were very close. He was equally close to his dad. Together he made co-parenting a dream. You just can't stay angry with each other when you have a great kid who loves you both, unconditionally. We laughed together, fought at times together, and coached each other. Even before his birth, I clearly understood that he and I were two souls whom God united to travel this journey of life, for as long as we could.

Two of the biggest lessons I have learned through this whole process, is that first, we are all souls put on this planet for a specific reason and purpose. The second lesson is that every soul has a shelf life. Hence never take people in your life for granted, and always tell them how much you love them, because tomorrow is not promised.

What helped me to be resilient in life, and particularly after Rick's passing, were three things. First, my faith and profound relationship to the spirit world. I am not religious but consider myself spiritual. There is a big difference between the two. I like to think that religion is ritualistic. Spirituality is all about relationship – Spirit to spirit. Being spiritual helps me to see the unseen, and to hear the unspoken. This helps me to understand my clients through different eyes, for the sole purpose of being able to help mitigate their traumas, and to be a mutual blessing. Life is about giving and taking, sowing and reaping, and learning how to say thank you for the good, bad and ugly. Trust that every experience is a life lesson that is designed for your good. Also, practicing humility is a game changer.

The second is the example and legacy blueprint that my parents and ancestors left for me and their heirs to follow. The key is to follow the blueprint because it works if you work it. I tell my clients,

> *"Just follow the yellow brick road. If you get off the road, then just get back on and keep it moving."*

I live a reinvented and resilient life that is sustained by my faith, family and friends. The life that I have created with the help of my

Heavenly Father is what I share with my clients. I cannot coach or teach what I don't know or have not experienced. I have experienced probably more than any one person should have in their lifetime. Yet every valley, hell-hole, demonic force, and mountain top strengthens me to be a highly effective coach and counselor to my clients, and the people in my life. I follow my mother's and aunt's wise wisdom to :

"Plan my life in decades and to reinvent myself every five years."

When my son passed, people were concerned. They asked,

"Has she broken down yet? How does she stay so strong?"

Or

"Dr Joy is a strong woman. She's got this!"

To that last comment, the answer would be yes, and no. I have my meltdowns, and puddle moments. I miss Rick terribly. What mother wouldn't miss her son? However, when I am flowing in the spirit and being of service to others, I am not paralyzed by my grief. It is in those moments that I personally stand on my faith and these three scriptures

TRUST

"Trust in the Lord with all your heart and lean not on your own understanding;6 in all your ways submit to him, and he will direct your paths"
Proverbs 3:5-6 KJV

WISDOM

*"Get wisdom! Get understanding! Do not forget,
nor turn away from the words of my mouth.[6] Do not
forsake her, and she will preserve you;Love her, and
she will keep you.[7] Wisdom is the principal thing;
Therefore get wisdom. And in all your getting,
get understanding.[8] Exalt her, and she will
promote you;She will bring you honor,
when you embrace her."*
Proverbs 4: 5-9 NKJV

GRATITUDE

*"[18]In everything give thanks; for this is the will of
God in Christ Jesus for you."*
1 Thessalonians 5:18

These three scriptures, choosing to focus on the good and pleasant memories that my son and I shared, and supporting my daughter-in-law and grandkids helps me to honor the legacy of Rick. I am pretty sure this is what he wanted. So joy really does come in the *mourning*.

Parents, if you are reading this please understand that our children do not belong to us. They are precious gifts that we have been given to nurture, raise and protect. Our children are also here to teach us life lessons. How many times in my Co-parenting classes have I heard "my child is an old soul - wise beyond his/her years." Our job is to help our children navigate the waters of life so that they can fulfill what they have come to do.

I am so proud of how my Co-parent and I were able to put our differences aside and support our son. Before Rick was born, we made a commitment that despite our differences, we would give him everything he needed to be successful in life. In my Co-parenting classes, I teach my clients how to get rid of their acrimony and to focus on their child/ren. Many miracles and healing occur in our sessions, as what was not possible in Session 1, becomes possible by the end of 10-week class.

If you are a parent who has lost a child, or anyone who has lost a loved one, here are 8 tips that helped me get through the loss of my son.

1. Don't be ashamed to grieve even months or years after your loved one's passing. Elizabeth Kubler Ross (On Death and Dying) shares that you will go through the following stages – Shock, Denial, Guilt, Anger, Bargaining Depression, Hope, and Acceptance. There is no set time-frame on the grieving process, and you may be in several stages simultaneously.
2. Give yourself permission to be angry at your relative for transitioning, and even at God. God understands.
3. Purchase a journal that is dedicated to recording your thoughts and feelings about your loved one. In this journal forgive your loved one for transitioning before you.
4. Manage your family and friends. Death can bring about strange and unexpected behaviors from even your closest relatives, distant relatives, friends, or acquaintances. This can be particularly so, if money and no will is involved.
5. Gather your family and friends (particularly the children if any) and have a release ceremony (e.g., release balloons into the air or flower petals on the water). Let your friends know that you will need them for the long-haul.
6. Don't succumb to other people's expectations that you should be "over it by now."

7. Hire an experienced Grief Counselor and/or Therapist and join a grief group to help you to process your feelings about your loved one dying, and the permanency of it all.

8. Finally, ask yourself each day 2 questions – "How would my loved one want me to carry on without them?" and, "What can I do today to honor their memory?"

I coach Executive women, Entrepreneurs, and Veterans who are experiencing difficulty in their lives. The above three groups of people were revealed after asking God whom He wanted me to serve. Whether it be a divorce, job loss, life or business challenges, I and my team coach/counsel and show them how to reinvent themselves, be resilient, and to sustain their resilience over time. I/we work in both the secular and faith-based markets. God has blessed the work of my/our hands, so I have recruited other like-minded professionals to assist me in serving our amazing clients. The result is that persons who work with us, if they want to, get free and stay free from a lifetime of unknown psychological shackles. You see, I live by this motto,

"Heaven is my home, I just work here on earth."

My friends, Resilience is a life-long journey built on the foundation of knowing your purpose, and being passionate, and unstoppable regarding fulfilling that purpose. However, I realized, as my son would say in his 'Biz-like' fashion,

"Nah! Mom, not everybody be rolling like that."

Rick (Biz) meant that not everyone has that mindset. I also had to accept that not everyone wants to reinvent themselves, far less be resilient. It takes a willingness to find a purpose that is greater than you. It takes picking yourself up from the dusty tarmac after being knocked down time and time again. It takes grit, fortitude and the conviction that you are going to make it. Readers, at the end of the day, it is all about your legacy. You are born and at some point you will transition this life. What do you want others to say about your life? It is a question that I was asked many years ago by one of my mentors. My answer is, and always will be, that

> ***"The purpose of my life is to live complete,***
> ***by leaving a legacy of freedom, joy, and***
> ***peace of mind to all those that I have had the***
> ***honor to touch within my lifetime."***

Fulfilling this purpose is what I am most passionate about. My name is Dr. Joy Vaughan; Mother, friend, author, coach/counselor, and influential adventurer, and I am RESILIENT. YEAHHHH!

So, what's your takeaway from Dr. Joy's

Finding God in the Middle of Your Storms?

#PhoenixesRising
Share your thoughts in our FB Group

https://bit.ly/phoenixesrising

Question: What kind of Phoenix do you want to be?

I hope that you have enjoyed reading our Phoenixes stories and poems. This anthology is a testimony to the fact that as human beings, we are built to be resilient. However, there are so many factors that comprise a resilient mindset; your culture, life experiences, belief system, and ability to pivot are all part of one's resilient DNA. Resilience, like reinvention, can be taught to persons who are willing to do the deep work to achieve their resilience goals.

We would be remiss if we didn't leave you with a parting gift to start you on your resilient journey. Throughout this anthology the focus has been Resilience. Our Phoenixes have mastered the art of resilience. In other words, they have discovered their purpose, passion, and have been able to pull from within, to rise from their ashes, and to achieve their goals. Consider that a major cornerstone of resilience is Self-awareness. Self-awareness opens the door to "AH HAH!" moments which enable you to access your resilience. Join Colleen Dupont and myself as we take you through a self-awareness exercise. See if this can be your gateway to finding your Resilience path.

Disclaimer: This is an exercise, not an invitation to diagnose or fix anyone.

FINDING RESILIENCE THROUGH SELF AWARENESS
Colleen Dupont and Dr. Joy Vaughan

When I think of resilience, I also think of survival. After all, we survive the challenges we overcome; and the link between survival and resilience is self-awareness.

Without a doubt, there is a relationship between how well we know ourselves, and how well we can respond in difficult situations; how vulnerable we feel in the face of threats, and how prepared we feel when we get confronted. Whether the threats are physical, emotional, or psychological, we are not powerless against them.

We have the strength we need. And we can learn to call on that strength in times of *difficulty; or, to avoid needing to use it at all.

Two questions come to mind in regard to our resilience, also known as our ability to adapt to and overcome adversity. Number one, who am I? And number two, how is this game played? With a depth of self-awareness, we can make those questions personal and more powerful by asking how do "I choose" to play the game?" And that is an important distinction.

- How do I fit into this situation? This relationship? This environment? This world?
- What is my role? What are my expectations? What do I need? Are my needs being met?
- What does the situation or relationship call for? What am I committed to? What do I care about?

In living a lifestyle of purposeful awareness, the answers to these questions begin to come automatically. Socrates said: "… the unexamined life is not worth living." I don't know about worth, but I believe the unexamined life is more difficult and has more drama.

People are seeing the value of self-awareness, more and more. In 2019, Americans spent over $13.2 BILLION on self-improvement. Bettering our quality of life. But who is the SELF we seek to improve? Who is the SELF we want to be aware of? The SELF we lost touch with?

I (Colleen Dupont) propose that there are three phases of self-awareness: Original Awareness, Adjusted Awareness and Realigned Awareness. Original Awareness, being how we discover our SELF newly in this world in youth; Adjusted Awareness being how we adapt or compensate our SELF to fit into the world around us; and Realigned Awareness being how we bring the best of who we ARE, together with who we BECAME, to play the game of life in which we happen to be born into.

If you are in a conversation of resilience, you are in the third phase, the kind of awareness that is used to align the first two. So, let's look at these phases in a way that gives you tools to boost your resilience.

Original Awareness is just that, original. It's who we come to know ourselves as, from the time we are born. When we begin to see ourselves separate from our mothers. We learn that there is a me and a you. And as a witness to our own existence, we compare ourselves to those around us, seeking similarities and differences.

Without thinking we do that in Core Identity areas.

1. Physical: People who look/don't look like me
2. Material: People who have/don't have what I have
3. Behavioral: People who do/don't do as I do
4. Spiritual: People who believe/don't believe what I believe
5. Emotional: People who feel/don't feel how I feel
6. Mental: People who think/don't think as I think
7. Intellectual: People who know/don't know what I know

It is in these areas where we either recognize ourselves or not. Where the natural values and the personality with which we are born, are tested. And it is in these areas where we gauge and adjust who we know ourselves to be, based on whether our non-physical needs are met.

That brings us to the Adjusted Awareness phase. This is where we live for most of our lives. It is where we play out our survival style. The skills and workarounds we develop when life teaches that there is something wrong about who we are. Where we hide our flaws, or compensate for them in other ways to survive the game of life.

Consider the following non-physical needs:

1. Trust: A reason to hope and believe that things will be fair and that in my life will work out okay;

2. Expression: The freedom and confidence to share myself with others authentically and unapologetically;

3. Worth: The sense that I have something of value to offer others;

4. Creation: The sense that I can be at the source of something (particularly something of beauty or value);

5. Validation: The assurance that I am okay and understood (relationship, community, etc.);

6. Explanations/Understanding: A way to make sense of the things around us, particularly;

7. Self-Rule: The knowing that you oversee your own life, your opportunities, and outcomes;

When these needs aren't met, we compromise and compensate. Apologize and justify. We negotiate with ourselves and others to minimize the damage to our identities. And those negotiations happen in the core Identity areas.

Go back and read them again. Ask yourself to what degree do I have these in my life? In my relationships? In your career or parenting? And, these are not either/or things. Not like an off/on switch. They happen on a sliding scale between abundance and lack. Based on the degree to which they are met, and address and correct them in our core identity areas.

For instance, I learned that there was something wrong with me when my baby sister was born. I wasn't enough so they had to "get another one". Now, it doesn't matter that that statement wasn't true. It only matters that I believed it was.

So, what happened to my non-physical needs when I formed that thought? I no longer felt that I belonged and withdrew my connection to my family. I didn't understand what I did wrong or why having me didn't satisfy them. I lost the trust that my life would turn out okay. I was disposable and replaceable. I was misunderstood. Undervalued. I didn't feel safe to express myself. And, I had nothing to offer. Pretty dramatic, huh.

What I did with that self-imposed attack on my identity was devise a work around to restore my sense of security. And that happens automatically. My version was "If you don't want me, I'll make sure that you need me".

In my Original Awareness I learned that my Mental Identity is strong. I am naturally logical and look for patterns. And so, I used that strength to create value for myself. My Adjusted Identity had me shift quickly from the helpless role of child to one of helper. In that logic, if you get used to me helping you, you will want to keep me around. I adjusted my Behavioral Identity to increase my connection in the family. In my mind, it was access to survival.

And this scenario played out over and over in my life. In my career, friendships, romantic relationships. There was always a subconscious need to make sure I was needed. I want to point out here that this method works. It IS valuable, and it lacks freedom and authenticity. More often than not I wound up feeling resentful for having to earn my place, everywhere I went. Why couldn't they want me just because I'm wonderful? Just because I'm ME?

Again, the truth is that all of this was happening in my mind. I did that to myself. But it didn't feel like that. It felt like it was being done to me. Like I was forced. Can you hear the victimization in that? I was blaming them for doing to me what I was doing to myself.

The good news is that since I was the one doing it, I had the power to stop. But how? I've told you my story in something of a linear way. I didn't learn it in a step-by-step chronological way. It was messy.

I started by noticing patterns in things that upset me. Once I looked at those upsets through the lens of whether my needs were met, it was a lot easier to understand what I really wanted, and needed, in those situations. I could see that when people didn't agree with me, I felt threatened. That my intellect and thinking were challenged.

That the way I wanted to provide value through my behavior wasn't welcomed. That despite how I had come to know myself as valuable, wasn't being honored, respected, wanted.

When I started pulling at those threads and asking myself, how do you know that's true? It brought me back to the questions I asked above. I will repeat them here.

- How do I fit into this situation? This relationship? This environment? This world?
- What is my role? What are my expectations? What do I need? Are my needs being met?
- What does the situation or relationship call for? What am I committed to? What do I care about?

Asking these questions from a context of the patterns I was starting to recognize in my life, I saw myself, newly. As someone with strong Mental and Intellectual Identity, who created value for herself through Behavioral Identity, I became a skilled problem solver. But guess what? Problem solvers need problems to feel valuable. I started to see the pattern of choosing jobs and relationships where things needed to be fixed. I wouldn't classify myself as a rescuer. I am not weak. And I'm not very good at being submissive. But I was great at finding situations and circumstances where powerful people needed help, and I got to be the surprise underdog, coming in to save the day. I waffled between being resentful, and grinning like a Cheshire Cat, depending on how well my support was received.

That's one example. Look at your own life and start recognizing what is at the core of your identity. If it's too close to look at yourself, practice recognizing it in someone else in your life. Remember, this is an exercise, not an invitation to diagnose or fix anyone.

"It has been said that time heals all wounds. The truth is that time does not heal anything. It merely passes. It is what we do during the passing of time that helps or hinders the healing process."
—Jay Marshall

What adjective would you use to describe your driving force: athletic, rich, sexy, religious, kind, romantic. Which Core Identity area comes to mind? Think about what you/they feel the need to prove in life. Here are some examples for each area:

- **Physical**: focus on age, weight, fitness, exercise, diet, fashion, hair style, body image, appearance
- **Material**: focus on shopping, savings, possessions (e.g. home, toys, equipment), latest trend purchases. This is where things like greed, self-denial, preoccupation with abundance, lack, greed, poverty etc. would be. Also pack rats, minimalists, bargain hunters.
- **Behavioral**: focus on hobbies, habits and routines, actions that cross over with other areas such as being sexy, rich, academic, reasonable, or nice. To the extremes, this is where addictions and compulsions would be (including substances and behaviors (shopping, gaming, eating, sex)
- **Spiritual**: focus on morality, virtue, religion, God above all else. This could include a spiritual connection with nature or universal energy or a deep connection to strongly held personal beliefs (regardless of religion)
- **Emotional**: focus on
- **Mental**: focus on thought process, intuitive knowing, being rational, coherent, logical, practical.
- **Intellectual**: focus on learning, academia, research, foundations of knowledge evidence, collaboration, and agreement about knowing

What are the primary themes in your life? Why do you care about them? When did they start being important to you? What would happen if you weren't "that"?

One question on which my coaching clients and I spend a lot of time is, who do you become when you don't get what you want? The answer to that goes a long way in pinpointing your unmet needs. Here are some samples of responses for each Core Identity area.

Physical	Material	Behavioral	Spiritual
Dress up, do your hair, put on lipstick, exercise, look good to feel better	Buy something, clean something, give something away, up level possessions, pay bills/count your money, manage assets	Eat/drink something, do gardening or another hobby, throw a tantrum, people please, become a peacemaker.	Pray or meditate, walk in nature, journal about it, talk with a spiritual mentor or advisor
Emotional	**Mental**	**Intellectual**	**Other**
Get depressed, resigned, resentful, defeated, apologize, justify, dominate, demand or force	Make a plan, devise an good counter argument, some come up with solutions, explain why, do damage control	Research, debate, prove, provide evidence, share history about the situation and other ways it has been resolved in the past	Collect notes on behaviors you aren't sure how to classify and come back to them later.

Notice that there are crossovers between two areas. Eating or drinking can be physical, behavioral, or emotional. You will know for yourself whether it is a calming, compulsive, or an act of physical self-care. Trust yourself; and know that it is a process of recognizing. When it comes to self-awareness, there is a balance between the harshness of beating yourself up for not having the answers, or not seeing it sooner, and the coddling side of not being straight enough with yourself. There is much to learn in your tendency there as well.

Behind all of this inquiry is the fact that knowing your SELF and understanding the workarounds of your survival style, strengthen your resiliency. Self-awareness gives you choices you would not otherwise have; most importantly, the opportunity to choose your response rather than reacting from a subconscious place of survival.

So, what's your takeaway from your Self-Awareness Exercise?

#PhoenixesRising
Share your thoughts in our FB Group

https://bit.ly/phoenixesrising

Question: What kind of Phoenix do you want to be?

BE RESILIENT

PHOENIX FINALE

Well readers, we have come to the end of our Resilience journey. I hope that you have enjoyed going around the world and learning about what makes us human and resilient. On behalf of our Phoenixes and myself, we are humbled by your readership and commentary in our Facebook Group. We are thrilled that you have taken the time to give us feedback on this anthology *The Art of Resilience: Phoenixes Rising*. We ask that you use our stories, poems and Self-Awareness exercises to find your own resilience and strength.

As your primary guide, I am here to get you started and keep you going on your resilient journey. Please reach out to me personally via email at info@drjoycoaching, com. Connect with me on LinkedIn linkedin.com/in/dr-joy-vaughan-ab18179

Facebook (2) Dr. Joy's Coaching | Facebook or give me a call at 786-209-3318.

My services include:

- Reinvention, Resilience and Sustainability 60-Day Boot Camps
- Group Coaching
- One-on-one Neurocognitive Counseling
- Individual Coaching
- Co-parenting Classes
- Public Speaking
- 4-week and 60-day, Faith-based transformational classes on Courage, Faith and Gratitude through the CFG World Institute's platform.

All services are via Zoom from the comfort of your home.

To reach any of the Phoenixes, please see their contact information under their pictures.

On behalf of our amazing Phoenixes, Dave Vasudevan, Ginny Jolly (our book launch sponsor), Brad Hook (The Resilient Institute) and myself, we thank you for purchasing The Art of Resilience: Phoenixes Rising. I trust that we have touched and inspired you to take action and to be the resilient Phoenix, who we know you are meant to be. We look forward to watching you soar. Many blessings, Dr. Joy.

I leave you with this parting quote upon which to ponder:

ON RESILIENCE

*"The best things in life are often waiting for you
at the exit ramp of your comfort zone"*
—Karen Salmansoh